FOREIGN POLICY OF INDIA

Volume 1

K.R. Gupta
Vatsala Shukla

ATLANTIC
PUBLISHERS & DISTRIBUTORS (P) LTD

Published by

ATLANTIC

PUBLISHERS & DISTRIBUTORS (P) LTD

7/22, Ansari Road, Darya Ganj,
New Delhi-110002
Phones : +91-11-23273880, 23275880, 23280451
Fax : +91-11-23285873
Web : www.atlanticbooks.com
E-mail : info@atlanticbooks.com

Branch Office
5, Nallathambi Street, Wallajah Road,
Chennai-600002
Phones : +91-44-64611085, 32413319
E-mail : chennai@atlanticbooks.com

Printed in India at Nice Printing Press, A-33/3A, Site-IV, Industrial Area, Sahibabad, Ghaziabad, U.P.

Preface

Foreign policy can be defined as a set of principles adopted and followed by a nation for securing the objectives of national interest during the course of its relations with other nations. It is the key element in the process of efforts by which a state translates its ideals and broadly conceived goals into concrete courses of action according to the prevailing international environment.

The foundations of India's foreign policy were laid during the freedom movement when our leaders—even while fighting for Independence—were engaged in the cause of protecting the country's territorial integrity and abolition of slavery and colonisation from the world. They cooperated with the oppressive British rulers and joined hands with them in fighting against the fascist forces during the First World War as maintenance of international peace was a more immediate task than ousting the British from India. Recognizing India's high ideals of peace, security and universal brotherhood it was given the pride of place among the founding members of the United Nations in 1945 although it was not a free nation at that time. India was the first country to raise the question of racial discrimination in South Africa in 1946. It was due to India's initiative that apartheid came to an end in South Africa and the blacks started enjoying equal rights in that country. India's Independence itself played the role of a catalyst in removing the vestiges of colonialism in other parts of the developing world.

Panch-sila became the basis of India's foreign policy when our first Prime Minister, Jawaharlal Nehru embodied it in a treaty with China on the issue of Tibet in May 1954. The five principles mentioned therein were: (i) mutual respect for each other's territorial sovereignty; (ii) non-aggression; (iii) non-intervention in each other's domestic affairs; (iv) mutual benefit and equality; and (v) peaceful coexistence. Several countries including the erstwhile Soviet Union, China, Poland, Saudi Arabia and Laos have commended Panch-sila as worthy of universal respect.

Non-alignment is considered another cornerstone of India's foreign policy. In the pre-Cold War era, non-alignment stood for keeping away from power blocs and military alliances and yet participating actively in the international relations through independent decision-making based upon the world view and national interests of India. Before the disintegration of the USSR, when the world was virtually divided into two blocs, the Indian policymakers thought it well to keep away from Cold War and concentrate on securing the national interests of security, social upliftment and economic prosperity. In the bipolar world, India's good relations with both Russia and America continued. However, these relations have never been at the cost of core principles of international peace and security. Mrs Indira Gandhi openly criticized the presence of Russian troops in Afghanistan in 1980. India was equally vocal in expressing its displeasure of American attempts to make military bases in the Indian Ocean.

The end of Cold War and the disintegration of Soviet Union drastically changed the power configuration in the world and added to the perplexities of the international situation. Today, the world faces a new situation and so does India. Many of the old hypotheses have become victims of the march of history. Countries like China, though still communist, have given up rigidity in controlling economic activities and are embracing more open policies in the present scenario of globalization, liberalization and free flow of goods, services, technology and capital from one country to another. The economic struggle has become far more crucial than before with direct implications for foreign policy. The United States, with its overwhelming powers has become the chief architect of almost all the major decisions. Terrorism has become a major threat to civilized societies across the globe. Widespread expansion of technology and possession of nuclear weapons by rogue states have brought the danger of such weapons falling into the hands of terrorists, which may have catastrophic consequences. India's foreign policy aims at addressing such serious problems in cooperation with the international community and agencies. India's joint military exercises with America are a measure of India's concern for fighting the menace of terrorism. India has been actively participating in the United Nation's peacekeeping operations across the world.

A notable feature of India's foreign policy has been its strong advocacy of general and complete disarmament, with nuclear disarmament being accorded the highest priority. In August 1999, the Government of India released a draft of Indian Nuclear Doctrine. The use of weapons of mass destruction (WMDs) including nuclear weapons is the gravest threat to humanity and to peace and stability of international systems. Unlike biological and chemical weapons which have been outlawed by international treaties, nuclear weapons remain the instruments for national and collective security, the possession of which on a selectire basis was sought to be legitimized through permanent extension of Nuclear Non-proliferation Treaty (NPT). Nuclear weapons states have asserted that they will continue to rely on nuclear weapons, with some of them adopting policies to harness nuclear power to fill the gap between demand and supply of energy required for industrial development. These developments amount to virtual abandonment of nuclear disarmament. In the absence of global nuclear disarmament, India's strategic interests require effective credible nuclear deterrence and adequate retaliatory capability, should deterrence fail. Our foreign policy provides for this, being consistent with the UN Charter, which sanctions the right of self-defence. The policy carefully weighs the design of Indian nuclear forces as well as the strategy to provide for a level of capability consistent with maximum credibility, survivability, effectiveness, safety and security.

The policy of 'retaliation only' is an integral part of India's doctrine of credible minimum nuclear deterrence. This is a dynamic concept in which the protection of our arsenal has been considered critical. The actual size of components and the deployment of nuclear forces is to be decided as per prevailing circumstances. India's peacetime posture aims at convincing any potential aggressor that any threat of use of nuclear weapons against India shall invoke measures to counter the threat, and any nuclear attack on India and its forces shall result in punitive retaliation with nuclear weapons to inflict damage unacceptable to the aggressor. Despite the escalation of tension between India and Pakistan in 2001-02 India remained committed to its nuclear no-first-use policy.

India is among the countries which need to pursue nuclear energy options for peaceful purposes. The global prices of petrochemical products have risen sharply during the last six months. The developing countries like India which cannot bear the burden of higher oil import bill have to cut down their import, leading to an energy crisis. But since India has not signed the Comprehensive (Nuclear) Test Ban Treaty (CTBT), it could not receive nuclear fuel from the Nuclear Suppliers Group (NSG)—a body of 45 nations including America. But the Indo-US Nuclear Deal is going to solve this problem. The NSG has already given its waiver to India for the supply of nuclear fuel. Despite opposition from some quarters, the deal can be termed as a reward for India's impeccable nuclear non-proliferation record and a worldwide recognition of India's strong foreign policy.

Another important principle of India's foreign policy has been the strengthening of regional cooperation. India is an active member of the South Asian Association for Regional Cooperation (SAARC), which *inter alia* aims to accelerate economic growth, social progress and cultural development; promote collective self-reliance and contribute to mutual trust, understanding and cooperation between the nations and institutions of South Asia. South Asian Preferential Trade Arrangement (SAPTA), which became operational in 1995, and South Asian Free Trade Area (SAFTA) in 2001 have emerged as two major instruments of cooperation under the auspices of SAARC with the active support of India. Today, India is implementing a 'Look East' policy which is underpinned by significant economic considerations. Some important steps in pursuance of this policy have been taken with India's admission as a full dialogue partner of Association of South East Asian Nations (ASEAN) as also of the ASEAN Regional Forum.

With China and Pakistan, the aim of our foreign policy has been to develop a relationship of friendship, cooperation and good neighbourliness, exploiting the potential for growth wherever it exists — even as we seek to find a mutually acceptable solution to the outstanding issues. To realise this, a series of high-level visits have been exchanged, bilateral trade is growing and confidence-building measures are continuing.

Although it is difficult to express the achievements of a country's foreign policy in exactly quantifiable terms, yet a fair evaluation is that India's foreign policy has stood the test of time and sought to preserve with conviction and consistency the principles that were enunciated by the founding fathers of the Republic. That our views have won worldwide recognition and respect bears testimony to the fact that our foreign policy is built on strong foundations.

The book in two volumes provides illuminating insights into various aspects of India's foreign policy such as core values, salient features, determinants as well as the external forces like changing international scenario influencing it. I am grateful to Vatsala Shukla for allowing me to use some insightful material from her book *India's Foreign Policy in the New Millennium* which has enriched these volumes. The book comprehensively covers India's global orientation analysing the country's role in international bodies like the UN, its supreme position in the subcontinent as well as Asia and its quest for major power status. It will be immensely useful to students and teachers of foreign policy, international relations and political science and researchers in these fields. It will serve as a reference source for policymakers. The common readers who want to know about India's foreign policy will find it interesting and informative.

K.R. Gupta

Contents

1

Foreign Policy

WHAT IS FOREIGN POLICY?

Foreign policy can be broadly defined as a set of goals that seeks to outline how a particular country will interact with other countries of the world. Generally, foreign policies are designed to help safeguard a country's national interests, national security, ideological goals, and economic prosperity.[1]

Foreign policy plays a prominent part in the peace and progress of every country in the world today. Every nation aspires to be self-reliant but it has to depend upon other countries for many things. In other words interdependence is an essential factor. It leads to healthy international relations. For giving a meaning and direction to its behaviour at the international level each nation adopts a set of principles, a rational guide — the foreign policy. Through the foreign policy the nation formulates, it adopts to secure the goals of its prime interest. In short, the behaviour of each nation is always conditioned by its foreign policy.

Many definitions have been given for the term 'foreign policy' by many writers. In simple words, foreign policy can be defined as the set of principles adopted and followed by a nation for securing the objectives of national interest during the course of its relations with other nations.

According to George Modelski, "Foreign policy involves all activities of a nation by which that nation is trying to change the behaviour of other nations and to adjust its own behaviour in the international environment." He further adds that "foreign policy always aims at successfully changing the behaviour of other nations." Norman Hill defines foreign policy, "as the substance of a nation's efforts to promote its interests *vis-à-vis* other nations."

According to Padelford and Lincoln, "Foreign policy is the key element in the process by which a state translates its broadly conceived goals and interests into concrete courses of action and to attain these objectives and preserve its interests." In other words, foreign policy involves both a formulation of objectives and the attempts to achieve these objectives. Cecil V. Crabb offers a simple yet very effective definition of foreign policy when he writes: "Reduced to its most fundamental ingredients, foreign policy consists of two elements — national objectives to be achieved, and — means for achieving them." As Mahendra Kumar puts it, "Foreign policy is a throughout course of action for achieving objectives in foreign relations as dictated by the ideology of national interest."

Foreign Policy and Its Contents

The following are its main contents:

1. General principles adopted and followed by the nation.
2. The objectives or aims of national interest which are to be attained.
3. The nature of means that are to be used for achieving the objectives.
4. The guidelines for understanding relations with other nations.
5. The assessment of the gains and failures of the nation.
6. Attempts to maintain continuity and change in relation as the case may be.

Crabb says, "The study of foreign policy includes both the study of national objectives and the means used for securing these. Since the national objectives are always stated with the help of set of national principles one has to study the principles of foreign policy on the basis of these actions of the state and the international level."

Elements

The policymakers are mainly responsible for the formulation and implementation of the foreign policy of a nation. No doubt it is a complex affair because they have to take into account the interest of the nation, the internal and external environment and the national values. Hence, J.N. Rosenau refers to these as "the Foreign Policy Inputs". Let us discuss the factors which determine the foreign policy of a nation. James N. Rosenau, K.W. Thampson and Roy C. Macrides have mentioned the following three as important:

1. The relatively permanent material elements, i.e. Geography and Natural Resources.
2. Less permanent material elements, i.e. Industrial Establishment, Military Establishment and changes in Industrial and Military Capacity.
3. The human elements, i.e. Quantitative (population) and Qualitative (policymakers and leaders). Ideology and Information also play an important role.

Indeed this is a very useful and systematic classification. The major characteristics that influence the foreign policy of the nation are enumerated below:

(1) Size; (2) Geography; (3) Economic Development; (4) Culture and History; (5) Power Structure; (6) Treaties and Alliances; (7) Technology; (8) Social Structure; (9) Public Opinion; (10) Political Accountability; (11) Government Structure; (12) Situational Factors; (13) The Values, Talents and Experiences; (14) Leaders; (15) Ideology; and (16) Diplomacy.

Size

The most important factor of foreign policy is the size of the state. Size influences the psychological and operational environments within which the foreign policy makers and public respond. It includes, as Rosenau says, "both human and non-human resources".

Nations with large human and non-human resources always try to be big powers and they have better chances of being big powers in international relations. Foreign policy of a big sized state is bound to be different from the foreign policy of a small-sized state.

Public and foreign policymakers of big sized states are definitely governed by their desire to be big powers in world politics. Size has been a factor in the foreign policies of USA, USSR, China, India, etc.

However, size alone is not an independent determinant of foreign policy. Resources of the state are always not dependent upon size. Middle Eastern countries, even with small size but with the largest quantity of oil resources, are playing an influential role in international politics. Before 1945, Britain with a small size could play the role of a superpower. Large size poses the problem of defence, security and maintenance of communications. In the absence of natural boundaries, the large size of a nation very often creates problems in maintaining smooth relations with neighboring states.

Geography

Geography of the state is relatively the most permanent and stable factor of foreign policy. The topography of land, its fertility, climate and location are the major geographic factors which influence the foreign policy of a nation. These factors determine both the needs and the capability to fulfill the needs of the people of a nation. Suitable geographical conditions can help and encourage the nation to adopt and pursue higher goals.

The role played by English Channel in the development of England as major naval power and consequently as an imperial power is well known. The influence of the Atlantic Ocean on American foreign policy of isolationalism is again an example. India's Indian Ocean policy definitely bears the influence of its geographical location as the largest littoral state of the Indian Ocean. The relatively unhelpful geographical conditions of Canada have been a limiting factor in the determination of the foreign policy of Canada. The large territory of Soviet Union makes it difficult for other nations to think of scoring an outright military victory over Russia. The location of Pakistan too has influenced its foreign relations with India, China and USSR. The geographical separation from Pakistan has been a factor influencing the foreign policy of Bangladesh.

The natural resources and the food production capacity of a nation are directly linked with its geography. These factors are also important in the formulation and implementation of foreign policy. Existence of adequate vital natural resources — minerals, food production and energy resources has been a helping factor for American and the erstwhile Soviet Union foreign policies. Food shortage was a cause of limitation on Indian foreign policy in the fifties and sixties. Large quantities of oil have made it possible for the West Asian nations to adopt oil diplomacy as a means of their foreign policies.

Geography, as such, is an important and forceful factor of foreign policy, yet it is not a deterministic factor. The revolutionary developments in communications and modern warfare, the ability of nations to overcome geographical hindrances have tended to reduce the role of geography. English Channel now cannot materially help England to recover its old colonial status. The geographical conditions of both India and China have not changed yet both of these are now playing a vigorous role in international politics.

Economic Development

One of the main reasons why America's foreign policy is very often successful in securing its national objectives, particularly in relation to the poor and economically lowly placed states of the world, is the country's high degree of economic development. Both America and the former Soviet Union were highly industrialised and economically developed states; they could use foreign aid as a tool for securing their foreign policy goals. The global perspectives and policies of the two superpowers were again governed by their vast economic and industrial resources. For similar reasons, economically and industrially developed nations are playing a more vigorous role in international politics than the least developed and developing nations. The low commitment of the foreign policies of the least developed and developing nations to the cause of new international economic order is again a proof of the role of economic factors in the foreign relations.

The level of economic development also determines the scope of relations that a nation wishes to establish with other nations.

The foreign policy of Japan in the post-war period is directly and fundamentally related to its economic development. The military preparedness and capability of a nation is again directly related to the factor of economic development and industrialization. Only industrially and economically developed nations can hope to become major and strong military powers.

Thus, the level and nature of economic development, industrialization and modernization are important factors of foreign policy. But here again we must say that these factors are in themselves related intimately to natural resources, manpower and even ideological commitments of the nation. In spite of big industrial and economic constraints Pakistan's foreign policy has been a very active policy. Islamic world has been helping it to overcome its economic and industrial backwardness.

Culture and History

The cultural heritage and the history of a nation are again important and valuable factors of its foreign policy. The norms and traditions that characterize the relationships of its people are highly influential factors. The foreign policy makers of the nation, during the process of interpreting and formulating the objectives of national interest, are always governed by their cultural links, historical traditions and experiences. Strong cultural unity of the people is always a source of strength for them. It materially influences their ability to secure the objectives of national interest during the course of international bargaining.

Historical experiences and cultural links further help them to analyze and assess the nature and scope of relations with other nations. In the words of Rosenau, "Effectiveness in foreign affairs depends on a multitude of variables, but one of them is surely the support which officials enjoy from the people for whom they are conducting external operations and extent of this support is significantly affected by the degree to which basic values are shared in the society." Indeed, the weakness of the foreign policies of most of the Asian and African states is due largely to the presence of internal dissensions and conflicts among their peoples.

Bitter experiences with the policies of imperialism and colonialism have been a near determining factor of the anti-imperialist and anti-colonial contents of the foreign policies of most of the newly emerged sovereign states. History is an important factor in determining the relations among nations and particularly among the neighboring nations. The foreign policy interactions between India and Pakistan are mostly the legacies of the past history. The shadow of the history of 1962 still influences the course of Sino-Indian relations.

However, cultural values and links are subject to perpetual changes and adjustments. Historical experiences too are forgotten in the face of national interest. The existence of conflict among the European nations, despite their cultural links and the development, and continuance of strong US-Japan friendship and relations bear ample proof that cultural and historical factors have collusion with other factors before influencing the course of foreign policy.

Power Structure

The foreign policy of every nation is influenced by the nature of power structure in international politics. The power vacuum caused by the weakened power of the formerly powerful European states, because of their involvement in two World Wars within a short interval, made USA come out of its isolationism and assume a new global role in international relations. The change in US foreign policy and its attempt to influence the European states brought into operation Soviet foreign policy of keeping close the East European friendly socialist nations. The emergence of USA and USSR as the two superpowers, with Cold War in between them made it imperative for the new states like India to adopt a policy of keeping away from the Cold War and yet attempt to have friendly co-operation with both the superpowers for securing the much needed help and aid for meeting the needs of its people. The bipolar system that emerged after World War II and the multi-polar or polycentric system that presently exists have been very influential in the making of foreign policy decisions of all nations.

In the 19th century, the foreign policies of nations were always regulated by the 'balance of power' system as constituted by the big powers of that time. Even now, a particular conception of the 'balance of power' system guides the foreign policy making of nations belonging to a particular region. The foreign policies of India and China bear the impact of power structure in Asia. Indo-Pak foreign policy interactions are governed by the consideration of 'Balance of Power' in South Asia. The power structure in Middle East and West is an input factor of foreign policy of the USA. Rosenau has included great power structure as a foreign policy input. We have, however, regarded it more worthwhile to analyze power structure in general as a factor in foreign policy making.

Alliances and International Treaties

Alliance is a means by which some nations pool their powers or agree to pool their powers in the event of a particular situation. Alliances as such serve as a source of foreign policies. The system of alliances that has emerged in the post-war period has been a source of considerable influence on the foreign policies of all the nations. Both the United States and Soviet Union recognized alliances as the means for consolidating their respective positions. Their own foreign policies as well as those of their allies were governed by the goal to secure new partners in alliance and to maintain and consolidate the alliance partnership. However, many other nations, which have come to be known as non-aligned nations, record alliances as a source of tension and distrust and their foreign policies are governed by anti-alliance principle.

Recently, another factor has become an influential factor in foreign policy making. The realization for mutual inter-dependence has given birth to a large number of international treaties and agreements. The foreign policy of a nation is always conscious of these treaties and agreements and it tries to uphold those which it favours and to overcome the hindrances caused by the unfavourable treaties. The pressures of Non-Proliferation Treaty on India's relations with America are a well known fact. Hence, international treaties and alliances constitute a factor of foreign policy.

Technology

The application of the knowledge of scientific inventions to practical and useful purposes leads to technology. The level of technological development and the nature of know-how are important elements of foreign policy. Highly advanced technology has been a major factor of the strength of the foreign policies of the two superpowers in the past, when the world was bipolar. The ability to provide technical know-how to lowly developed and developing nations has been an instrument of influence, rather power, with the foreign policies of the developed nations. India's dependence on developed nations for getting technological know-how has been a limiting factor of Indian foreign policy.

The level and nature of industrial output and military preparedness of a nation are dependent upon technology. These in turn are important components of foreign policy. Rosenau writes: "Technological changes can alter the military and economic capabilities of a society and thus, its status and role in the international system." The rise of France, China and Japan are the present classic examples of the change that technological development has brought about in their roles at the international politics. Technology is, however, a relatively less stable element of foreign policy because technological changes always and continuously take place in every society. Moreover, it is only in relation to scientific and industrial developments that technology becomes a factor of foreign policy.

Social Structure

The structure and nature of the society for which the foreign policy operates is also its important input. The nature of groups and the degree of conflict and harmony that characterize their mutual relations are determined by the social structure. A society characterized by strong internal conflict and strife is a source of weakness for the foreign policy. A society of united, enlightened and disciplined population with a high degree of group harmony is a source of strength for the foreign policy. The democratisation of the process of policy-making in recent times has increased the importance of social structure as an element of foreign policy. The linkages between the domestic and international environments have tended to strengthen the role of this element in the making and implementation of foreign policy.

Moods of Opinion (Public Opinion)

Public opinion, both national and international is another important input of foreign policy. The foreign policy makers of each nation have to accept and give due place to the opinion of the people they represent as well to the world public opinion. Undoubtedly, the decision-makers as leaders have to lead the public, yet they also have to accommodate the demands of public opinion. American Senate's refusal to ratify American membership of the League of the Nations, the opposition to Vietnam War by the Americans and other people had a big impact on the foreign policy of USA. The strength behind the objectives of disarmament, arms control and nuclear disarmament, anti-colonialism and anti-apartheid policies of various nations have been public opinions.

Political Accountability

According to Rosenau, "The degree, to which public officials are accountable to the citizenry either through elections, party competitions, legislative oversight, or other means, can have important consequences for the timing and contents of the plans that are made and the activities undertaken in foreign affairs." A political system which is both responsive to and responsible before the people works in a different environment than the political system which is a closed system, i.e. a system which is not accountable to the people. As such the foreign policy of an open political system is more responsive to public opinion and public demands than to the foreign policy of a closed political system. The difference between the foreign policies of a democratic state and a totalitarian or authoritarian state is largely due to this factor.

Government Structure

The organisation and structure of government, i.e. the organisational agencies which handle the foreign policy making and implementation is another important element of foreign policy. The shape of the foreign policy is also determined by the fact whether the government agencies handling it are democratically constituted or not, whether the authority relations are centralised or decentralised. In a democratic and decentralised system, the foreign policy decision-making is free and open, since it takes into account the views of various personalities and agencies. It has to adapt to the environment. In a centralized and authoritarian system, the foreign policy can and often does remain isolated from the domestic environment. The nature of legislative-executive relations too is an influential factor in foreign policy decisions. The harmony between the two, as is there in a parliamentary system, is a source of strength for the Prime Minister, Foreign Minister and in fact the foreign office. The checks and balances relationship between the two, as is there in a presidential system can be a source of hindrance for the President and the Foreign Minister of the State. Similarly, the nature of party system elections and electorate are other influential factors. The continuity in Indian foreign policy has been also due to the single party dominant system of India. The existence of military dominated governmental system of Pakistan has been largely responsible for military-security oriented foreign policy of Pakistan. Centralised authority system of Communist China has helped the Chinese foreign policy decision-makers in frequently changing rather reversing many of their former foreign policy decisions.

Situational Factors

External

Foreign policy has to operate in the international environment which is subject to many frequent and important situational changes. As such, it has always to adapt to these changes. Consequently, these situational changes become foreign policy inputs. For example, socialist revolution in a neighbouring state or a military coup, or the emergence of dispute between two friendly nations or the rise of a controversy in the United Nations or the nationalisation of industry by a major nation or the devaluation of a popular currency, or the aggression or intervention by a nation against another nation, etc. are some of the situational changes that keep on taking place in the international environment. These changes are always instrumental in bringing changes in the decision-making and operationalisation of a foreign policy.

The emergence of Sino-Soviet rift had been a factor in changing the US foreign policy towards China. The Bangladesh war and its impact on the power structure in the South Asia had produced changes in Indian foreign policy. The overthrowing of Bhutto's Government in Pakistan, the rise of military dictatorship of General Zia-ul-Haq, the murder of Mujib-ur-Rehman in Bangladesh, the crisis in Afghanistan, the supply of advanced technology F-16, AWACS to Pakistan by USA, etc. had been the external situational inputs of Indian foreign policy in South Asia.

Further, the foreign policy of a nation is always made and implemented with an eye on the situation in various regions of the world. A situational change in West Asia or South-East Asia or Africa necessitates a change or modification of foreign policy. Similarly, international issues and crises are also important factors of foreign policy. The issues of new international economic order, the distribution of international resources, the recurring international crises — like the Lebanon crisis, the Iran-Iraq War, were other important external situational inputs of the foreign policies of various nations.

Internal

Like the external situational factors, sudden changes, crises, disturbances, etc. that occur within the internal environment of a nation also influence the nature and course of foreign policy. The resignation of President Nixon over the issue of Watergate Scandal considerably limited the foreign policy of USA under President Ford. The internal opposition to the present military regime of Pakistan was a determinant of Pakistani foreign policy. Similarly, the declaration of emergency in India in 1975 did materially affect the relations of India with other countries. A change of government, sudden or otherwise, is also a source of change in foreign policy. The death of Mao and Chou within a short duration and the rise of new leadership in China had been an important input of Chinese foreign policy of the post-Mao period.

Values, Talents and Experiences

Since the foreign policy of a nation is made and implemented by men, naturally it bears an imprint of the values, talents, experiences and personalities of its leaders. The ideas, orientations, like, dislike attitudes, knowledge, skill and the world view of the leaders are influential inputs of foreign policy. The differences between the foreign policy decisions of various US Presidents and their Secretaries of States have been due to the differences in their attitudes and personalities. John Foster Dulles, who was a highly power-conscious statesman and who believed in the policy of "massive retaliation" and President Eisenhower inducted America into a Cold War and alliance-oriented foreign policy. President Reagan's idea of making America as number one power had been a source of increased competition and armed race between the two former superpowers.

Indian foreign policy till 1964 was often, and rightly so, described as Nehru's foreign policy. 'Non-Alignment' and 'Panchsheel' as principles of Indian foreign policy and India's attempt to forge ahead her solidarity with Asian and African nations were determined by Nehru's thinking. The support at home and the popularity that Nehru enjoyed as a world leader were sources of strength for Indian foreign policy in the Nehru era. Under the leadership of Khrushchev the Soviet foreign policy underwent a change because of his rejection of war and acceptance of peaceful coexistence as an ideal.

Leaders

However, this does not mean that this factor is an independent determinant of foreign policy. Leaders are always guided by the dictates and demands of national interest and are committed to securing it. The vital interests of the nations are a source of continuity if the personalities and attitudes of the leaders are a source of change. The two have to be balanced before these serve as foreign policy inputs. The Janata leaders, particularly Morarji Desai and Vajpayee, had to reconcile their rightist ideology with India's national interests and give up the talk of 'Genuine Non-Alignment' in favour of 'Non-Alignment' as before.

Ideology

Foreign policy is a set of rational principles and a strategic plan adopted by a nation to fulfill the goals of national interest. It has always an ideological content. For securing support for its goal as well as for criticising the foreign policy goals of other nations, it needs and adopts an ideology. Therefore, it always tries to use as well as popularize the ideology. The ideology of communism is an important factor in the foreign policies of communist nations. Anti-Communism and pro-Liberal Democracy orientations are influencing the shape and course of foreign policies of non-communist Western nations. Ideological conflict had been a determining factor in the Cold War policies of both the superpowers. Similarly, ideological commitments are sources of affinity in the foreign policies of some nations.

Diplomacy

Diplomacy is the means by which the foreign policy of a nation travels beyond its borders and establishes contacts with other nations. It is diplomacy which tries to secure the goals of foreign policy during the course of relations with other nations. Besides being a means, diplomacy is also an input of foreign policy. The world view sketched by diplomacy and the reports prepared by the diplomats are valuable instruments of foreign policy making. The modes of operation and quality of diplomacy always affect the operational quality and efficiency of a foreign policy. In the late sixties the contacts between Indian and Chinese diplomats helped the emergence of a definite trend towards normalization of Sino-Indian relations.

FOREIGN POLICY AND NATIONAL INTEREST

There is a close link between foreign policy and national interest. Foreign policy acts for securing the goals of national interest. But at the same time, it is foreign policy which selects, formulates or concretises and defines the goals of national interest and then attempts to secure these goals. If national interest is a determining element of foreign policy, the latter is the director of national interest. National interest is often characterised by ambiguity and vagueness and it is foreign policy that sorts out and defines the real nature of national interest of the nation and formulates concrete goals which are to be attained in foreign relations. Thus, both foreign policy and national interest are intimately related. National interest is the objective of foreign policy and foreign policy is the protector of national interest.

The exact role of national interest in the formulation of foreign policy is subject of great debate among scholars. One set of scholars advocates that foreign policy is and should always be based upon national interest.

A former US Secretary of States, Hughes once observed, "Foreign policies are not abstractions but the results of practical concepts of national interest." Morgenthau also holds that foreign policy always "seeks to defend national interest".

While formulating foreign policy, the decision-makers of a nation are always guided by the demands of national interest. National leaders as a rule never pursue national policies that are in the interest of any nation other than their own.

Analysing the process of foreign policy decision-making, Ivo D. Duchacek remarks, "In planning, formulating, adopting and executing foreign policy, national leaders and their aides are confronted with a veritable spider's web of conflicting claims and values. Yet priorities, that is, the practical and not the ideal content of national interest, must finally be established in terms of preferred goals and in relation to power of one's own nation and that of other nations. Both national goals and national means must simultaneously be related to dangers or opportunities on the international scene; not only other nations' power but also their intentions must be properly evaluated." Thus national interest is the basis for the formulation of foreign policy.

The other set of scholars, however, does not accept such logic and is of the view what it is not always possible to base the foreign policy only on the national interest of the state. National interests of a state are general, vague and often lack clarity. For example, security is regarded as the primary interest of a state and yet no member of the government can precisely define the nature of security that is actually required by the state. National interests cannot be precisely identified and concretised. These have to be related to values of the people as well as to the interests of other nations. Hence, national interest alone cannot be accepted as the basis of foreign policy.

In actual practice we find that very often the leaders of the state try to give priority to their selfish interests in domestic policies over the national interests of the state. They sometimes construct interest in such a way as to make their way of ruling the state easier.

Pakistani rulers have very often, rather always, used Pakistani interest in Kashmir as a means for securing their positions in domestic politics. They have even resorted to wars with India for maintaining their power and control over the government.

All this makes it clear that national interest is not the only basis of foreign policy.

Both these views offer divergent interpretations of the relation between foreign policy and national interest. The reality lies in between these two views. No one can deny the importance of national interest as a basis of foreign policy but at the same time no one can deny the role of foreign policy in giving meaning and shape to national interest. A foreign policy not based on national interest is inconceivable. Likewise, national interest can never get rid of its ambiguity if it is not perfected and concretized by foreign policy.

DIPLOMACY AND FOREIGN POLICY

There is a close connection between diplomacy and foreign policy. In common usage these are very often used as synonyms. The statement 'British diplomacy in Middle East lacks vigour' equates diplomacy with foreign policy. However, this is not an acceptable proposition in international politics. Diplomacy and foreign policy are related but have different concepts.

Foreign policy is the plan and the programme formulated for securing the goals of national interest of the nation, whereas diplomacy is the means and the tactics employed for implementing the foreign policy. Foreign policy of a nation travels to other nations on the wheels of diplomacy. It is the substance of foreign relations. Diplomacy is the process by which foreign policy is implemented abroad.

In the words of J.R. Childs, "Foreign policy is the substance of foreign relations, whereas, diplomacy proper is the process by which policy is carried out."

Policy is made by many different persons and agencies. Diplomacy provides the machinery and the personnel by which foreign policy is executed. One is the substance, the other a method. Diplomats do not determine the principles of their government's foreign policy but with their reports they render important help in policy formulation. During the course of the determination of foreign policy, the reports of the diplomats are always taken as raw-material.

While analysing the distinction between foreign policy and diplomacy, Harold Nicholson observes: "Both are concerned with adjustment of national interest. Both aim at the planned achievement of national interest. Foreign policy is based upon a general conception of national requirements.... Diplomacy, on the other hand is not an end but a means; not a purpose but a method. It seeks, by the use of reason, conciliation and the exchange of interests, to prevent major conflicts arising between sovereign states. It is the agency through which foreign policy seeks to attain its purpose by agreement rather than by war. Thus, when agreement becomes impossible, diplomacy, which is the instrument of peace, becomes inoperative; and foreign policy, the final sanction of which is war, alone, becomes operative." While disagreeing with Nicholson's thesis that diplomacy ends when war breaks out, we do accept his overall view of the relation between foreign policy and diplomacy.

Sir Victor Wellsely has beautifully analysed the relations between foreign policy and diplomacy by observing: "Diplomacy is not foreign policy, but is the instrument for implementing it. Both are supplementary to each other because without one, the other cannot work. Diplomacy has no separate existence apart from foreign policy." It is bound to behave like an aimlessly drifting rudderless ship without being guided and conditioned by foreign policy. Similarly, foreign policy, howsoever well formulated and rational it may be, can become neither operational nor successful without being carried out by diplomacy. "Both together determine executive policy. Foreign policy is strategy, diplomacy is the tactics.... Foreign policy is the soul of foreign relations; diplomacy is the activity through which foreign policy is enforced." "In order to have successful relations with other nations, a nation must combine rational foreign policy with subtle diplomacy."

Diplomacy and foreign policy are two vitally important instruments of nation's behaviour in international relations. International politics is the process of interactions among the foreign policies of various nations and diplomatic activity, particularly diplomatic negotiation, forms the core of these interactions. Foreign policy and diplomacy have been rightly described by Mahendra Kumar as the two wheels of international relations.

STUDY OF FOREIGN POLICY

Different theories have been put forth for the study of foreign policy by different writers in different times. In other words there are different approaches for the study of foreign policy. Baljit Singh groups these theories/approaches into two categories:

1. General Theories; and
2. Middle Range or Partial Theories.

In the first category he includes:

- Analytical;
- Structural-Functional; and
- Decision-making theories.

The middle range theories, he writes, are more of the nature of analytical tools and include:

- Study of public opinion and related field of mass communication;
- Official factors such as specific government agencies; and
- Unofficial individuals or groups often called pressure groups acting in the process.

Such a classification is indeed very broad. On the basis of popularity of various approaches, K.W. Thompson and Roy C. Macridis, however, suggest a discussion of two approaches to foreign policy which have been very popular and are two contending approaches of modern times. These are:

Analytical Approach

The Analytical Approach to the study of foreign policy concentrates upon the study of the elements and objectives of foreign policy and considers them to be the results of a variety of factors, attitudes and circumstances.

This approach holds that means, methods, techniques that the foreign policy makers adopt may change while the interests and objectives before them are relatively constant.

The foreign policy of a nation is based upon the view and determination of the priority order of various aspects of national interests and international obligations. It is as such based upon national interests which are vital and must be defended at all costs and at all times. The non vital or variable interests are to be adjusted and safeguarded under particular circumstances. The analytical approach, as such emphasises the study of all the elements and factors, domestic as well as foreign, which are the inputs of a foreign policy.

According to Baljit Singh, "Foreign policy is a system of activities evolved by nations for influencing and changing the behaviour of other states and for adjusting their own activities to international environment." Foreign policy is not the product of the ideas and ideologies of the policy-makers. On the contrary, it is a complex social process in which the following play an interactive and related roles:

1. Policy-makers,
2. Principles of foreign policy,
3. Policy aims, interests and objectives,
4. Power inputs and outputs, and
5. The context of foreign policy.

At the heart of this approach is the view that policy rests upon multiple factors. To understand foreign policy, the students must, therefore, study and analyse all these factors. As such, this approach seeks to study foreign policy by analysing input, interests, objectives and outputs of foreign policy. It also seeks to analyse the process by which policy-makers process the inputs into output.

Ideological Approach

As against the Analytical Approach, the Ideological Approach seeks to study foreign policy in terms of the prevailing political, social and religious beliefs which are considered to be the determinants of the policies of states *vis-à-vis* other states of the world.

In this approach, as Thompson and Macridis write, "Foreign policies are classified as democratic or totalitarian, libertarian or socialist, and peace-loving or aggressive."

In other words, the Ideological Approach holds that foreign policy of a nation is the product of the belief and ideological commitments of the leaders and policy-makers. Each foreign policy is either for or against various ideologies like Liberalism, Totalitarianism, Communism, Socialism, etc. It is with the help of ideological principles and preferences that policy-makers give shape and meaning to national interest and the foreign policy that is formulated to secure the national interest. Foreign policy in this approach is considered as the function of the preference or convictions of political leaders who carry out the programme of the system.

This approach, however, offers a limited and oversimplified view of the foreign policy. No one can ignore the importance of ideology as an input of foreign policy yet no one can accept that foreign policy is determined by ideological beliefs. In the post-war period the foreign policy of no nation has been faithfully following the professed ideological commitments. The US foreign policy, with professedly strong commitment to liberalism, has been actively maintaining warm, friendly and highly co-operative alliance relationships with dictatorships like Pakistan and many other such countries. Soviet Union, though a strong champion of communism, has been maintaining more friendly and cooperative relations with non-communist India than with communist China.

Hence, the Ideological Approach is definitely a limited approach. No doubt, ideological factors of the foreign policy have to be studied and analyzed by a student of foreign policy yet ideology cannot be accepted as the approach to the study of foreign policy.[2]

NOTES

1. Foreign Policy: http://en.wikipedia.org/wiki/Foreign_policy
2. N. Jayapalan (2001). *Foreign Policy of India,* Atlantic Publishers and Distributors Pvt. Ltd., New Delhi, pp. 1-21.

2

India's Foreign Policy

ORIGIN

Prior to independence India started participating in international affairs and the nature of her relations with other nations were a source of influence on her foreign policy in the post-independence period. Hence, it is worthwhile to examine the nature of the Indian participation in international affairs in the pre-independence period.

In the opinion of Charles Heimsath, "No other fact of Independent India's political tradition has the impress of British ideas and institutions stronger than its foreign policy." The very fact that India does not try to reverse or fundamentally change the pre-1947 structure of its external relations tends to prove the worth of this observation. It can also be stated that in its administrative structure for conducting diplomacy, in some of its definitions of the national interest and formulation of policies on some important subjects and in its style of diplomacy, the Government of India as led by Pt. Nehru followed some of the precedents of the British Indian Government.

The reason why India could keep up certain pre-independence precedents was that Britishers had tacitly accepted India as a quasi-independent entity in international political scenario before 1947, in fact since 1917. After the First World War, Indian participation in international policies as a separate but non-sovereign entity was accepted by the British, of course largely for strengthening the imperial voice in international relations and partly for giving some place to Indian nationalism. Some limited objectives of Indian nationalism were pursued by the pre-independence Government of India and those objectives were naturally retained by the Government of Independent India. India's experience in the sphere of international relations of the inter-war period did help independent India to analyse and understand the post-war changes in international relations.[1]

Relation with Imperial Rulers

The foreign relations of India before 1947 were linked to and governed by the interests of British Empire. The Imperial government committed the entire empire to war in 1914 without any formal consultations with the dominions or India. But during war, because of its own needs and dependence upon the resources of India and other dominions, it started the practice of holding consultations with dominions and India on matters of defence and foreign affairs. India was denied the dominion status but it was linked with other dominions because of the Indian contribution to the imperial war efforts. The August 1917 Montague Declaration, accepting the establishment of responsible Government in India as the final objective of the British, was made to ensure Indian help during the war.

In 1917, Lloyd George's Government agreed to India's participation in the war conferences. Indian participation in war conferences of 1917 and 1918 did strengthen India's position in relations with the imperial government and consequently, its participation in international politics increased.

An Indian delegation participated in the Paris Peace Conference and India got original membership of the League of Nations. Thus, India was in a position to achieve a recognised international entity, status and to participate in international relations during the inter-war period. The experience that India gained during this period was utilised by the foreign policy makers of free India.

People of Indian Origin

The issue of status, rights and welfare of the people of Indian origin, living in many other countries of Asia and Africa, which were previously parts of British Empire, has been an important issue in the Indian Foreign Policy since 1947.

In the pre-independence period too the Government of India was actively concerned with this issue. The discrimination against Indians on the grounds of colour and race was being practised by a number of dominions of British Empire.

The British India Government tried hard to secure assurances from the Imperial Government for checking this discrimination. The Imperial Government, however, failed to provide this assurance. The anti-racialism, anti-apartheid content of Indian foreign policy as such had its origin in the pre-independence period.

Economic and Trade Relations

A study of pre-independence economic and trade relations of India with Britain and other countries also bears out the existence of quasi-independent character of India in international affairs.

In the twenties and thirties of the 20th century India was in a position to establish economic and distinct trade links with many countries. However, the tilt in favour of the imperial master Britain existed. In 1919, British Government agreed fiscal autonomy to India. As a result, an Indian Fiscal Commission was established and this commission recommended tariff protection for certain Indian industries. In 1923, a tariff board was established. In 1924, Steel Industry of India was granted protection. In 1931, India signed, at Ottawa, the Indo-British Trade Agreement. This agreement provided for preferences in tariff rates for Indian and British goods entering markets in other countries.

In the post-independence period, Indo-British trade relations and India's economic and trade relations with the Commonwealth countries have been influenced by the pre-independence economic and trade relations of India with Britain and other countries.

India and International Organizations

Further, Indian participation in international organisations had its beginning in the inter-war period. India signed the Treaty of Versailles and other peace treaties and became an original member of the League of Nations. India also became a member of the International Labour Organisation and the International Court of Justice.

In 1928, Indians started leading delegations to the sessions of the Assembly of the League. India could, however, assert some measure of autonomy only in social, economic and technical matters. Besides participation in the affairs of the League, India took active part in the organisation and deliberations of various international conferences/conventions. Particularly, India played active role in the drafting of Opium Convention. It could also subscribe to the convention on traffic in women and children and the slavery convention. India fully supported and adhered to the means of peaceful settlement of disputes. India was in a position to participate actively in the working of International Labour Organisation. India used ILO as a forum for voicing its grievances against economically more powerful states. Indian leaders and the Congress also never hesitated to criticize the failures of the League. Later on, India participated in the San Francisco Conference, 1945 and signed the Charter of the United Nations as an original member.

This participation in international organisations stood in good stead to Indian foreign policy makers when they settled down to formulate the foreign policy of free India.

Foreign Policy and Security of India

The defence and security policy of India too started taking shape during the pre-independence period. The Government of India and Indian leadership very often differed on the subject of defence policy, yet when the national leaders assumed power in 1947 they preferred to build upon the past rather than try to upset it. The system of having military barriers along the frontiers, the northwest land frontiers and the creation of Indian navy with the responsibility of coastal defence were undertaken. Indian foreign policy got oriented towards security of India as a vital part of India's national interest. The British practice of looking to Himalayas as the impenetrable barrier too was accepted. This, however, proved to be a costly mistake in the subsequent years.

In another way, the India's role in international relations during the 1919-46 period helped the process of foreign policy making in the era after Independence. The training and experience that many Indians received during this period gave valuable help and support to the leaders of free India in their attempts to formulate the foreign policy.

Heimsath has rightly observed: "The training and personality of Indians in government service before independence set the style and contributed in some measure to the ideals which characterised Indian foreign policy after 1947. The British legacy, the continuity of tradition had the advantage of providing a ready model from which a quick copy could be made." The ideas of Congress, particularly of its leader Nehru, of course added, adjusted, reshaped and amended the legacy and made it to suit and uphold the Indian national interests. Yet, we must admit that the British legacy and the relations which India could establish during 1919-46 period did contribute to the origin and initial course of Indian foreign policy.

BASES

We can categorize the bases of Indian foreign policy for the study of convenience as under:

1. Historical Basis;
2. Philosophical Basis;
3. Ideological Basis.

Historical Basis

The history of Indian foreign policy is short but very active. It was after the establishment of Indian National Congress as the political party of Indian people that the politicisation of the people and formulation of policy orientations had its origin. The Indian nationalist leaders showed great interest in world affairs. As early as in 1885, i.e. in its very first session, the Congress deprecated the annexation of upper Burma by the British. In 1892, it objected to the military activity around the natural defence lines of India. The use of India, by Britain as a base for political manoeuvering or military moves against India's neighbours like Tibet, Burma, Afghanistan and Persia was opposed by the Congress. In 1904, it opposed the British involvement in Tibet. As N.V. Raj Kumar has said, "These were the earliest expressions of India's dislike of getting involved in unnecessary foreign entanglements and favouring a neutral stand on matters that did not concern her."

However, it was after the First World War that Indians led by Congress started taking more active and articulated interest in foreign affairs. In 1920, the Congress sent a message of sympathy to the Irish people who were struggling for their independence. It was in 1921 that AICC in its Delhi meeting adopted a complete resolution on foreign policy and affirmed India's desire to establish good neighbourly and friendly relations with neighbouring and other states. It criticised the Government of India for adopting a policy governed by the imperial interests of Britain over and above the interests of India. This was the first significant declaration made by Indian leadership.

In Madras session (in 1927), Congress passed a resolution against the use of Indian troops in China, Mesopotamia and Persia. The Calcutta Congress of 1928 directed the AICC to open a Foreign Department for developing contacts and organising the anti-imperialist movement of the dependent people. Congress also sent greetings to the people of Egypt, Syria, Palestine and Iraq who were struggling against Western Imperialism. Pt. Jawaharlal Nehru came to head this department and became the director of the foreign policy of Congress. It was this experience that made him retain and act with precision and efficiency the role of the architect of Independent India's foreign policy.

In 1930, the Congress came out with a thorough condemnation of the aggressive acts of Nazis and Fascists. It warned against the outbreak of an imperialist war and declared that India would not be a party to this war in 1939. At the Tripura session, the Congress asserted the right of India to have and direct its own foreign policy. It again strongly condemned the forces of Imperialism and Fascism in international politics.

When Second World War broke out and Britain made India a party to war on its side, the Congress strongly attacked the British policy. Later on, it demanded the recognition of right of India to be a full state on the basis of the letter and spirit of the Atlantic Charter.

During 1945-47, the Congress, through a number of declarations spoke out strongly "for the freedom of all countries and for the elimination of all traces of imperialist control by whatever name it may be called." It welcomed the formulation of United Nations but expressed its dissatisfaction with the big power domination of its organisation. In 1946, the Congress voiced concern and apprehensions regarding the consequences of the Atom Bomb and of the continued power struggle among the imperialist powers. It further demanded an end to the foreign domination of Asian and African countries.

These historic declarations of the Congress were instrumental in providing roots to the anti-Cold War, anti-imperialism, anti-racialism, anti-power politics and pro-neutralism, good-neighbourliness and solidarity with Afro-Asian states, principles of Indian foreign policy. The resolutions adopted by the Congress clearly reflected the desires and commitments of the Indian people. The foreign policy of independent India has drawn ideas, principles and strength from these declarations and resolutions of the Congress.

Philosophical Basis

The study of philosophical basis of Indian foreign policy includes an account of such moral ideals and values of Indian society which have influenced its nature and content. Indeed the vast difference in the ideals and values of India from the western values has been responsible, to a significant extent, for the difference that exists between the Indian and the western foreign policies. Whereas power-politics, war and domination have been the western values, India stands for peace, non-violence and peaceful adjustment. India's policy of non-alignment derives strength from these values.

The high importance that we give to the ultimate good of life is different from the 'immediate good life approach' of the western societies. Consequently, love for and faith in world peace and friendship with all are regarded as possible and practical values by India, whereas these are regarded as Utopian values by the West. The five principles enunciated by Buddha are writ large in the five principles of Panchshila. Indian foreign policy of peace and the policy of taking independent decisions on the basis of the merits of the individual cases definitely have their basis in the Indian values of peace, non-violence and truth. We, in India regard non-alignment, anti-imperialism, anti-racialism, and anti-war principles as practical, egalitarian and realistic principle because of our faith in human goodness, equality of all men, universal brotherhood of man, unity in diversity, secularism and spirit of sacrifice, accommodation and tolerance. The land of Gautama, Guru Nanak, Gandhi, Asoka, Akbar has faith in all these values. However, in the West dominated foreign relations system, India has to accommodate western values along with its own values. Here also Kautilya's realism and his *Arthasastra* come to our help. Thus, Indian foreign policy has some of its roots in the Indian philosophy and culture.

Ideological Basis

Like the foreign policy of other nations, Indian foreign policy too has its source of strength in some well established and popular ideologies. In the main it derives strength from Gandhism, liberalism, democratic socialism and internationalism. In these are included the ideologies of secularism, nationalism, anti-imperialism and anti-racialism.

In their struggle for independence Indians were guided by Mahatma Gandhi. His ideals of *ahimsa* (non-violence), *satya* (truth), *satyagrah* (fight for truth), universal brotherhood, unity of man and complete faith in peaceful means guided the people of India in this struggle. After independence, these very ideals of Gandhiji influenced the ideas of the policy-makers of India.

The faith in the principles of world peace, total opposition to apartheid and a firm commitment to peaceful coexistence and peaceful means are some of the major principles of Indian foreign policy. These clearly reflect the influence of Gandhism. The direct approach to peace through such positive devices as mutual respect, mutual socio-economic and cultural cooperation among nations is a valued objective of Indian foreign policy. The preference for Marxism minus violence in economic and political institutions and the desire for a peaceful world order which our policy-makers are trying to secure also bear an influence of Gandhiji. The followers of Gandhism, as Indian policy-makers, could not think otherwise.

Nationalism, as the love and respect for the nation, has been a key characteristic of Indian political thought. It stands for positive attitude of love and sacrifice for the country. It bears no negative or extreme postures. It neither stands for imposition of national interests upon others, nor for Hindu-Nationalism, and nor even for racial superiority complex and expansionism. The principles of non-alignment as "one of the fundamental," rather the most fundamental principle of Indian foreign policy, has its roots in such a view of nationalism. Non-alignment stands for the upkeep of freedom of action for securing India's national interest without involving India into power politics and Cold War. Thus, nationalism is a source of Indian foreign policy.

The political ideals of Indian leaders like Gokhale, Surendra Nath Bannerji and many others were governed by the ideal of liberal Internationalism — the ideology which stands for love and respect for humanity, faith in universal brotherhood, secularism, self-government and opposition to imperialism, colonialism, and use of force and domination.

Indian foreign policy stands for the objective of free and intimate co-operation among the nations. It opposes, tooth and nail, imperialism, colonialism, neo-colonialism, racial discrimination, other unnatural inequalities and war in international relations. The faith in the sovereign equality of states, the right of national self-determination, the right to an independent foreign policy, and a firm commitment to the spirit of the Charter of United Nations is an important and valued feature of Indian foreign policy. All these principles are based upon the ideology of liberal internationalism.

The Constitution of India in its Part IV — Directive Principles, under Article 51, clearly mirrors India's commitment to liberal internationalism. It states as its objectives:

> To promote international peace and security, to maintain just and honourable relations among nations, to foster respect for international law and treaty obligation in the dealings of organised peoples with one another, and to encourage settlement of international disputes by arbitration.

Thus, the ideology of liberal internationalism is also a source of Indian foreign policy.

Indian national leaders were highly influenced by the 1917 Socialist Revolution of Russia and also by the ideology of Marxism upon which this revolution was based. However, along with this they were influenced by the ideas of Fabian Socialists. Their own love and respect for democracy and the values of Indian culture were influenced by these two ideologies; the result came to be in the form of commitment to democratic socialism.

This integration of love for democratic means and socialist goals has been a fundamentally important ideological orientation of the Indian people and their leaders. Their policies, including the foreign policy bear a clear imprint of a faith in democratic socialism. In the realm of foreign policy, this has led to the struggle for securing the rights of the Third World, particularly for securing a new international economic order based upon an equitable distribution of resources and wealth among all nations and fairer economic relations between the developed and the developing countries. The Indian commitment to work for friendly and co-operative relations with both the communist and non-communist countries also shows commitment to both democracy and socialism.

Thus, the ideology of democratic socialism too is a source of Indian foreign policy. Besides these key ideologies, it also stands influenced by the ideologies of peace, United Nations, self-determination, anti-imperialism, anti-racialism and secularism.

NOTE

1. N. Jayapalan (2001). *Foreign Policy of India*, Atlantic Publishers and Distributors Pvt. Ltd., New Delhi, pp. 21-32.

3

India's Foreign Policy—Core Values

India is an old civilisation, but a new state. With freedom, India changed from being an object of world politics to the status of its creator. Thus free India was reasonably imagined to be a maker of world peace and prosperity, if not its prime creator.[1]

Geo-physically, India forms 1/41 portion of the Earth with an area of 3.3 million square kilometers out of Earth's total area of 133.9 million square kilometers. It is a part of the landmass called the continent of Asia.[2] In fact foreign policy is never original, it is determined by a certain order of facts, geographical, historical and economic. "One characteristic of our foreign policy", Jawaharlal Nehru once said, "is that it is not foreign."[3] What he was emphasizing was that India's foreign policy (and for that matter the foreign policy of any country) is rooted in the domestic determinants — history, traditions, culture, geography, economic resources, level of economic development, military strength, political institutions — and of course the international milieu at a given time. The foreign policy aims of the British rule were neither a guide nor relevant to India's needs and status after 1947. Moreover, the partition of the country had created a new set of problems. Therefore, the foreign relations, that India had to forge after independence were essentially to be evolved in a new setting and the process was one of learning by making mistakes or avoiding them.[4]

Prior to the transfer of power, Jawaharlal Nehru, who was already a factor in world politics could organise an Asian Relations Conference in March 1947. In his address he observed: "For too long have we of Asia been petitioners in the Western courts and chancelleries. That story must now belong to the past."[5] He declared that after independence it would be India's task...to chart a new course in world politics for all states which wished to join in breaking with political alignments centering on the established great powers. He had the vision of an independent India playing its rightful role in Asia and the world.

Besides, India's historical experience is too long and too varied and therefore, in the making of India's foreign policy the Indian leaders were deeply influenced by the philosophy and traditions of their ancient civilisation. In this regard the two most influential streams of thought in the country were of great importance — the positivistic philosophical framework of Kautilya and the moralistic philosophy enunciated and practiced by Buddha and Ashoka. Of these two, the latter — the moralistic philosophical tradition — had a deep impact on a whole lot of India's nationalist leaders, including Jawaharlal Nehru, whose role in shaping the country's international behavior was singularly important.[6] However, the foreign policy of a nation is a complex and dynamic political course, which must include the prevailing pattern of its interests as well as principles and ideas in its conduct towards other states. Thus, the task of statesmanship lies in arriving at a balanced integration between idealism and realism as represented by the above two streams of thought.[7] Furthermore, "the central message of India's philosophical tradition, dating from Buddha has revolved around the rejection of absolutes and extreme positions; on the contrary, it has stressed philosophical relativity, intellectual Catholicism and coexistence of good and evil; in short the golden middle path of compromises and tolerance of opposites."[8] This philosophical tradition has yielded "the idea of the independence of the two power blocs in making up her own mind as to the rights and wrongs of a given problem, the use of methods that relax inflexibility and counter-flexibility."[9]

The international environment also influences foreign policy considerably. The pre-Second World War era had a different story. Foreign policy then was largely a matter of military strength and alliances.[10] But India's problem of underdevelopment, poor per capita and poverty situation were the compulsions, which avoided the luxury of defense spending slicing away from funds meant for economic development. As far as political institutions are concerned India adopted the parliamentary form of government of the British type with which the ruling political elites in India were familiar and they were trained in that system too.[11]

The name of Mahatma Gandhi and the method of moral persuasion to gain independence gave the country a special international standing. Furthermore, the independence of India was a watershed in human history for two important reasons. First, it signaled the beginning of the end of colonialism, thus opening the possibility of a democratic world order based on the sovereign equality of all nations. In fact, India is the first of such nations that cast away their shackles of colonial slavery. With the independence of India started the process of decolonisation on a global scale. The implications of this development are far reaching. It brought a new element in the concept of foreign policy of every nation — it could no longer be confined to the exclusive club of monarchs and caucuses. Foreign policy has become a matter of interest and concern for the people, the new nations suddenly emerging into freedom. Diplomacy could no longer be confined to the well-groomed diplomats; it had to take into account the urges and aspirations of the demos — both on a world scale and within every country. It is unthinkable today that a government — even if it is not democratic — can follow a foreign policy without taking into consideration the mood and outlook of the people in a country, because the common people provide the ultimate sanction for any foreign policy. On a global scale, too, the arrival of this element could be felt with the emergence of what is called the Third World, which commands overwhelming majority in the United Nations.[12]

The second major development was India's articulation of an alternative world order to the one being fashioned by the rival power blocs. This alternative world order found expression in the philosophy of Non-alignment. It means, India would no longer be the camp follower of any power. It would decide its foreign policy on the basis of its own understanding of India's national interest. In other words, the transfer of power from the British to Indian hands meant clearly that this country would no longer be guided by the foreign policy of Britain.

In this politico-military-economic, historical, geographical, cultural and international environment, elements of independent India's foreign policy were evolved. These elements are: pursuit of non-alignment, maintenance of world peace, pacific settlement of disputes, peaceful coexistence of nations of diverse social/political/economic systems (especially cooperative relations with immediate neighbors); opposition to the remnants of colonialism (since largely vanished) and neo-colonialism; anti-Apartheid; promotion of both its own economic development (and that of other Third World countries); development of an 'Asian-identity' and intra-Asian co-operation; working for disarmament; and support to, strengthening of, international organisations — the United Nations in particular. These elements reflected not merely "official policy"; they represented the foreign policy of the people of India as such.[13]

Indeed, these are the elements, which constitute the 'core values' of India's foreign policy.

There are very few countries in the world, which have displayed such a degree of consistency, coherence and tenacious loyalty to the elements (ideals) underlying their respective foreign policies, as India has done. There has not been a single major instance when India has deviated from the core values of her foreign policy.[14]

India commanded admiration when it defied the Cold War hypothesis. India's respect was at its highest when it fearlessly followed non-aligned principles and played a sagacious role during and after the Korean War (1951-53), during the crisis over Suez (1956). Although, it was the ability of Jawaharlal Nehru, to keep the Indian image at center stage when world crisis emerged, that enabled this sub-continent to play such a significant role. India was looked upon as the leader of the developing continents in Bandung (1955) and Belgrade (1961) and was obvious choice for the biggest UN peacekeeping operations in Congo (1960).

As a visionary Nehru looked into the post-War environment with full involvement. He understood that the problems of the underdeveloped countries could not be solved on a regional basis. "Nor could they be solved only by the pushing back of imperialism. Their solution required that the paramount question of global confrontation be tackled. He also understood that with the power distribution in the world, the two blocs could only engage in mutual destruction and this, in turn, would mean the destruction of the entire human race."[15] The lack of communication between the two sides of the Cold War at its inception provided India with an opportunity to provide good offices in conflict and crisis situations. In fact, Nehru advocated non-aligned technique to tackle Cold War situations. His techniques included dialogue, discussion, negotiation, compromise and respect for other's point of view. Peacekeeping took India to Congo, Cyprus and the Middle East. Thus, two of the most striking aspects of the Nehru era were the high visibility of India in UN efforts to intervene in international disputes (*viz.* Korea, Suez, Congo and so on) and the complete dominance of Pt. Nehru himself in the formulation of foreign policy, at least up to 1962.[16]

"If Mahatma Gandhi stood for the self-respect of individuals, Pt. Nehru asserted the self-respect of people."[17] Though India was economically and industrially backward and could be rated as middle power throughout 1950, yet it could be pushed to the front rank of nations because it could exhibit self-respect and rational and constructive attitude in international politics. The Gandhian message that India should have certain mission in the world prompted the Indian administration to avoid entanglement in the conflicts of big powers and at the same time play a major role in world affairs. As an outcome of the dual urge the policy of Non-alignment was given high priority in foreign policy formulations. Thus India played a serious global role in the fifties.[18]

Despite, Nehru era was not above criticism. "The constant desire to adhere to general principles without realizing the difficulty of applying them to practical situations, was indeed a general weakness running through the entire gamut of India's policy under Nehru."[19] India refused to accept military assistance, which was available from both the groups. The Indian leadership thought that by accepting the assistance the policy of Non-alignment adopted by India would be questioned. Even Marshal Tito and Col. Nasser, the other champions of Non-alignment could make their countries militarily strong by receiving external military aid. Had India been militarily strong China would not have dared a military action in 1962. In the same vein when India appealed for military help in 1962 it became a laughing stock. Again the principles of 'panchsheel' covered the Chinese deeds in Tibet. Too much of adherence to the principles was not good. It prevented the Indian leadership to assess Chinese mood and ambitions. Further, the Goan episode damaged the reputation of India. Since Prime Minister Nehru had always given importance to peaceful settlement of disputes without taking resort to forcible means. Thus, when force was used, the whole world was practically shocked and condemned India.[20]

The Sino-Indian war damaged India's reputation, true, but it could preserve and protect the non-aligned image of India. Failure of Non-alignment in India would have invited death to a cause, a mission and a technique.[21] Idealism without the kernel of self-interest may sound hypocritical and hollow. The foreign policy of a nation is a complex and dynamic political course, which must include the prevailing pattern of its interests as well as principles and ideas in its conduct towards other states. Thus, the task of statesmanship lies in arriving at a balanced integration between idealism and realism. After 1962 India's global role began to recede. The post-Nehru years witnessed injection of greater realism in India's foreign policy. Indira's Gandhi used Non-alignment as an instrument in a manner, which reflected her positivistic thinking. During her stewardship of the nation, she made the policy more purposeful and dynamic. Her realisation was that India was on the threshold of becoming a great world power and had to survive and play its due role in making the globe safe for humanity to survive and struggle in. It was the pursuit of this goal that brought her into conflict with the US and to a friendship and co-operation treaty with the Soviet Union. She linked the march of our country to its great world power status with world peace and development.[22] Two important developments, one, the help to the liberation of

Bangladesh (1971) and the other one is peaceful nuclear explosion (1974), exhibit legendary courage of Indira Gandhi and it was the courage to use power, when the nation needed it. These developments enhanced the regional image of India. At the same time, the fact of regional dominance gave India a global status and prestige.

In 1976, the US Agency for International Aid organised a seminar on the re-examination of the US policy towards India. Participants were of the view that:[23]

"India has made substantial, perhaps even extraordinary progress. India left its colonial era poorly equipped to preserve its national integrity and freedom of action in a difficult and hostile world environment. Since then India has built a domestic base of political, economic, technological and trade capabilities consistent with a large and growing international role. The first 30 years of independence saw India laid the foundation for its goal of growth to major power status. The second 30 are likely to see that aspiration realised." The participants spoke highly of the development of science and technology in India and of the fact that India now had the third largest pool of scientific and technologically trained manpower.[24]

However, in concise, the policy pursued by India in her external affairs has injected a moral tone in world politics. Nehru, Shastri and Indira Gandhi firmly believe that, however, deep the crisis and however obstinate the opponent, the doors of negotiation, peaceful parleys and conciliatory approach should never be closed. In this respect India herself set an example, with regards to Pakistan, in spite of her bellicosity, aggression and terrorist activities, India never broke diplomatic relations with Pakistan, but continued talks with her in a spirit of accommodation. On both the occasions in 1965 and again in 1971, Pakistan received the conquered territory back. In 1972, India even returned 5000 square miles of territory in Sind to Pakistan. In 1965 conflict, India restrained its victorious march to Lahore, so as to spare Pakistan a further humiliation. In her hour of victory, India displayed generosity with a view to laying down the groundwork of conciliation. Pt. Nehru in 1948 was conciliatory to Pakistan and Shastri readily agreed to

Tashkent Agreement; Indira Gandhi displayed statesmanship and spirit of generosity in 1972 and concluded the Simla Agreement. The same may be said about China when both countries were engaged in hostilities in October-November 1962. Since 1972 the process of normalisation between China and India has gained momentum.

Among the elements of India's foreign policy, the Non-alignment is the one, which encompasses all the other elements of foreign policy. It is the struggle for the removal of poverty, illiteracy, health and nutrition problems of the neglected millions, for which Non-alignment is striving. It is a humanitarian approach which is much more acceptable than cut-throat competition policy approach. This campaign should continue. The issues of the New Economic Order, an equitable relationship between the needs for environment and development, a comprehensive understanding of the place of human rights in vulnerable societies, terrorism, etc. call for the articulation of our positions in forceful language. Here Mikhail Gorbachev's sound suggestion that the chairman of NAM must always be a member of the Security Council by virtue of his position is quite valuable and NAM ought to insist that its chairman must be on par with the delegates of the other five permanent members.[25]

Thus, never before in history, the thrust of foreign policy is felt in all fields of human affairs. "Men learn slowly" wrote Donald G. Bishop, "but one lesson that they should have learned in the 20th Century is that foreign affairs are infinitely the most important branch of politics."[26]

PURSUIT OF NON-ALIGNMENT

The polarised post-War politics of the Cold Warriors had no attraction for the newly emergent nations. The ideological strife and the struggle for hegemony were alarming for them. It was opulence for the powerful nations. The free but militarily weak nations viewed the expensive power game as anti-peace and destruction-oriented. The strong nations also tried to carve out the political support of the newly independent nations of Asia and Africa by persuasion, cajolery, threat and temptation. "Thus, the most remarkable feature of international politics when these new nations were toddling into world scene was the crystallisation of the Cold War into polarised struggle for power between two blocs."[27] The international environment provided difficult choices for the new nations, which were emotionally charged with their concern for economic development. They were interested to pursue foreign policies, which would ensure international peace and internal development. Their economic development was dependent upon foreign assistance. Therefore, in this type of international environment, the rational choice paved way for the policy of non-alignment.[28]

Specific Meaning of Non-alignment

"Non-alignment is the courage of true independence," said Indira Gandhi, in the Colombo Non-aligned Summit Conference (1976), "it was the only practical policy for the preservation of newly won independence of many countries. To us, choice between one military bloc and another seemed irrelevant and unreal. Our choice was between independence and dependence, between progressing through co-operation and perishing through confrontations."[29] Thus for India, non-alignment not only meant maintenance of independence, sovereignty and equality in foreign policy and relations; it also meant certain specifics: opposition to division of the international community into blocs/groups of any kind — political, economic or ideological; opposition to Great Power hegemony and the Cold War between and among them and their allies; freedom of foreign policy and relations, consistent with the increasing interdependence among nations; refusal to accept the stationing of foreign military forces or bases or facilities on one's territory, since they impinge on one's freedom of policy/action; and peaceful coexistence of nations of different political, economic and social systems. In general, non-alignment meant avoiding any dependence on other nations for large-scale economic and or military assistance, except on the basis of capability and mutual interest.[30] Moreover, 'non-alignment' has generally been used in two distinct though related senses. In its first sense it is a world view or ideology concerning how the global state system should function. It purports to describe a broad movement, the Third World Non-Aligned Movement (NAM), which initially sought to play the role of an international buffer between the two Cold War blocs. Non-alignment as a normative principle undoubtedly had a certain moral cast. It was supposed to represent an alternative to 'balance of power' and 'alliance' politics.[31] In its second and more important sense, It is a description of the specific foreign policy orientation of a particular non-aligned country. As such, it becomes a loose synonym for the traditional policy of effective pursuit of national interest through the expansion of national power.'[32]

When India became independent, Jawaharlal Nehru declared, that since India coveted nobody's territory nor had claims against any foreign land, India would remain aloof from all the conflicts and wars that arose only from such claims. This was a doctrine, which happened also to suit a rather underdeveloped and ill-armed country, which though vast in size was yet to emerge as a state with material resources and armed forces of any significance.[33] However, although India pioneered the policy, it was not done solely to serve India's interests. It was, from the beginning, conceived as also serving the interests of world peace. That would explain why the policy was opted for by many other nations also. In connection, Prime Minister Morarji Desai remarked: "It is recognised by other commonwealth nations, that the policy of non-alignment, as enunciated, and practiced by India not only serves our interests, but makes India a coveted partner in their own network of relationships and their views of a stable world order."[34]

Characteristic Features of Non-alignment

The basic characteristics of non-alignment, as evolved by India, though not codified into a charter, which are openly practiced in inter-state relations and approach to international issues[35] are summarized below:

1. Non-alignment stands for a plurality and democratic equality within international community. It affirms faith in self-determination and total end of colonialism. It opposes all forms of pressures and outside interventions in the internal policies of a nation. It stands for international co-operation and functional relationship in an interdependence world.
2. It opposes all forms of racialism and discriminations and champions the cause of fundamental human

freedoms. Economic and social justice is the motto of Non-alignment.

3. "Non-alignment through its ideological agnosticism in determining international relationships stood for the freedom of nations to determine their own internal socio-political philosophies. It upheld the validity of differing and opposing socio-economic concepts and opposed the imposition of an external ideology. In effect it argued that a nation must have the right to evolve from its own civilisational roots and economic circumstances."[36]
4. Non-alignment rests on the presumption that the national security is linked with national strength. It negates the validity of military power in ensuring internal legitimacy; even less is it prudent to surrender to outside protection.
5. Lastly one of the major characteristics of non-alignment is that it asserts, that international peace is an inalienable prerequisite for accomplishing national aspirations and the exercise of sovereign independence. It therefore pleads for peaceful coexistence and avoidance of confrontation that will lead to international strife. In the face of weapons of mass destruction and the potentialities of nuclear war, it pleads for the peaceful resolution of international disputes.[37]

India pushed the non-aligned concept into an international doctrine in the Bandung Conference in 1955 and had stuck to these basic postulates since her independence.

Policy of Non-alignment — Origin

However, this is nothing new. The United States and Britain followed such a policy for long and then only they could manage the heavy task of nation building and overhauling of their economy. Until these complex tasks were accomplished, USA kept herself in complete isolation from the rest of the world. Thus it was non-alignment with neutrality or isolationist policy.[38] It is only after, that they managed to become a completely developed nation; they followed the policy of engagement in world affairs.

In India this policy is not merely a creation of Jawaharlal Nehru, but "it flows from our historical as well as our recent past." As Jawaharlal Nehru, in his unique style and imbued with humility, once said, "I have not originated the policy of Non-alignment. It is a policy inherent in the circumstances of India, inherent in the past thinking of India, inherent in the whole mental outlook of India, inherent in the conditions of the Indian mind during our struggle for freedom and inherent in the circumstances of the world today. I came in by the mere accidental fact that during the few years I have represented that policy as Foreign Minister, I am quite convinced that whoever might have been in charge of the foreign affairs of India and whatever party might have been in power in India, they could not have deviated very much from this policy. Some emphasis might have been greater here or there because, as I said, it represents every circumstance that goes towards making the thought of India on these subjects."[39] "Indeed, Indian spokespersons were in the habit of emphasizing the indigenous roots of the policy,[40] while the beginnings of Non-Alignment can be traced to Afro-Asian resurgence — a reaction against European colonial system (1919-1945) and even prior to that in the struggle of small and weak states against the hegemony of great European powers since the birth of the sovereign nation system in the middle of the seventeenth century Europe. These oppressed, suppressed and dominated states struggled hard for freedom from colonialism, imperialism and great power domination to choose their own path in internal development and external policies.[41] Their common commitment to world peace, justice, security and co-operation, to the elimination of imperialism, colonialism and neocolonialism, to the eradication of apartheid, racism and all forms of foreign domination, aggression, intervention, occupation and pressures, to the acceleration of the process of self-determination of peoples under colonial and alien domination and the consolidation of the national independence, sovereignty and territorial integrity of states and to the social and economic development of their peoples constitute an irreversible factor in world history.[42] The

Non-alignment with its emphasis on independent judgment, independent decision-making and independent action provided them a suitable foreign policy alternative. Again the Cold War as a dominant theme of post-World War II international politics certainly influenced and shaped the emergence of Non-alignment, but it was by no means the cause of that emergence, because it was just a coincidence that when these countries began to gain independence (in 1940s) they found themselves in a bipolar world.[43]

Non-alignment — A Need

However, the policy of Non-alignment does not imply pacifism or isolationism. Jawaharlal Nehru, summing up his attitude in *The Discovery of India* said, "It is surprising how internationally minded we grew in spite of our intense nationalism. The policy of Non-alignment was not isolationism, but rather a condemnation of the powerful countries and their policies of imperialism and wars."[44] Besides, the Herculean task of building up a country of 360 millions, as India then was, with its legacy of poverty and the worldwide nature of war, could not allow India to follow U.S. line non-alignment with the policy of isolation.[45] India was comparatively backward and economically weak country at that time. She had yet to stabilise her economy. Its agriculture and industries were in the early stages of development. Thus India was in urgent need of foreign aid in building up her economy. She has to build up her strength in peace and under the condition of Non-alignment. The basic rationale of Non-alignment was that a climate of peace was necessary to optimise development, which was desperately urgent after centuries of foreign rule and retarded progress. Therefore, India followed Non-alignment with the policy of co-operation and has established diplomatic relations with almost all the independent states[46] and welcomed aid from all quarters — USSR, UK, USA, Germany and Japan. India commanded respect in the West for embarking on a massive social and economic transformation through the democratic political system. As a consequence, for almost three decades, in spite of its 'irritating' non-aligned positions, India was the biggest recipient of economic aid from the West.[47]

Furthermore, India's policy of Non-alignment rests on "Panchsheel", which is a set of five principles. Since a guarantee, says that a war, except in your country, has no meaning today when war is worldwide, therefore the guarantee must be to avoid war and going a step further to avoid interference with any country.[48] Sukarno, addressing the Investigating Committee for Preparation of Independence on 1 June 1945, referred to the five rites of Islam, five fingers and the five Pandavas. The five principles of international conduct were first included in the preamble of Sino-Indian Agreement on Tibet on 29 April 1954.[49] These are: mutual respect for each other's territorial integrity and sovereignty; non-aggression; non-interference in each other's internal affairs; equality and mutual benefit; and peaceful coexistence. Jawaharlal Nehru introduced the term "Panchsheel" into the domain of international relations on 23rd of September 1954 at a banquet given in honor of the Prime Minister of Indonesia. The Bandung Conference held in April 1955 and attended by countries of Asia and Africa, further elaborated and reinforced these principles.

Crisis Situation and India's Non-alignment

In a conflict situation during the Cold War era,[50] the peaceful negotiation of a non-aligned nation had some meaning. The nation conducted negotiation free from pressure. The diplomatic technique adopted by India in crisis situations provided ample testimony to that effect. Through peaceful negotiation a desirable solution might not be arrived at. But Non-alignment helped to establish an attitude and approach that made those solutions possible. "It is not our intention to be a part of...a third bloc, or to tell the world how to establish peace," asserted a leader of the Indian delegation to the General Assembly: "In our circumstances, in light of our history and in the great traditions of the man who made our national independence possible, we think it is always necessary to talk to one's opponent and to seek the basis of reconciliation and negotiation becomes necessary."[51]

Korean Crisis

The Korean crisis was a legacy of the Second World War and its post-war military occupation. The military understanding developed at the Potsdam Conference decided the future of Korea, which was previously under Japanese occupation. Japan surrendered. Korea was divided at the 38th parallel. The artificial division of the country and the military occupation of both the parts by the then superpowers, who had already entered into a phase of Cold War in the Eastern Europe, gave birth to several problems. The US-USSR rift forced the Americans to place the matter for discussion in the UN Agenda. On 14 November 1947 the General Assembly passed a resolution, which recognised the right to independence of the Koreans. It further established a UN Commission for Korea (UNCOK) for facilitating a program for that country having a national government and withdrawal of all occupying forces. The Soviets reacted sharply to the resolution and called that illegal. It refused to accept the UN proposals. Ultimately, the war in Korea broke out on 25 June 1950. The North Korean forces crossed the 38th parallel. This action of the North Korea led to a serious apprehension that the tension might lead to superpower confrontation in the Far East.[52] Korea was treated by the USA as a test case for the so-called domino theory, that if the UN/USA allowed the USSR/China to overcome Korea, this would lead to other countries like Vietnam to fall into Communist hands.[53] The North Korean attack upon the South Korea was under the active Soviet support, which was trying to test the firmness of the American policy of containment.

From the beginning of the conflict the Indian position was quite distinct from that of two superpowers. The sole objective of the Indian policy on the other hand was to help maintain world peace and reduce international tensions. As per the Indian action it recognized neither North nor South Korea as the aggressor and asking it to withdraw behind the 38th parallel and to cease hostilities.

The Truman Administration had enough faith in the institution of the United Nations as an instrument of international action during the war in Korea. India had and experience of the United Nations which was able to arrange a ceasefire between India and Pakistan over Kashmir in 1948-49, but was not successful in enforcing the vacation of the Pak-occupied areas of Jammu and Kashmir State as a preliminary to holding a plebiscite. Therefore, when President Truman appealed to the United

Nations to organise an international force under the UN flag to oppose the invasion, India did not offer to send any troops, but instead sent a Red Cross contingent to work among the UN forces in South Korea.[54] The diplomatic action thus taken was to keep the options open. India was interested to get out of the situation once large-scale conflict got in. "India from the beginning wanted to localize the conflict and that in case of its spread she wanted to be out of it."[55]

Thus, despite India's public condemnation of the aggression by North Korea, it stood outside the US camp. Because of this attitude and action it was also accessible to the other bloc. "A major declaration of its aloofness form the western position regarding the conflict came by way of its withdrawal from the sponsorship of the Eight Power Resolution of the General Assembly which established the UN Commission for the Unification and Rehabilitation advocating unification by force, if necessary."[56] The Indian decision to abstain from voting was based upon reason. It had all faith in the UN. In the Korean crisis how could UN take resort to force to unify the two Koreas and that too the action supposed to be taken against North Korea, which had crossed the 38th parallel with the intention of unifying both the Koreas, further the UN action might invite PRC to intervene. This would have resulted in the extension of the conflict in the region. India was careful not to pre-empt the UN forces from crossing the parallel until all other possibilities had been exhausted.

The Indian apprehension came true. The crossing of the 38th parallel by the UN Forces immediately provoked the armed action by PRC. The Chinese forces crossed the Yale River from Manchuria to aid North Korean forces and the war in Korea developed into a serious conflict between China and the USA. Attlee, the Prime Minister of UK came to USA to advise Truman that instead of relying on the domino theory, the USA should negotiate with China on the assumption that China would behave like Yugoslavia and might be weaned off the alliance with the USSR. This advice was not heeded.[57]

India advocated peaceful negotiation to diffuse the tension. It tried its best to arrange for a ceasefire without publicly denouncing the Chinese action. It piloted a draft resolution along with twelve Asian nations for the constitution of a ceasefire group and presented the proposal to the UN First Committee. It also appealed to both China and North Korea to declare that they had no intention to cross the 38th parallel. The appeal was rejected by China and the Soviet Union. The draft resolution piloted by India was presented to the First Committee of the General Assembly on 11 January 1951 and was accepted on 13 January 1951 with overwhelming support. The proposal had five principles[58] enclosed to settle the crisis. The PRC rejected these principles. The Chinese action was treated as a total defiance of the UN by the USA. The situation was further aggravated by a UN resolution on 1 February 1951 branding China an aggressor. India, Burma and the Communist bloc strongly opposed the resolution. The American action for a military settlement was resented in the Western world. An opinion was created that it was undesirable to defeat China. This resulted in the historic decision taken by President Truman in dismissing Gen. Mac Arthur, the Commander of the UN Forces from his post. Both USA and USSR then agreed for a ceasefire negotiation, which commenced from July 1951.[59]

India's role in the war in Korea was her first assay in international affairs. But China and the USA used the Indian Ambassador in Beijing for negotiations and passing on messages and warnings to each other since they had no other mutually acceptable contact. An Indian proposal regarding the repatriation of the Prisoners of War (POWs) was accepted. The Armistice Agreement was signed on 27 July 1953. India was made a member-chairman and executive agent of the Neutral Nations Repatriation Commission (NNRC) consisting of India, Czechoslovakia, Poland, and Sweden as members and Switzerland as Chairman. Despite several bottlenecks and controversial developments General Thimayya, of India, did a marvelous job and finally succeeded to persuade both the groups to accept the procedure for repatriation. The prisoners were given the right to exercise their choice whether they wished to be repatriated to the Communists or stay in South Korea. India won all-round praise for carrying out this difficult task with impartiality.[60]

Thus, during the Korean crisis it was evident that India pursued a neutralist track, but it was positive and not elusive in character. It never gave support to just one side and opposed the other side forever. India followed an independent policy that was, by and large, independent of the decisions of the other powers. Jawaharlal Nehru always insisted on taking 'decisions on merits'. India always gave importance to the solution. Mahatma Gandhi told that in order to arrive at good end you must adopt good means. The Indian diplomacy in the Korean crisis just reflected the Gandhian way of settlement of disputes.

Moreover, in 1954, France arranged a nine-power conference in Geneva to deal with the question of the successors of France in Vietnam and to arrange the modus vivendi between North Vietnam held by Ho Chi Minh and South Vietnam. Krishna Menon played an active role at the Conference as a "tenth power".

Suez Crisis

In the Suez crisis, India played both visible and invisible role. The 101-mile long Suez Canal extends from Port Said to Port Suez. On 30th November 1854, the then Khedive (Viceroy) of Egypt gave a concession to a Frenchman Ferdinand de Lesseps to establish an international company under the name Universal Company of the Maritime Canal of Suez to build a canal. It was leased out for 99 years and after the completion of the leasing period the canal was to be handed over to Egypt. The construction of the canal started in April 1859 and the completion of the work took nearly ten years. The canal was opened to traffic in November 1869. The canal was within the Egyptian territory, but it was an international waterway, built and owned by an international company.[61]

Prior to that, due to financial crisis the Khedive had sold the shares of the Suez Company to Britain in 1875. That brought in the British to begin its dominance in the region. In 1882, Britain temporarily occupied Egypt in order to ensure 'stability and peace' in the region and to protect her share in the Company. The temporary occupation developed the tendencies of taking a permanent character and continued up to 1922 when Egypt was granted independence. Despite this new development the British forces stationed there continued. In 1936, Britain imposed a Treaty upon Egypt by which Egypt gave the British people the right to defend the Suez Canal. The Treaty came to an end in 1951 by the unilateral abrogation by Egypt. The abrogation of the Anglo-Egyptian Treaty followed great changes in Egypt leading to the military supremacy.[62] Britain agreed to withdraw its forces by 1956. The British withdrawal process was initiated. But meanwhile a Baghdad Pact was signed which brought the Anglo-American forces nearer to the Egyptian soil. Israel was already an enemy of the Arabs. To counter the military developments, General Gamal Abdel Nasser, the then Army Chief of Egypt, made an arms deal with Czechoslovakia and Russia. In July 1956, USA abruptly broke off negotiations with Egypt, which was expecting big finance from USA for its ambitious project—the Aswan Dam that was second largest in the world. Nasser countered by expropriating the shares of the Suez Canal Company and asserting Egypt's sovereign right to operate the canal itself. The objective was also to raise additional sources of revenue to finance the dam. However, the main purpose of the nationalisation was indeed to find money for the dam. Nonetheless, it did affect the power equations in the area and the world.[63]

The US Administration's withdrawal of economic aid from Egypt had caused the nationalisation. Egypt also refused to take part in the US inspired alliance system in the region (Middle East Defense Organisation). Of the Western powers Britain and France, who were also members of NATO, were visibly upset by the steps taken by Gen. Nasser. Both of them were controlling parties of the erstwhile Suez Canal Company. The Suez crisis was thus initiated which experienced the superpower involvement and UN intervention.[64] India played a crucial role. Its participation was active and extensive. Britain and France were the allies of USA. Naturally, the US reaction could not be as sharp as non-aligned India's.

Israel attacked Egypt on 29 October 1956. The inevitable happened when Franco-British forces launched a military attack on Egypt. Along with India the two superpowers denounced the Franco-British military action on Egypt.

Factors Behind India's Stand

Indian stand in the Suez crisis was dictated by its following attitudes and interests:

(a) India was against colonialism. Jawaharlal Nehru denounced the attack as a "flagrant case of aggression by two strong powers against a weaker country."[65]

(b) India was determined to support a neutral country in its attempt to make the nearby region of its own country a Cold War free zone.

(c) It was also interested in supporting progressive Arab nationalism as practiced by Egypt as a means of minimizing the danger of unqualified Muslim support for Pakistan and an anti-Indian course.[66]

(d) The most important single factor attributable to India's stand with regard to Suez was "the inclusion of Pakistan in the Baghdad Pact, which aroused the fear that the Cold War had been brought close to her door."[67]

(e) In the words of V.K. Krishna Menon, the then Minister without Portfolio: "India was concerned in the Suez Canal as a lifeline in her economy...76 per cent of her exports pass through the Canal. The fulfillment of India's Five-Year Plans depended upon traffic through it. India did not approach the problem in a legalistic way but with a full sense of the reality of the importance of the canal for many countries of the world who used it."[68]

The Security Council could not take any positive step due to Anglo-French veto. Both the superpowers demanded immediate cessation of hostilities. Yugoslavia suggested convening of the General Assembly under 'Uniting for Peace Resolution'. The Assembly met on November 1956. The British Premier Anthony Eden charged India for its clandestine role to present the proposal through Yugoslavia. "India and Canada, both suspicious of the motives of the two superpowers and fearful that simple ceasefire may not be enough, proposed, that there be an International Emergency Force, under the UN, to be constituted of the willing contribution of small powers only."[69] It was at that point that

India came to play a role in the UN for the first time with regard to the issue. A ten-member (including India) International Force was formed on the basis of resolution adopted on 5th November 1956. On November 6 Britain declared that it would be willing to order a ceasefire from the midnight. But it was a victory for Arab nationalism as the proposal put an end to Anglo-French imperialism—colonialism.

In essence, the Indian stand was a novel kind of neutralism. It never helped either of the parties, but could put a check on both. It checked the growth of colonialism. Further, it encouraged the Afro-Asian nations to pursue neutralism. India also secured the support of a Muslim State in its future conflicts with Pakistan. Egypt also joined the Indian mission for the Non-alignment cause. Sarbadhikari observed: "India's stand during the crisis therefore measured up with the principles guiding her foreign policy in that area. Her efforts towards the withdrawal of foreign troops stemmed both from her anti-colonial policy and the fear that the intervention of the Great Powers, which was in the logic of events, would spark off a major war. The impact of the crisis in strengthening the non-aligned policies of some Arab governments such as Egypt and paving the way for others to follow suit such as Iraq, was a success for India's rationale, that neutralism was the most logical policy for the developing slates. Moreover, the support of a secular India for a Muslim State on the basis of colonial intrusion was an acute embarrassment for Pakistan, wedded as she was to Western alignments; it revealed that diplomacy on the basis of religion was unsuited to modern relations of States."[70]

Hungarian Crisis

At this very time, the Hungarian crisis also emerged. The revolution in Hungary was against the Soviet occupation by stationing Russian troops in that country. The revolution occurred about the same time as the nationalisation of the Suez Canal. The revolt was fierce and the measures taken by the USSR were ruthless. Pt. Nehru had been outspoken about the Suez Canal issue, but kept his own counsels in regard to the events in Hungary. This was taken note of by the liberal elements both in India and abroad, who felt that Nehru had shown discretion to be the better part of valour where Russia was concerned. The silence of Pt. Nehru was also adversely commented upon by the Western powers that pointed out that the liberation movement in Hungary was a test for those who stood for liberty and freedom and India had failed in that test. Nehru had spoken out in favor of Egypt against the USA, but not for Hungary against the USSR.[71]

Congo Crisis

In the Congo Crisis, India's position was anti-colonialist. The second part of the 20th century experienced awakening in Africa. Africa was the unfortunate scene and example of the arrogance of the Western countries. Exploitation in Africa knew no limits. Colonial powers adopted the policy of racial discrimination (apartheid). It was observed through physical and cultural segregation of the Black community. Congo, situated in tropical Africa was under the Belgian control for decades. Belgium ruled over Congo in a paternalistic-colonial way and had not cared much for the welfare and real interests of the people of that country. Rather it was busy to exploit the land commercially, which had rich mineral resources. Meanwhile, the two developments stirred nationalistic sentiments in Belgian Congo (Leopoldville): One, the neighboring French-occupied Congo (Brazaville) attained independence and the other that an All African People's Conference was held in Accra which urged for the end of colonial system.[72] In the Round Table Conference between Belgian government and the Congolese leaders between January to March 1960 the demand for immediate freedom was accepted and 30th June 1960 was fixed for the commencement of Congolese sovereignty.

Joseph Kasavubu and Patrice Lumumba assumed offices as the President and Prime Minister of Central Republic of Congo respectively. But within hours after independence, a wave of unrest began sweeping across the country. There was another competitor for power, Moise Tashombe who was the Premier of the Province of Katanga. The region was rich in minerals. Without Katanga's financial support Congo could not think of progress. But on 11th July 1960 Katanga announced its secession from Congo and formed a new state allied with Belgium.[73] Prior to that P.M. Lumumba had asked the Belgians to vacate Congo. On July 12, 1960 the Belgian troops from Katanga, had already marched into Leopoldville. The situation became chaotic. "Faced with that kind of circumstances Lumumba looked for assistance from President Eisenhower, Premier Khrushchev, as well as to Beijing and on 12th July sent urgent appeal to the UN Secretary-General for the UN assistance in maintaining the national integrity of his country against the aggression being hatched by foreign interests."[74] The Secretary-General Dag Hammarskjoeld took the matter immediately to the Security Council. The Secretary-General threw the resources of the UN into his effort to save Congo from becoming an East-West battleground.

The Congolese crisis took a new turn when President Kasabuvu dismissed Premier Lumumba and the latter did the same to the former. Seeing an opportunity, pro-Western Colonel Joseph Mobutu took command of the armed forces through a coup, thus making it possible for the Belgians to return to Congo as unofficial advisers. Both the superpowers reacted sharply. As expected, the USA supported Kasabuvu-Mobutu faction for their claim to have legitimate government and the Soviets gave moral and material support to Lumumba. Both the superpowers remained adamant on their stand. "This helplessness was mitigated to a degree by the action in the emergency session that followed it, of an overwhelming majority including India, which supported the US position; and therefore the Secretary-General's position...."[75]

An irritated Khrushchev presented his Troika Proposal, which would have three-man committee replacing one Secretary-General who shall be representing three worlds (both the superpowers and Third World) India opposed the Troika proposal, but suggested for the reform of the Secretariat by having an advisory Committee from different geographical areas. In December, India along with seven non-aligned nations asked for immediate convening of the Congolese Parliament. In a debate on this resolution Indian representative Krishna Menon emphatically observed that, "his government considered the Kasabuvu regime as unvarnished, unashamed and unconstitutional dictatorship."[76]

The death of Patrice Lumumba in a mysterious situation shocked the conscience of the world. The Soviet Union demanded that Gizenga, who was Lumumba's deputy, be the head of the lawful Congolese government. But later on, the Soviet Union had to change its stand and it supported the UN decisions. For this Pt. Nehru played a significant role.[77] India took leadership with Afro-Asian members passing a resolution calling upon Belgium to accept its responsibility as a member of the UN and the proposal demanded the withdrawal of all military and non-military personnel from Congo. That led to a UN resolution rejecting Katanga's claim as a sovereign nation and authorised the Secretary-General to take all possible steps to make the area free from foreign action.[78]

In the Congolese crisis, apart from the support or opposition to proposals in the UN, India had a share of 5600 strong force in a 30-nation pool of 20,000 forces. It also contributed $ 105,000 to UN Fund for Congo. Rajeshwar Dayal, an Indian diplomat, served as Secretary-General's personal representative in Congo. He was instrumental in bringing the UN to a stage for strong action through his reports. India's military contribution was politically important for the UN.[79]

As per the views of a researcher, the Secretary-General who was accused as the agent of the Western colonialism could function strongly because he received the support of the neutral powers and India was one of the prominent supporters.[80] Another observer said that the successful conclusion of the UN operation in Congo-depended to a large extent on two powers — India and USA.[81] "In a real sense India and the USA were two countries the UN operation most depended upon, both for political support in New York and for military in Congo. Despite some differences in interpreting the mandate, the US-India partnership remained solid throughout the Congo drama. The Congo operation would probably have collapsed if either New Delhi or Washington had withdrawn its support before the integration of Katanga."[82]

Crisis in Goa

Immediately before the third general election in India (1961), the Indian forces entered Goa, drove out the colonial Portuguese regime and incorporated Goa, Daman and Diu into the Indian Union. Since Portugal and South Africa were the only powers to display obstinacy and intransigence, the Portuguese imperialism refused to retreat from Goa. At first India fought the costly litigation in the International Court of Justice at The Hague for six years from 1955 to 1960. When Portugal refused to abide by the advice of the World Court, India resorted to police action in 1961 under the effective guidance of Krishna Menon.[83] The forcible liberation of Goa was perfectly justified as the final step in eliminating colonial rule in India, but it further eroded the moral credibility of India and Prime Minister Nehru as apostle of non-violence.[84]

Border War with China

India's China policy popularly known as *Hindi-Chini Bhai-Bhai* folly was not successful. In 1962, there was a thirty-one day border war with China in which India suffered a humiliating defeat. Its forces had to withdraw in the north-east. In the north, China managed to advance still further beyond Aksai Chin region, which it had occupied earlier. The Indian authorities sought aid from the USA and the UK. At this moment the Chinese withdrew in the north-east beyond the McMahon line and announced a ceasefire unilaterally. Indian Non-alignment had been exposed as a non-workable basis for international relations.[85] Nevertheless, China's humiliation of the Indian armed forces in the border war, did not cause India to abandon Non-alignment, though it forced it to seek active support form the west (particularly the USA), to give up the wider global pretensions of the Nehru era and to pay much more attention to developing its own military powers.[86] Henceforth, strengthening Indian Non-alignment would mean strengthening the Indian capacity to pursue its national interest. This shift away from international pre-occupations also meant a sharper definition of Indian 'interests,' which were now seen to be essentially, indeed almost entirely, regional in character. Non-alignment was still a valid framework for policy-making because it was the only approach compatible with the effort to make India an independent and respected power in the region.[87]

Following the humiliation suffered by India at the hands of the Chinese in October-November 1962 when they pushed back the Indian forces in Himalayas, it began to be pointed out that the nation's relatively unarmed foreign policy had failed to ensure the security of the country and that the policy of Non-alignment, though based on noble idealism, was no substitute for realism. What was more obvious the reverses suffered by India's armed forces had damaged India's military establishment and its image abroad."[88] The Indian foreign policy became a policy of double alignment when India began to take military aid from both the superpowers.[89] To compensate for the Sino-Indian imbalance, India sought support from the USA, USSR and Western Europe. Its great success story was its developing link with the USSR.[90] In 1963, US President Johnson sent General Maxwell Taylor to India regarding India's needs for defense aid. After this trip Taylor recommended a five-year $ 500 million program for India for the defense plan drawn up by the Indians. The US had given supersonic aircraft F-104s to Pakistan; they were denied to India. Six Indian mountain divisions were to be equipped with better communications, transportation and air defense, for the defense of the northern frontier.

As the US refused to provide F-104s, the Indians took up a Soviet alternative. The USSR agreed to provide 45 MIG-21 and to set up factories to assemble another 400.

War with Pakistan

Another shock was yet to come and it came in 1965, when the nation's much smaller neighbor, Pakistan, considered itself strong enough to mount an attack on India. Though, then India was three times the size of Pakistan and the Indians numbered five times as many as Pakistanis; and though since 1962, India had been engaged in improving its defense capabilities by spending more and more on defense and by acquiring sophisticated weapons from wherever the country could get them, yet militarily, the outcome was a stalemate. But politically it represented a victory of sorts for India.[91] The Pakistani assumption that the war would spark off a rebellion in Indian-occupied Kashmir was belied. Indian Non-alignment had resulted in the while providing aid to India while the USA remaining neutral.

Although, Lal Bahadur Shastri succeeded in teaching Pakistan a salutary lesson in 1965, yet due to lack of political will, India surrendered her military and political gains at the Tashkent Conference.[92] The Soviet role during the war and at the Tashkent

Conference, held in January 1966, made it clear that India no longer enjoyed a privileged position in Moscow's South Asia policy. In fact, since 1963, the Soviet leaders had been working towards achieving a balance in their policy between India and Pakistan and had achieved some success in improving their relations with Pakistan.[93] On the other hand, Pakistan's membership of the SEATO (it withdrew after the 1965 war) got it nothing. With the USA increasingly bogged down in Vietnam, it was the USSR that emerged as a truce-maker. The Soviet Prime Minister Kosygin used his good offices in arranging talks between the Indian Prime Minister Lal Bahadur Shastri and President Ayub Khan of Pakistan. Ayub Khan accepted the position and Lal Bahadur Shastri decided it would be in the long-term interest of their mutual relations to give up the two important positions it had wrested in the operations, *i.e.* Haji Pir Pass and Tithwal. The agreement was signed on January 10, 1966 and unfortunately Lal Bahadur Shastri died on January 11, 1966.[94] One of the paradoxes of the Indian misfortune in 1965 was that none of the superpowers was willing to accord even the position of a predominant regional power.[95]

Nevertheless, one lesson that was not lost on Washington or Moscow was that the Indian military performance (in contrast to 1962) suggested that the country would soon emerge as the dominant power in South Asia. In the last years of the Johnson administration such a realisation was beginning to dawn and was expressed in policy re-examination in the State Department. The 'no arms' policy to both India and Pakistan embodied the new perception.[96] The two wars had weakened India considerably and had thus increased its dependence on others. However, the major source of foreign aid had dried up when the United States and Britain suspended both military and civilian aid as soon as the 1965 war began.

Thus, when Indira Gandhi assumed the office of the Prime Minister on 24th January 1966, she not only faced serious economic problems and shortage of foodgrains but also the fact that both Washington and Moscow considered India a power of little consequence, a "plaything of circumstances" which could be controlled by the big powers and "harassed by smaller countries."[97] Therefore, in the beginning of her rule, she at first tried to strengthen bonds of friendship with the US (1966 Indira-Johnson Joint statement, branding China as a threat to peace and supporting the US position in Vietnam; 1966 devaluation of the Indian rupee, etc.). But later, the compulsions at home (to defeat the rival Congress-group through leftist slogans and with communist help) and the continued US support to Pakistan, induced her to tilt her foreign policy towards the USSR.[98] In the 1968 Czechoslovakian crisis when the Russian armed forces went into action against the people in Prague, India remained quiet.

At home, the steps taken (like the bank nationalisation) and promises made, like *garibi batao* (abolish poverty) in 1969-70 to bring about the much needed socio-economic changes won her the support of the people who rallied around her in the March 1971 election. The result was that the Congress Party won 350 out of 518 Lok Sobha seats. By this time Congress was back in power in most states. Political uncertainty thus came to an end and it appeared that India had found in Prime Minister Indira Gandhi a leader who was tactful, forceful and effective enough to carry out the promised social and political reforms.[99]

These events and what happened in Pakistan between 1969 and 1971[100] made Moscow realise that the assumptions on which it had adopted the policy of equating Pakistan with India were wrong. The happenings in Pakistan made it abundantly clear that the reported Soviet view that Pakistan was more stable politically and sounder economically than India[101] had proved to be wrong. On the eve of the Bangladesh crisis, therefore, India was back in favor of Moscow.

Bangladesh Crisis

In the wake of the gruesome events in East Bengal, refugees started pouring in from all parts of East Pakistan. They literally flooded the adjoining states of Assam, Tripura and West Bengal. By the end of May 1971, 335 camps had been set up; and the refugees continued to pour in at the rate of sixty thousand a day. This created a tremendous strain on India.[102] Indira Gandhi told Parliament:

> So massive a migration, in so short a time, is unprecedented in recorded history. About three and a half million people

> have come into India from Bangladesh during the last eight weeks. They belong to every religious persuasion—Hindu, Muslim, Buddhist and Christian. They come from every social class and age group. They are not refugees in the sense we have understood this word since partition. They are victims of war who have sought refuge from the military terror across our frontier.[103]

The growing burden of the refugees put intolerable strain on India's meagre resources. The Indian economy could not bear the burden indefinitely, nor would the people tolerate inaction for any length of time. The opposition pressure for strong action mounted daily. However, attempts were made by Pakistan to give the tragic happenings a communal turn. Despite the emotional strain and provocations from Pakistan, India presented a picture of absolute national unity. Communal harmony was maintained throughout the country.[104] Gradually, the world opinion began to turn against Pakistan. Jayaprakash Narayan was deeply moved by the happenings in East Bengal and came out of his Sarvodaya "shell". He organised a World Conference on the issue of East Bengal in New Delhi that played an important part in moulding international opinion. Further, his tour abroad evoked good response.[105] Ultimately, Indira Gandhi assured Parliament that the Government would be guided by its own "independent assessment of the situation."[106]

Besides, there was a threat from President Nixon to the region when he ordered Kissinger to "tilt" the US actions towards Pakistan. Resentment of India's independent attitude particularly over war in Vietnam was the cause. In this situation, India and the USSR signed a treaty of friendship to come to the aid of each other in case either country was attacked by another.[107] Nixon's action was in contrast to Russia's role at Tashkent in 1966 when Kosygin had maintained an equanimity and patience, which brought about peace. On the other hand, Nixon in 1971 created a threat of enlarging the risk and scope of a war by ordering the carrier Enterprise to move to the Bay of Bengal. Nixon had thus tried to use the massive armed strength of USA for a show of force.[108]

Despite political stability, increased production and healthy economy made it possible for Prime Minister Indira Gandhi to face the Bangladesh crisis with courage and determination.[109] As a result, she handled the situation tactfully; refused to be rushed into premature recognition or to be pressurised into accepting UN observers all along India's frontier with what was then East Pakistan; ensured Soviet support by concluding a 20-year treaty of peace, friendship and co-operation in August, 1971; and led the country to victory some four months later.[110]

The emergence of Bangladesh as an independent nation has been described as "a second liberation for India", for it made the nation "more secure than it ever was"[111] and shattered all Pakistani hopes of achieving parity with India, at least in economic strength and military might. Additionally, many countries praised India's diplomacy and capability demonstrated in 1971; New Delhi was thus able to rehabilitate India's image in Asia where it began to be recognised as a great power.[112]

Following the liberation of Bangladesh, one of the major aims of Indian diplomacy was to improve India's relations with its neighbors and to make South Asia free from outside interference. For this, it was necessary to assure the subcontinent nations that India did not have expansionist designs, though it had become the dominant power in the region.

Testing Time for India's Non-alignment

By concluding the 1971 Indo-Soviet Treaty of Friendship, India's Non-alignment was put to severe test as the August 1971, 20-year Treaty of Peace, Friendship and Co-operation with the Soviet Union initially raised many questions at home and abroad, about India's continued Non-alignment.[113] But India managed to push aside any Western doubts and anxieties. First, India had managed to insert a particular provision in the Treaty (Art. 4), which ensured the Soviet Union's continued respect for India's policy of Non-alignment. Second, the Article IX, which provoked suspicion about the Treaty being a *de facto* military alliance, was treated in practice as an enabling provision for mere "consultation" in the event of a threat to the security of either nation. Third, the Treaty provided substantially for continuing economic and scientific cooperation the two nations.[114]

Another test for India's Non-alignment came, when USSR President Brezhnev spoke about the Soviet proposal of an Asian

Collective Security system, to Members of the Indian Parliament in November 1973. Obviously, India could not have accepted such a proposal, largely because it involved a political and/or military alliance among Asian nations, including the Soviet Union, during the Cold War period. It was also the Indian perception, that the proposal was directed against China and the United States. The Indian response not only avoided a straight answer, it was also a highly constructive one,[115] said Swaran Singh:

"Our own thinking is that an adherence to such principles as renunciation of the use of force, peaceful coexistence, respect for sovereignty of all countries, non-interference in internal affairs and broad development of economic and other co-operation on the basis of equality and mutual benefit will assist such peoples."[116]

Once again, India triumphed over the suspicions and anxieties of other states and critics who thought that India had compromised its non-alignment by an alleged military alliance with a superpower. India remained a genuinely non-aligned nation, as before.

Allegations against India's Non-alignment

Throughout the Cold War years, India was persistently buffeted by allegations, both domestic and external, that it was tilting either towards the United States, or the Soviet Union; Western propaganda was especially insistent that India was friendlier, at least towards the Soviet Union (and Warsaw Pact countries) than towards Western bloc states. In response to these criticisms, Prime Minister Indira Gandhi asserted that friendship with the Soviet Union would not be at the cost of India's friendship with any other country (the United states?).[117]

Some months later, she told the Commonwealth Conference, "It is absolutely ridiculous to suggest that we (India) are under Soviet or any other influence. We have been scrupulously trying to keep out of power rivalries and we feel that a country of our size and background cannot be in anybody's orbit."[118]

Besides, the fact of the matter was that:[119]

1. Soviet bloc countries followed foreign policy postures parallel to India's in some respects, such as anti-

colonialism, anti-racialism, and promotion of economic development of the so-called Third World and developing countries.

2. They were very helpful to India commercially, especially by supplying military stores and sophisticated technology.

Despite this, India never conceded any favors to the Soviet bloc countries, which would compromise its non-aligned stance. Indeed, it is fair to say that it remained throughout an exemplar of Non-alignment, as it was a pioneer of policy.[120]

When Soviet military forces invaded Afghanistan in late 1970s, India was again criticised for not making a harsh reaction against the Soviet Union. The Minister for External Affairs, P.V. Narasimha Rao, told Parliament that the Government was "deeply concerned and vitally interested" in the security, independence and territorial integrity of this "traditionally friendly neighbor" (Afghanistan). "We are against the presence of foreign troops and bases in any country. We have expressed the hope, that Soviet forces would withdraw (soon) from Afghanistan." This was consistent with the policy of Non-alignment.[121]

Tasks in the New Millennium and India's Non-Aligned Policy

Non-alignment, by definition, represents a global, universalist policy and outlook. It is true that some of the parameters of Non-alignment developed during the Cold War period, but it would be misplaced to think that Cold War or block politics was its sole reference point.[122] The policy of Non-alignment as formulated by Jawaharlal Nehru in 1946 was primarily meant to serve the Indian national interests and security. It is only after the July 1956 Brioni Island Conference (Yugoslavia) that the Non-aligned Movement as launched by Pt. Jawaharlal Nehru, Marshal Tito of Yugoslavia and Col. Gamal Abdul Nasser of Egypt and institutionalised at the Belgrade summit in 1961, was conceived in the context of the Cold War. From India's point of view the Belgrade Summit was pleasant and useful but not vital. Individual countries like India without the necessary backing of a movement could effectively pursue the non-aligned policy.[123] However, Indian leaders were quick to realise that in case a war broke out, the chances of the domestic development of their poor and backward societies would become further distant. Hence, Cold War and bloc politics were considered anti-thetical to their hopes and aspirations of better conditions of living for their people. In this way there was established an organic link between promotion of national interests and international peace. On the other hand, the policy and movement of Non-alignment are enduring factors in the conduct of international relations, while Cold War and detente are transient factors. These transient, superficial vagaries of the international system and of superpower relations do not affect the continuing validity and relevance of the policy and movement of Non-alignment.[124]

Besides this, what is equally significant is that, the scope of Non-aligned Movement's concerns has greatly expanded; they now cover practically the whole gamut of international affairs (somewhat like that of the United Nations).[125] While the other view is that the end of the Cold War and the disintegration of the Soviet Union have serious repercussions for Third World countries and, for that matter, for Non-aligned Movement. In fact, the end of the Cold War is a fatal blow to some Third World nations, which used to get economic and military aid either in the name of containing communism or opposing imperialism.[126] Today NAM summit meetings have been reduced to mere rituals where resolutions are adopted which have no relevance to the emerging international situation. As usual, the leaders of these countries indulge in high eloquence and empty rhetoric. Their membership has been swelling as though it is a United Nations of Third World countries.[127] Even during its heyday, the Non-aligned Movement achieved nothing except for making some noise against imperialism, colonialism and neo-colonialism. PM Jawaharlal Lal Nehru, Marshal Josef Tito and President Abdul Nasser—the high priests of the Non-aligned Movement—were quick in their condemnation of both imperialism and colonialism. At the same time, they remained silent when the Soviet Union intervened and crushed democratic movements in Hungary, Poland, East Germany and Czechoslovakia. Peaceful settlement of disputes had been a major tenet of the NAM and yet, failure to comply with this tenet (and of UN Charter obligations too) on the part of some members and blatant use of force against each other (for example, Iran and Iraq) brought a bad name for the movement. Thus, its efforts to promote peaceful settlement in some cases (for example, Iran-Iraq war) were a demonstrable failure. When hostilities broke out between India and China, the Non-aligned Movement remained a silent spectator. In effect, Non-alignment and the NAM have remained irrelevant to the security of non-aligned states. Therefore, a major failure of the NAM has been its inability to ensure some security in all its three senses—politically, militarily and economically. When Soviet troops marched into Afghanistan, a loyal non-aligned nation, NAM did not raise a finger. The non-aligned nations had conflicts among themselves.[128]

Despite all this, many of the seeming failures cannot altogether be placed at the doors of the NAM. They are also the failures of the world organisation and the international community generally.[129] Just as we all desire the continuing functioning of the World Organisation, in spite of its limitations, so should we desire the continuance and effectiveness of the largest intergovernmental organisation next only to the World Organisation in size and in similarity of objectives. Further, the NAM can at least claim that it is the only active movement having as its regular agenda the promotion of many of those proposals and constantly urging their implementation. If they have not been achieved (or at least fully), they are not due to lack of its efforts, but some other reasons, including the international environments in which the movement has to operate unavoidably. Therefore, the future of the NAM depends only partly on its own success or failure; it depends on many other factors outside its control.[130] Another consideration that needs to be taken into account is assessing the future of the NAM. Many of the important objectives/demands of the NAM are of a long-term nature such as establishing the New International Economic Order (NIEO), disarmament and the true democratisation of the international system and its functioning and so their non-fulfilment appear to be failures. Surely, no one can expect the achievement of these large, worldwide objectives in the foreseeable future. But they are worth fighting for and waiting for![131]

Rajiv Gandhi, in an address to the Ninth Non-aligned Summit at Belgrade (1989), opined, that an end to dominance was what we sought, an end to the outdated belief, that it was in any way legitimate for nations with muscle to impose any kind of hegemony—military, political or economic—on other nations. We set out to persuade the world to change its world view by bringing to a close the dangerous and ultimately self-destructive pursuit of military domination, by ending "policies of pressure in the economic sphere," and by working towards an international order in which there is no "intimidation, interference or intervention."[132] Our endeavors began in the human mind, for it is the human mind that is at once the repository of the detritus of the past and the engine of change for the future."[133] In Belgrade, at the time of first NAM summit in 1961, Jawaharlal Nehru said:

"The power of the nations assembled here is not military power or economic power; nevertheless it is power. Call it moral force."[134]

There have been successes. There have been setbacks and the path ahead is strewn with problems.

Critical Global Issues

There is nothing legitimate about a system, which mortgages the long-term interests of all to the short-term gains of some. There is nothing legitimate about a system, which marginalises the developing countries in the management of the global economy. There is nothing legitimate about a system, which cannot offer the prospect of rapid development to the developing countries.[135] The major economic powers are determined to perpetuate their dominance over the global economy. That is not acceptable. It is the developing countries that suffer most the deleterious consequences of the structural imbalances, which afflict the world economy. They must be party, therefore, to decisions, which affect the world economy. International security rests not only on disarmament, arms reduction and confidence building. Ultimately, it must rest on the elimination of the real scourges of humankind: hunger, disease, illiteracy, poverty, exploitation, conflict and war. There is no lasting security to be found in a world segmented into the rich and the poor, the developed and the developing, North and South.

Furthermore, there are certain global problems, which are not only serious and urgent, but the rich and the industrialised nations alone cannot tackle them and they must seek the co-operation of the developing countries. These comprise the threats presented by the massive increase in international drug trafficking, environmental destruction, the regional crisis and the increase in terrorism (also state sponsored).

In concise, in the new millennium, tasks for a non-aligned country like India, are manifold. These are:

(a) Non-aligned movement must give substance to the political sovereignty through true economic sovereignty.

(b) Continuous struggle against domination, exploitation, war, poverty, illiteracy and women subjugation.

(c) Commitment to one world and one humanity translates into a struggle to end the iniquities of a system in which the prosperity of the prosperous is pursued in disregard of the problems of poverty of the poor.

(d) Struggle for the establishment of a system of international economic relations based on the interdependence of the global economy—a system in which the common interest of all prevails, as much the interest of those who fall within the charmed circle of the developed countries as of those who fall without.

(e) Call for revolution, but revolution of a different kind —not to bring down those who have climbed the ladder of economic success but to enable those who remain at the bottom to climb the rungs of opportunity.

DEVELOPMENT AND SELF-RELIANCE IN ECONOMIC FIELD

Before we can play a significant role in world politics, we have to make the home front very strong and sound—both physically and economically.[136] As Pt. Nehru once remarked that "he was in spite of his being Minister in-charge of External Affairs, interested in external affairs so much as in internal affairs, because external affairs would follow internal affairs; but there was no basis for external affairs if internal affairs were wrong.[137] It is for the most part due to British imperialists, that India is so industrially backward. They have left us in a pitiable economic position. Therefore, the first and foremost problem is of economic development. To devise ways and means, to improve the living standard of teeming millions.

"Nobody can bear our burdens for us; we have to bear them ourselves—this is what, we understand by the term self-reliance", said Jawaharlal Nehru. It means paying our own way, standing on our own feet,[138] we hold ourselves responsible for our own development. On the other hand self-reliance does not mean autarchy; it does not mean isolation from the international community or the global economy. That is why we have willingly sought — and given — economic and technical cooperation. We have stressed that such cooperation can only be on terms compatible with our honor as a nation, our independence as a State and our self-reliance as an economy.[139] Thus, it was realised that if India was to find her rightful place in the comity of nations, it had to reduce her dependence on aid from abroad. And by the 1960s, India had achieved considerable success in its own economic development enabling it to, in turn, help other, less developed countries of the Third World. This was of course, partly due to the fact, that most of the less developed Third World countries realised that the Indian experience and intermediate technology were more relevant to their economic conditions than the experiences of developed countries using advanced technology. Thus, beginning from the 1960s, India developed extensive economic cooperation with both the developed and the developing state, of course, at different levels and in different directions; by and large, it was a beneficiary of the former as the latter was of India.[140] "This approach to our foreign policy has already paid some handsome dividends in as much as it has greatly increased the goodwill, friendship and trade between us and a large number of countries of Africa and Asia."[141] India gave extensive financial, economic and technical assistance to a large number of Asian, African[142] and other countries, including the smaller neighbors.

India played a leading role in international forums (especially in the Group of 77, the UNCTAD and NAM Conferences) in persistently making proposals and putting forward ideas and suggestions for promoting economic cooperation between the developing and the developed countries and among the developing countries themselves. While recognizing the essential interdependence of the economies of the world, Jawaharlal Nehru described enlightened self-interest, as realizing that if some parts of the world do not progress, remain backward, they have an adverse effect on the whole economy of the world and they tend to drag down those parts that are at present prosperous.[143]

MAINTENANCE OF WORLD PEACE

Since independence, it has been India's conviction that its plans for economic development raising the living standards of its people and fulfilment of the people's aspirations cannot be achieved without both world and internal peace. Thus, the maintenance and promotion of world peace became India's primary objective in world affairs. Besides, India has been an old and persistent opponent of nuclear weapons, their proliferation and all that these new weapons of mass destruction represent. This applies not just to the conduct of war but also to the maintenance of international peace and security. Jawaharlal Nehru was the first to bring the problem of proliferation of nuclear weapons to the attention of the world and also of the World Organisation. India was opposed to both horizontal and vertical proliferation.

Not only does India strongly and persistently oppose nuclear weapons and their proliferation, while rejecting the nuclear weapons option for itself, for years it persistently urged the development of nuclear energy for peaceful, non-military purposes. It took seriously and sincerely the propagation, by the major nuclear weapon powers themselves, the idea of developing Peaceful Nuclear Explosion (PNE) technology for use for economic and medical purposes. Nor did India object to PNEs being made by the nuclear weapon powers.

While explaining the rationale and significance of the Indian PNE, Sardar Swaran Singh made a statement in Parliament, that, it was "a step forward" on the road to peaceful uses of nuclear energy for the welfare of the Indian people, an important landmark in the development of nuclear technology for peaceful purposes.[144]

Since India took a global view with respect to foreign policy and relations, it naturally viewed the security of the world as indivisible. It is this larger perspective that determined India's approach to peace zone proposals. It backed the UN resolution on the "Indian Ocean as a Peace Zone", because it covered and affected the large number of states on the periphery of the ocean, which had big powers' military presence. Further, India conceived of Peace not only in the conventional political/military senses, but also and perhaps especially, in its economic and social dimensions.[145] Peace cannot coexist with violence and tyranny, or when justice is trampled upon. The one real threat to the maintenance of peace is the problem of poverty and economic underdevelopment.... The problem is that two-thirds of the human race living in areas well-endowed with natural resources and populated very often by people inheriting ancient culture and high technical skills, are wallowing in extreme poverty; while one-third of the humanity has become rich through a misdistribution of the wealth of this world.[146] The social dimension of international peace visualised by India, relates to maintenance and promotion of human rights and fundamental freedoms, in particular racial equality. India firmly believes in the equality of all human beings.

Thus, India was concerned not only with the obvious causes and symptoms of hostilities, but also with deeper, potential causes poverty, violation of human rights, racial discrimination, narrow national interests, non-commitment to the purposes and principles of the UN Charter and other sources of international conflict.

India regularly reiterated the need for peaceful settlement of disputes and conflict situations; avoidance of confrontation between nations; pursuit of cooperation in order to obviate the use of force by any of the parties concerned. It particularly urged, as it did in the Delhi Declaration with the Soviet Union,[147] the creation of a non-violent and non-nuclear world. The new approach to international relations enunciated in the Delhi Declaration requires a change of doctrines, policies and institutions to build and sustain a nuclear weapons free and non-violent world. This needs demilitarisation, democratisation and humanisation in international relations.[148] It expounds the new world order, which India at least envisages in the post-Cold War era.

Furthermore, peace demands an end to the fanning of conflicts by proxy. Peace means an end to terrorism, whether by States or individuals. Peace requires the diversion of resources from armaments to development. Peace needs a world free of the menace of drugs. Peace demands a wholesome environment and the conservation of nature's gifts to life on planet Earth.

WORKING FOR DISARMAMENT

Indian foreign policy is based on non-violence and truth, as enunciated by Mahatma Gandhi and Jawaharlal Nehru. These, of course, are moral principles that when translated into political terms, mean disarmament and open diplomacy.[149] For years, India has been in the forefront of the campaign for general and complete disarmament, both in India and in many forums abroad — the United Nations, the NAM conferences, the Commonwealth forum and so on. For years, it has repeatedly expressed dissatisfaction with the poor progress in any international disarmament measure; while, on the contrary, the armaments race was constantly spiralling upwards, with grave consequences to world peace and economy.[150] The NPT had failed to arrest the growth of nuclear armaments either qualitatively or quantitatively. In addition, India has been opposed for years to the development, production and stockpiling of chemical weapons. India has also been for years urging the holding of a World Disarmament Conference.

DISARMAMENT

Meaning

In a general sense, it connotes the idea of the limitation or control or reduction of armaments. It acquires a definitive meaning only when some adjective is added to it. For disarmament may be unilateral/multilateral, general/local, total/partial, and controlled/uncontrolled.

- *Qualitative disarmament this*: This refers to the limitation or prohibition of only certain types of weapons.

- *Quantitative disarmament*: This refers to the control of the weapons of all categories.
- *General disarmament*: When all or most of the great powers participate but not necessarily with a commitment to do away with all types of weapons.
- *Comprehensive disarmament*: This refers to the control or prohibition of all armaments of all categories. It is also called total disarmament.
- *Total disarmament*: It implies the ultimate achievement of a world order in which all human and material instrumentalities of warfare will have been abolished. There will be no weapon of any kind whatsoever. Armies would be completely disbanded. Military training centers, war ministries and ordnance factories will also be closed.

Therefore, it is clear that in a generic sense, disarmament may mean anything from a simple limitation to complete abolition of armaments. But it is to be noted that disarmament is concerned with the reduction or abolition of only existing weapons. And weapons technology is always on the move and this movement is likely to lead to the development of new types of armaments. The criterion of reduction/abolition cannot be applied to those weapons, which may be developed in future. In fact, the term disarmament does not cover control of the weapons of the future. This control is designated by the expression — arms control. Therefore, disarmament refers to the control of existing weapons and arms control to that of future weapons. In other words, disarmament seeks to control armaments, while arms control tries to check arms race.

From the point of view of international peace, disarmament and arms control are complementary to each other. As the mere reduction or abolition of existing weapons would not serve the basic purpose of peace if nations are allowed to acquire new and improved types of weapons in future. The purpose of disarmament is to deprive nations of the very instruments of fighting. The only direct cause of war admissible in disarmament approach is the existence of armaments. Armaments cause war, while disarmament leads to international peace.

Quincy Wright has, however, a different opinion, in this regard. He says disarmament probably tends to increase the frequency of war. For, if states are lightly armed, they may regard war as a manageable instrument of policy. What led to First and Second World War was not the armament competition, but the lack of it.

Arguments in favor of disarmament:

1. It promotes international security and reduces international tension.
2. It promotes economic prosperity.
3. It promotes moral objective.

In theoretical terms, there can be conflict between the security, economic and moral objectives. For, there can be a disarmament policy, which guarantees economic prosperity and is in conformity with moral principles but which may not ensure security. Further, the concept of national security, national prosperity and national morality differs from nation to nation. But today the prime need is international peace and disarmament is viewed as a step in that direction. Therefore, primary basis of disarmament is the concern for avoidance of war. Human survival is much more important than economic prosperity and moral values. Disarmament has to be accepted at least as an element of the solution of the problem of war and as a necessary condition of the evolution of a peaceful international order. Armaments cause war, not that war is caused by armaments. Disarmament can prevent wars that arise from armaments but other ways would be required for preventing wars emanating from other sources. Since peace is a matter of avoidance of all kinds of wars, disarmament is only a partial solution to the problem of war.

Different Ways for Disarmament

Disarmament can be done in three ways:

1. Gradual disarmament in agreement with other nations.
2. Total disarmament in agreement with other nations.
3. Total disarmament by a single nation (unilateral disarmament).

On one hand unilateral disarmament may pave the way for others to follow suit, on the other it may also mean national suicide. Actually, the idea of unilateral disarmament is linked to the idea of non-violent defense. For a nation disarming unilaterally will have to take care of the problem of how to deal with aggression. The problem of non-violent defense is the problem of finding out an alternative to war that could replace war as a means of defending freedom and as a way of life against tyranny and aggression. This alternative has to be capable of providing the necessary protection without military armaments. In fact, unilateral disarmament does not ignore the problem of defense, but insists that defense should be sought by a non-military policy. Therefore, what the world needs today is not only disarmament but also what Theodor Ebert calls 'transarmament' by which is meant a complete change from a military defense system to a non-military defense system. This is what Gene Sharp calls a 'third approach'. However, a complete strategy of non-violent defense is yet to be developed. In any case, unilateral disarmament has to be logically followed by transarmament.

Major Steps Towards Disarmament

More serious and consistent efforts for disarmament were made after First World War. The important function of League of Nations was 'the reduction of national armaments to the lowest point consistent with national safety'. In Paris Peace Conference 1919, disarmament was declared to have been one of the 'war aims' of the Allies, i.e. to apply the principle of disarmament effectively to the states defeated in the war. Under the Treaty of Peace, Germany, Austria, Hungary and Bulgaria accepted an immense reduction and rigid limitation on their armed forces. The forcible disarmament of the vanquished by the victors was not new. In 1808, Napoleon had also compelled Prussia to limit its army to 42,000 men for ten years. But in 1919, it was carried out more completely than ever before.

World Disarmament Conference was organised in 1932 and was attended by representatives of 61 states. Germany withdrew from Conference and also from League of Nations. Conference met intermittently for sometime. But in 1934, UK acknowledged that disarmament was not practicable and that it would increase its own armament. However, efforts for naval disarmament outside the framework of League also continued. Washington Conference held in 1927, was a success in bringing about a limitation in battleships and battle cruisers. There was London Agreement in 1930. But with the withdrawal of Germany from the League and the failure of Disarmament Conference, Europe slid back to the pre-war days of unrestricted arms competition.

After Second World War, hopes, however, again rose about general disarmament. Great powers agreed on the basic principle for disarmament. Provisions for disarmament were written into the UN Charter, signed on 26 June 1945. On 11 January 1952, UN Disarmament Commission was established by General Assembly. In 1960, Ten-Power Conference, consisting of 5 western powers and 5 members of Soviet bloc, was convened, but Soviet delegates broke up the conference. Then Disarmament Commission was expanded by General Assembly in 1961 from 10 to 18 nations, to include 8 non-aligned nations, like Brazil, India, Ethiopia, Mexico, Nigeria, Sweden, and United Arab Republic. In 1969, the membership of disarmament commission increased from 18 to 26, in order to ensure better geographical and political distribution. It was renamed Conference of the Committee on Disarmament.

The protracted post-war disarmament negotiations produced a limited agreement in 1963. It was signed by US, Soviet Union and Britain. They sought to prohibit the nuclear tests and as such, this treaty came to be known as the test ban treaty. Apart from three principal powers India was among the first countries to sign this treaty. Eight NAM countries of the Disarmament Commission made a notable contribution to the conclusion of test ban treaty. The 'principal aim' of the treaty was the speediest possible achievement of an agreement on general and complete disarmament under strict international control. Preamble to the treaty acknowledges the fact that nuclear tests contaminate man's environment by radioactivity. Para-2 of Article 1 imposes an obligation on each of parties "to refrain from causing, encouraging or in any way participating in the carrying out of any nuclear weapon test explosion or any other nuclear explosion." It, however, permits the underground explosion, but with certain limitations. Underground explosions are permissible only if they do not cause radioactive debris to spread outside the territorial limits of a state. Therefore, theoretically speaking, the treaty permits the continuance of underground tests.

The disarmament negotiations after 1963 treaty have shown that world powers are interested more in nuclear non-proliferation than general and complete disarmament. The US advocated a program for nuclear non-proliferation and a draft of Non-Proliferation Treaty (NPT) was submitted to UN in 1968. India had been opposed to this treaty because it did not specify any guarantee for her security against China — a nuclear power and it would prevent India from developing nuclear energy for peaceful purpose for which she was sufficiently equipped because of her being in an advanced state of nuclear research. NPT was open for sign in 1968 and came into force in 1970. Besides, efforts have been made to control the use of nuclear and conventional weapons through Strategic Arms Reduction Treaties.

With India's initiative, a meeting of the heads of states/ governments representing Argentina, Greece, Mexico, Sweden, Tanzania and India was convened at New Delhi on 28 July 1985. This meeting, attended by, among others, the distinguished African statesman and former Tanzanian President, Julius Neyerere, launched what came to be known as the Six-Nation-Five-Continent Initiative on Nuclear Disarmament. The Initiative, urged the nuclear weapons states to halt testing and to conclude an early comprehensive test ban treaty. It also called for prohibition of development and use of all weapons in space. It urged that outer space must be used for the benefit of mankind as a whole — not as a future battleground.[151] Later on, regular meetings took place on nuclear disarmament in different places. Even while pursuing multilateral effort, India and Soviet Union bilaterally urged the need for "a Nuclear-Weapons-free" and non-violent world order. In Delhi Declaration 1986, specific and immediate action for disarmament was spelt out.

Besides, with the efforts of Rajiv Gandhi a time bound Action Plan for general and complete disarmament was submitted to the Special Session on Disarmament of the United Nations General Assembly. The essential features of the Action Plan are:

- There should be a binding commitment by all nations to eliminating nuclear weapons, in stages, by the year 2010 at the latest.
- All nuclear weapon states must participate in the process of nuclear disarmament. All other countries must also be part of the process.
- To demonstrate good faith and build the required confidence, there must be tangible progress at each stage towards the common goal.
- Changes are required in doctrines, policies and institutions to sustain a world free of nuclear weapons. Negotiations should be undertaken to establish a comprehensive Global Security System under the aegis of the United Nations.

The heart of the Action Plan is the elimination of all nuclear weapons, in three stages.

In 1996, comprehensive test ban treaty (CTBT) came into existence. But India refused to sign it, on the ground of its being discriminatory.

Thus, we see that disarmament is one of those phenomena of international politics, which were mooted as solutions to problems but became problems themselves. As the efforts made in this direction show how difficult has been the achievement of a state of disarmament.

PEACEFUL CO-EXISTENCE OF NATIONS

An inevitable corollary to Non-alignment is non-interference. A nation, which does not belong to a multi-military alliance, usually does not wish to interfere in the affairs of other nations and, in turn, this attitude generates mutual tolerance. This leads to co-existence and when nations co-exist for some time they begin to display an element of dynamic co-existence. By dynamic co-existence is meant that nations take active steps to forge cooperation first in non-political matters such as trade, commerce and cultural exchanges and later on this blunts the edges of political differences.[152]

This element of India's foreign policy has consistently remained the same in all the years since independence. In a sense, the pursuit of this element is unavoidable for a country like India. Both politically and in other respects, India has remained a highly pluralistic society and, therefore, its external policy as well as the domestic one calls for harmonisation of the outlook and interests of its diverse population. This is not only a desirable policy, but also unavoidable in an interdependent world — self-isolation no longer being a foreign policy option for the vast number of states. As both Pt. Jawaharlal Nehru and Indira Gandhi used to say, 'the alternative to peaceful co-existence among nations is co-destruction.[153]

"Unless there is genuine acceptance of the principle of peaceful co-existence, the desire to live and let live and the determination to convert Cold War confrontation into competitive co-operation, the process of detente will not show the desired results,"[154] observed Indian Foreign Minister.

Thus in the Indian view, peaceful co-existence compels tolerance of differing perspectives. "In a world of great diversities, it is obvious that tolerance of differing viewpoints and understanding of each others perceptions could alone constitute the general basis for amicable relations and co-operation among nations" — in an increasingly interdependent society.[155]

Asian Identity

One of the issues, intermittently raised with respect to India's foreign policy/relations (usually at a non-official level), is India's possible role in promoting an intra-Asian forum through which an "Asian identity," and intra-Asian co-operation are established.

In this regard, the question of India doing something about developing an Asian identity was raised in Indian Parliament in April 1975. The then Minister for External Affairs Y.B. Chavan, acknowledged the absence of institutional arrangements for consultations among Asian countries to promote their interests and said that they were "exploring various avenues to foster a sense of identity." "But," he added, "you cannot force the pace; there are certain regional and internal contradictions which cannot forcibly be solved."[156] India, too, like other Asian nations, has not made any serious effort to pursue this larger objective.

Regionalism

India has always been a votary of regional co-operation in South Asia. The Bangladesh proposal for a South Asian regional organisation was welcomed by India. At the inauguration of the South Asian Association for Regional Co-operation in New Delhi in August 1983, Prime Minister Indira Gandhi stated that India, as a matter of policy, did not want to interfere in the affairs of its neighbors. She stressed that whatever happened in any country within the region would affect the affairs of other countries, either individually or collectively. She emphasised that our co-operation in no way limited each others freedom of judgment. The co-operation was only aimed at development and strengthening of the economies of its members. "India was not", she said, "oblivious of differences among the nations of the South Asian region; these ought to be resolved by peaceful means."[157]

SUPPORT TO, AND STRENGTHENING OF, INTERNATIONAL ORGANISATIONS

The United Nations

India has been a founder member of most of the international organisations, especially the United Nations and its Specialised Agencies (as it was earlier of the League of Nations). Consequently, support to, and strengthening of the world organisations is an important element of India's foreign policy. The principal purpose of India's foreign policy *vis-à-vis* the United Nations is to pursue three closely related goals:[158]

1. A significant role in the shaping of international relations in 21st century.
2. A movement towards a non-violent and humane international system.
3. The promotion of conditions for a sustainable and relatively equitable pattern of international development.

Like most others, India has had its share of disappointments and frustrations regarding the functioning of the UN, its limitations and the constraints under which it operates. It has learnt to recognise these from its own, rather bitter, experience with respect to the handling of the Kashmir issue by the world organisation since 1948. Other disappointments have been the way the organisation handled the Hyderabad question in 1948, the Goa question in 1961, even the 1971 Bangladesh question and the Ganga water dispute with Bangladesh in 1974.

Despite all this, India has remained a steadfast supporter of the United Nation and its family of institutions.

India's Vijayalakshmi Pundit was elected President of the UN General Assembly as early as 1953. India is one of the few countries, which got elected six times as a non-permanent member of the Security Council. It is also a strong contender for becoming a permanent member when the expansion of the Council takes place. It sought to prevent the world organisation from being misused as an instrument of power politics. India played a notable role in the peaceful settlement of many disputes and conflict situations. India was for years a major participant in UN peacekeeping operations.[159] India became first chairman of the Committee on Decolonisation in 1962 and played a leading role in the promotion of colonial self-determination of peoples. Also India was the first chairman of the Economic and Social Council (ECOSOC). Further, securing a permanent seat in the Security Council is the easiest way for India to expand its influence within the UN system. It is also clear that the expansion of the Security Council will not be easy and even if it happens, India may not be an automatic choice.[160] Japan, Germany, Brazil and Nigeria are also there. However, India has always been in the forefront of reforming the UN system in order to strengthen it and to make it more effective.

The reason for India's continuing support to the UN despite disappointments and frustrations, is that the purposes/principles of the organisation broadly reflect the goals and objectives of India's foreign policy.

The Commonwealth

India has been a founder member of the modern Commonwealth of Nations since 1949. It is because of India's decision to become a Republic on 26 January 1950 and its desire to still continue association with the Commonwealth,[161] that the modern Commonwealth ceased to be a British entity, and became a multiracial, multicultural, independent association of nations.

Despite intermittent changes in the composition and functioning of the Commonwealth association, and India's non-aligned role in world affairs (and domestic political changes too), India maintained its Commonwealth membership. It remained for India, a supplementary forum for playing an appropriate role in world affairs and for promoting the goals of India's foreign policy (and in the relations of other members of the Commonwealth, including India's neighbors, Pakistan,[162] Bangladesh, Sri Lanka and the Maldives). India, for instance, regularly used the Commonwealth forum for carrying on its crusade against South Africa's apartheid. Membership of the Commonwealth also helped India maintain with the United Kingdom some old, historical pre-independence links of affinity and links of advantage.

Besides these explicit elements in India's foreign policy, there are some implicit, innate elements, embodied in India's tradition, values, culture and civilisation, that constitute foundation stone and are inner values of India's foreign policy. The continuity of Indian civilisation has been based on an implicit recognition of the entire gamut of values comprised in the single word "non-violence". The roots of the Indian concept of non-violence lie in the philosophy of the Buddha, further developed by Indian civilisation over the last 2500 years. The philosophy of non-violence originated in Indian civilisation as a moral precept for individual conduct. That is the reason why India represented a new point of departure in history. This was the first time ever that history had seen non-violence used successfully as a political instrument. Further, the continuing theme of Indian civilisation has been synthesis, *i.e.* the fusing of numerous cultures into a composite culture, where individual identities are retained while common traits are shared. It has bred in our thought processes a sense of tolerance. While, more than any other single factor, it is the Indian tradition, which has enabled her to face contemporary challenges.

In a broadcast made during a visit to the United States, Jawaharlal Nehru said:

"I have become more and more convinced that so long as we do not recognise the supremacy of the moral law in our national and international relations, we shall have no enduring peace. So long as we do not adhere to right means, the end will not be right and fresh evil, will flow from it. That was the essence of Gandhiji's message."[163]

While Nehru's vision of India encompassed India's millennial past and looked out to a millennial future, it was not conditioned by immediate problems and immediate concerns. Rather, it drew its inspiration from the essential continuities of India's civilisation. When Nehru looked to the future, he visualised resurgent India as giving the moral leadership to the world, of leading the world in thought and philosophy, in culture and the arts, in science and technology, in equality and justice, in human dignity and human rights, in morality in public life and probity in personal conduct.[164]

NOTES

1. Ram Manohar Lohia, 'India's Foreign Policy' in Verinder Grover (Ed.), *International Relations and Foreign Policy of India.* Vol. 1, Deep & Deep Publication, New Delhi, 1992.
2. R.P. Saraf (Ed.), *Political and Social Realities in Modern India,* Indian Bibliographies Bureau Co-Publisher Balaji Enterprises, Delhi, 1990.
3. K.P. Saksena, 'India's Foreign Policy: The Decision Making Process,' *International Studies*, Vol. 33, No. 4, 1996, Sage Publications, New Delhi.
4. Sahdev Vohra, 'India's Foreign Relations Part-I', *U.S.I. Journal,* Vol. CXXVI, No. 525, July-Sept. 1996.
5. For details see *Asian Relations Conference,* 1947, Inaugural Address.
6. *World Focus,* 'India at Forty', Vol. 8, No. 11-12, Nov.-Dec. 1987.
7. Niranjan M. Khilani, *New Dimensions of Indian Foreign Policy,* Westvill Publishing House, New Delhi, 1995.
8. Sachidanand Murty, *Indian Foreign Policy,* Calcutta, 1964, pp. 197-200.
9. K. Shridharani, 'The Philosophical Bases of India's Foreign Policy', *India Quarterly,* XIV, 1958-II, p. 197.
10. J. Bandyopadhyaya, *The Making of India's Foreign Policy,* New Delhi, 1980.

11. S.N. Mishra, *India — The Cold War Years,* South Asian Publishers Pvt. Ltd., New Delhi, 1994.
12. Nikhil Chakarvarty, 'Evolution of Foreign Policy', *World Focus,* Nov-Dec. 1987.
13. See N.D. Tiwari, *Foreign Affairs Record,* New Delhi, Vol. 33, 1987, p. 167.
14. Niranjan M. Khilnani, *New Dimensions of Indian Foreign Policy,* Westvill Publishing House, New Delhi, 1995.
15. Mohit Sen, Non-alignment and Non-bloc Politics, *World Focus,* 1989.
16. K.P. Misra, 'Foreign Policy Planning in India', in K.P. Misra (Ed.), *Foreign Policy of India,* Thompson Press, New Delhi, 1977 and S. Tharoor, *Reasons of State.* Vikas, New Delhi, 1982.
17. S. Gopal, 'Crusader for World Peace', *World Focus,* 1989.
18. Geography and history, however, ensure that regional affairs receive priority in the affairs of most nations. Since the sixties India has found this true.
19. M.S. Rajan (Ed.), *India's Foreign Policy during Nehru Era,* Asia, 1976.
20. S.N. Misra, *India — The Cold War Years,* South Asian Publishers Pvt. Ltd., New Delhi, 1994.
21. *Ibid.*
22. Mohit Sen, 'Indira Gandhi's Role,' *World Focus,* Nov.-Dec., 1987.
23. Girish Mathur, 'NAM and South-South Co-operation,' *World Focus,* Nov.-Dec, 1986.
24. *Ibid.*
25. Inder Malhotra. 'Harare to Belgrade,' *World Focus,* June, 1989.
26. Niranjan M. Khilnani, *New Dimensions of Indian Foreign Policy,* Westvill Publishing House, New Delhi, 1995.
27. Urmila Phadnis, 'Non-alignment as a Factor in Ceylon's Foreign Policy'. *International Studies,* April, 1962, p. 425.
28. C. Muraleedharan, 'Non-alignment at the Summits,' *Kerala Journal of Political Studies,* Vol. I, 1986, p. 55.
29. *Foreign Affairs Record,* Vol. 22, 1976, p. 238.
30. M.S. Rajan, 'The Goals of India's Foreign Policy', *International Studies,* Vol. 35, No. 1, 1998.
31. A.Z. Rubinstein, 'Does Non-alignment have a Future?'. *The Non-Aligned World,* July-September 1984, p. 396.
32. Achin Vanaik, *The Painful Transition—Bourgeois Democracy in India,* Verso, London, 1990.
33. Sahdev Vohra, 'India's Foreign Relations Part-I', *U.S.I. Journal,* Vol. CXXVI, No. 525, July-September, 1996.

34. *Foreign Affairs Record,* Vol. 23, 1977, p. 97.
35. S.N. Misra, *India — The Cold War Years,* South Asian Publishers Pvt. Ltd., New Delhi, 1994.
36. Jagat Mehta, 'Non-alignment — A Spent Force', *Seminar,* July 1983.
37. *Ibid.*
38. Compare from India which followed Non-alignment with the policy of co-operation.
39. Niranjan M. Khilnani, *New Dimensions of Indian Foreign Policy,* Westvill Publishing House, New Delhi, 1995.
40. *Ibid.*
41. H.D. Ghoshal, *International Relations,* Unique Publishers, 1996, p. 202.
42. M.G. Gupta, *Indian Foreign Policy—Theory and Practice,* Y.K. Publishers, Agra, 1985, p. 106.
43. H.D. Ghoshal, *International Relations,* Unique Publishers, 1996, p. 202.
44. Sahdev Vohra, 'India's Foreign Relations Part-I', *U.S.I. Journal,* Vol. 126, No. 525, July-September, 1996.
45. *Ibid.*
46. Besides, India has cultural and commercial relations on a very wide scale. It is one of the most enthusiastic members of the UN and is part of the Commonwealth of nations. It is one of the five Colombo Powers and plays a major role in the Afro-Asian organisations. It is the acknowledged leader of NAM. The solid basis of all this is not isolationism but co-operation.
47. Jagat S. Mehta, 'Forty Years of Foreign Policy' in Verinder Grover (Ed.), *International Relations and Foreign Policy of India,* Vol. 1, Deep & Deep Publication, New Delhi, 1992.
48. M.G. Gupta, *Indian Foreign Policy—Theory and Practice,* Y.K. Publishers, Agra, 1985, pp. 95-96.
49. *Ibid.,* p. 97.
50. The Cold War era began immediately after the World War II. Charles O' Lerche, an analyst of the Cold War era, had divided the period into four distinct phases and each phase had distinct crisis situations having all the requirements to usher in a global confrontation — (1) Berlin Blockade of 1948; (2) Korean War (1950); (3) Suez Crisis (1956); (4) Congo Problem (1960). Since India was a new entrant into the world scene in the late 1940, the Berlin Blockade was not a problem effecting India's immediate interests. That was a peripheral issue.
51. *The Hindu,* Madras, 23.10.1956.
52. S.N. Misra, *India — The Cold War Years,* South Asian Publishers Pvt. Ltd., New Delhi, 1994.
53. *Journal of the United Service Institution of India,* Vol. 126, No. 525, July-September, 1996.

54. K.P. Karunakaran, *India in World Affairs*, New Delhi, 1958, p. 102.
55. J.S. Kundra, *Indian Foreign Policy*, 1950-54, Groningen, 1955, p. 128.
56. S. Bhattacharya, *Pursuit of National Interest through Neutralism*, Calcutta, 1968, p. 83.
57. *U.S.I. Journal*, Vol. 126, No. 525, July-September, 1996, p. 347.
58. See *Year Book of the UN*, New York, 1952, pp. 209-10.
59. S.N. Misra, *India — The Cold War Years*, South Asian Publishers Pvt. Ltd., New Delhi, 1994.
60. Blema Steinberg, 'The Korean War — A Case Study in Indian Nationalism', Orbis VIII, Winter, 1965.
61. S.N. Misra, *India — The Cold War Years*, South Asian Publishers Pvt. Ltd., New Delhi, 1994.
62. J. Dasgupta and J.K. Ray, *The Web of International Relations*, Calcutta, 1961.
63. S. Bhattacharya, *Pursuit of National Interest through Neutralism*, Calcutta, 1968, p. 907.
64. F.L. Schuman, *International Politics*, New York, 1962.
65. *Lok Sabha Debates*, Vol. 9, Pt. II, No. 3, Cols. 260-67.
66. W.F.V. Eckelen, 'India's Foreign Policy and the Border Dispute with China', *The Hague*, 1964, p. 71.
67. Bahman Amini, 'India's Foreign Policy with Particular Reference to Asia and Africa (unpublished thesis), cited in S. Bhattacharya, *Pursuit of National Interest through Neutralism*, Calcutta, 1968, p. 93.
68. *Asian Recorder* (I), 1956, 994-95.
69. S. Bhattacharya, *Pursuit of National Interest through Neutralism*, Calcutta, 1968, p. 98.
70. P.R. Sarbadhikari, *India and Great Powers*, Calcutta, 1962, p. 44.
71. Sahdev Vohra, 'India's Foreign Relations Part-I,' in *Journal of the United Service Institution of India*, Vol. 126, No. 525, July-September, 1996.
72. S.N. Misra, *India — The Cold War Years*, South Asian Publishers Pvt. Ltd., New Delhi, 1994.
73. *Ibid.*
74. Marc Lee, *The United Nations and World Realities*, London, 1965, p. 119.
75. S. Bhattacharya, *Pursuit of National Interest through Neutralism*, Calcutta, 1968.
76. *Ibid.*, p. 110.
77. S.N. Misra, *India — The Cold War Years*, South Asian Publishers Pvt. Ltd., New Delhi, 1994.
78. *Ibid.*, p. 244.

79. *Ibid.*
80. E. Lefever, 'Crisis in Congo: A UN Force in Action', Brookings, 1965.
81. *Ibid.*, p. 107.
82. *Ibid.*
83. Niranjan M. Khilnani, *New Dimensions of Indian Foreign Policy,* Westvill Publishing House, New Delhi, 1995.
84. Achin Vanaik, *The Painful Transition — Bourgeois Democracy in India,* Verso, London, 1990.
85. Sahdev Vohra, 'India's Foreign Relations Part-I', *U.S.I. Journal,* Vol. 126, No. 525, July-September, 1996.
86. Achin Vanaik, 'India in the World' in *The Painful Transition,* Verso, London, 1990.
87. *Ibid.*
88. Vijay Sen Budhraj, 'Indian Foregin Policy' in Verinder Grover (Ed.), *India's Foreign Policy and International Relations,* Vol. 1, Deep & Deep Publication, New Delhi, 1992.
89. R.P. Saraf (Ed.), 'Indian Diplomacy-cum-Defence', in *Political and Social Realities in Modern India,* Indian Bibliographies Bureau, Delhi, 1990.
90. Achin Vanaik, 'India in the World', *The Painful Transition,* Verso, London, 1990.
91. *Ibid.*
92. Niranjan M. Khilnani, New *Dimensions of Indian Foreign Policy,* Westvill Publishing House, New Delhi, 1995.
93. Vijay Sen Budhraj, 'Indian Foreign Policy — The Indira Gandhi Era' in Verinder Grover (Ed.), *India's Foreign Policy & International Relations,* Vol. 1, Deep & Deep Publication, New Delhi, 1992.
94. Sahdev Vohra, 'India's Foreign Relations' Part-I, in *U.S.I. Journal,* Vol. 126, No. 525, July-September, 1996.
95. Even for this India had to wait for six years, when in 1971 both the US President Richard Nixon and his versatile Secretary of State Henry Kissinger recognised India as a regional power and thus made it the custodian of peace and stability in the region of South Asia.
96. Achin Vanaik, *The Painful Transition,* Verso, London, 1990, p. 239.
97. Vijay Sen Budhraj, 'Indian Foreign Policy — The Indira Gandhi Era', in Verinder Grover (Ed.), *India's Foreign Policy & International Relations,* Vol. 1, Deep & Deep Publication, New Delhi, 1992.
98. Madhu Limaye, *Problems of India's Foreign Policy*, Edited by Dr. N.C. Mehrotra, Atma Ram & Sons, Delhi, 1984.
99. Vijay Sen Budhraj, 'Indian Foreign Policy — The Indira Gandhi Era', in Verinder Grover (Ed.), *India's Foreign Policy & International Relations,* Vol. 1, Deep & Deep Publication, New Delhi, 1992.

100. Anti-Ayub Khan demonstrations in Pakistan in 1968-69 which ultimately led to his decision to step aside on 25 March 1969, in favour of General Yahya Khan, imposition of martial law, the results of the first general election held in December 1970 and the decision of the military junta to crush the demand for autonomy in March 1971 in what was then East Pakistan.
101. For details, see Vijay Sen Budhraj, *Soviet Russia and Hindustan Subcontinent*, Bombay, 1973, pp. 189-207.
102. Madhu Limaye, *Problems of India's Foreign Policy*, Edited by Dr. N.C. Mehrotra, Atma Ram & Sons, Delhi, 1984.
103. *The Years of Endeavour: Selected Speeches of Indira Gandhi,* p. 526.
104. Madhu Limaye, *Problems of India's Foreign Policy*, Edited by, Dr. N.C. Mehrotra, Atma Ram & Sons, Delhi, 1984.
105. *Ibid.,* p. 116.
106. *Ibid.,* p. 118.
107. Sahdev Vohra, 'India's Foreign Relations Part-I', *U.S.I. Journal*, Vol. 126, No. 525, July-September, 1996, p. 350.
108. *Ibid.*
109. Vijay Sen Budhraj,' Indian Foreign Policy: The Indira Gandhi Era', in Verinder Grover (Ed.), *India's Foreign Policy and International Relations,* Vol. 1 Deep & Deep Publication, New Delhi, 1992.
110. *Ibid.,* p. 346.
111. Pran Chopra, *India's Second Liberation,* Delhi, 1973, pp. 3-4.
112. Vijay Sen Budhraj, 'Indian Foreign Polity—The Indira Gandhi Era' in Verinder Grover (Ed.), *India's Foreign Policy & International Relations,* Vol. 1, Deep & Deep Publication, New Delhi, 1992.
113. See Appadorai and Rajan, *India's Foreign Policy and Relations,* New Delhi, 1988, p. 250.
114. M.S. Rajan, *The Goals of India's Foreign Policy in International Studies;* 35, 1, 1998, Sage Publications, New Delhi.
115. For details, see A. Appadorai and M.S. Rajan: *India's Foreign Policy and Relations,* New Delhi, 1988, pp. 569-74.
116. *FAR,* Vol. 19, 1973, pp. 512-13.
117. *FAR*, Vol. 20, 1974, p. 52.
118. *FAR,* Vol. 21, pp. 116-18; *FAR,* Vol. 24, 1980, p. 191. See also A.P. Thornton: 'The Security of South Asia, Analysis and Speculation, in Stephen Cohen (Ed.), *Security of South Asia,* New Delhi, 1987, p. 218. Rajeshwar Dayal, "The Super Power and India," Seminar, New Delhi, Feb. 1980, pp. 12-17, says he : "India's relations with Super Powers have been rather like those of a capricious and reluctant damsel towards the jealous lovers the one impetuous and immature, the other ardent exigent," p. 12.

119. M.S. Rajan, *International Studies,* 31, 1, 1998, p. 79.
120. *Ibid.,* p. 80.
121. See *FAR*, Vol. 24, 1980, p. 19.
122. *World Focus,* May 1996.
123. A.K. Damodaran (Ed.), 'NAM: The Road Ahead,' in *Indian Foreign Policy*, Vol. 1, FSI, New Delhi, 1997.
124. *World Focus,* May 1990.
125. *World Focus,* June 1989.
126. A.G. Naidu, 'India and the New World Order,' in K. Raman (Ed.), *Indian Foreign Policy in the 1990s*, Pillai, Radient Publishers, New Delhi, 1997.
127. *Ibid.*
128. *Ibid.*
129. M.S. Rajan, 'NAM—Still Very Relevant', *World Focus,* May 1990.
130. *Ibid.*
131. *Ibid.*
132. M.K. Rasgotra (Ed.), *Rajiv Gandhi's Worldview,* Vikas Publishing House Pvt. Ltd., 1991.
133. *Ibid.*
134. *Ibid.*
135. *Ibid.*
136. T.B. Mukherjee, 'India's Foreign Policy' in Verinder Grover (Ed.), *Introduction to India's Foreign Policy & International Relations,* Vol. 1, Deep & Deep Publication, New Delhi, 1992.
137. *Modern Review,* March, 1948, p. 184.
138. M.K. Rasgotra (Ed.), *Rajiv Gandhi's World View,* Vikas Publishing House Pvt. Ltd., 1991.
139. *Ibid.*
140. M.S. Rajan, 'The Goals of India's Foreign Policy', *International Studies,* 35, 1, 1998.
141. *FAR,* Vol. 19, 1973, p.165.
142. In 1983, India gave to African countries assistance of about Rs. 570 crores.
143. M.K. Rasgotra (Ed.), *Rajiv Gandhi's World View,* Vikas Publishing House Pvt. Ltd., 1991.
144. M.S. Rajan, 'The Goals of India's Foreign Policy', *International Studies,* 35, 1, 1998.
145. *Ibid.*
146. *FAR,* Vol. 23, 1977.

147. *FAR,* Vol. 32, 1986, pp. 380-82.
148. *FAR,* Vol. 34, 1988, p. 382.
149. Hugh H. Smythe, 'Nehru and Indian Foreign Policy', in Verinder Grover (Ed.), *Introduction to India's Foreign Policy & International Relation,* Vol. 1, Deep & Deep Publication, New Delhi, 1992.
150. See, for example, the lengthy statement of Ambassador P.K. Banerjee to the *Conference of the Committee on Disarmament,* Geneva, 12 Apr., 1973, FAR, Vol. 19, 1973, p. 150.
151. Text in *FAR,* Vol. 31, 1985, pp. 8-10.
152. Niranjan M. Khilnani, *New Dimensions of Indian Foreign Policy,* Westville Publishing House, New Delhi, 1995.
153. M.K. Rasgotra (Ed.), *Rajiv Gandhi's World View,* Vikas Publishing House Pvt. Ltd., 1991.
154. *FAR,* Vol. 24, 1978, pp. 124-25.
155. *FAR,* Vol. 28, 1982, p. 208. Excerpts from P.V. Narasimha Rao's *Speech to Parliament* on 13 Aug. 1982.
156. *FAR,* Vol. 28, 1975, pp. 138-39.
157. *Asian Recorder*, Vol. 29, 1983, p. 17316.
158. Amitabh Mattoo, 'India and the United Nations', in *Indian Foreign Policy,* Vol. 1, 1997.
159. However, Paul Diehl, an American scholar, has identified 16 different types of interventions under the rubric of 'Peacekeeping' in 'A Taxonomy of Peacekeeping', a lecture delivered at the School of International Studies, Jawaharlal Nehru University, Feb. 3, 1997.
160. Although even in the UN *Conference at San Francisco,* 1945, some other nations raised the issue of making India as permanent member of the Security Council.
161. See M.S. Rajan, *India and the Commonwealth*, New Delhi, 1990.
162. Pakistan left the Commonwealth in 1972 and rejoined in 1990. Again in 1999 after the military coup, Pakistan was threatened by Commonwealth, and it is only after the assurance given by its army chief that very soon state of democracy will be restored, that the membership of Pak continues.
163. M.K. Rosgotra (Ed.), *Rajiv Gandhi's World View,* Vikas Publishing House Pvt. Ltd., 1991.
164. *Ibid.*

4

Salient Features

EVOLUTION

During the British rule in this country, India had no foreign policy of her own. Everything was directed from the Whitehall. In spite of that, certain pronouncements were made from time to time by Indian leaders and the Indian National Congress about the foreign policy of the country. In a letter to Clemenceau, B.G. Tilak wrote: "India is self-contained, harbours no design upon the integrity of other states and has no ambition outside. With her vast area, enormous resources and prodigious population she may well aspire to be a leading power in Asia. She could, therefore, be a powerful steward of the League of Nations in the East for maintaining peace of the world."

At the Haripura session of the Indian National Congress, it was declared that the people of India desired to live in peace and friendship with their neighbours and all other countries. For that purpose, they wished to remove all causes of conflict with them. Striving for their own freedom and independence, they desired to respect the freedom of others. They also desired to build up their strength on the basis of international co-operation and goodwill. Such a co-operation could be founded only on a world order. Free India would gladly associate itself with such an order and stand for disarmament and collective security. World co-operation would be impossible so long as the roots of international conflict remained. If world peace was to be established on an enduring footing, imperialism and exploitation of one nation by another had to be ended.

Most of the resolutions of the Indian National Congress on foreign policy were drafted by Jawaharlal Nehru. In those resolutions, the cause of democracy was advocated and imperialism and colonialism were denounced. When Japan attacked China, the Indian National Congress not only condemned Japan but also sent a medical mission to China as a token of goodwill. The Congress supported the cause of the Republican Government of Spain against General Franco. In the Abyssinian War, the sympathies of the people of India and the Congress were on the side of Abyssinia and against Fascist Italy. After the Munich crisis, the Indian National Congress passed the following resolution in October 1938: 'The Working Committee send their profound sympathy to the brave people of Czechoslovakia in their struggle to preserve their freedom. Being themselves engaged in a war, though non-violent, nonetheless grim and exciting, against the greatest Imperialist power of earth, Indians cannot but be deeply interested in the protection of Czechoslovakian freedom.'

A few days after forming the interim National Government, Pandit Jawaharlal Nehru made his first official announcement on foreign policy over the All India Radio, on September 1946. In the course of his address he observed as under: "We shall take full part in international conferences as a free nation with our own policy and not merely as a satellite of another nation. We hope to develop close and direct contacts with other nations and to co-operate with them in the furtherance of world peace and freedom." We propose, as far as possible to keep away from the power-politics of groups, aligned against one another, which have led in the past to World War and which may again lead to disasters on an even vaster scale. We believe that peace and freedom are indivisible and the denial of freedom anywhere must endanger freedom elsewhere and lead to conflict and war. We are particularly interested in the emancipation of colonial and dependent countries and peoples and in the recognition in theory and practice of equal opportunities for all races. We repudiate utterly the Nazi doctrine of racialism, whosesoever and in whatever form it may be practised. We seek no domination over others and we claim no privileged position over other peoples. But we do claim equal and honourable treatment for our people wherever they may go and we cannot accept any discrimination against them.

The world, in spite of its rivalries and hatreds and inner conflicts moves inevitably towards closer co-operation and building up of a world commonwealth. It is for this one world that free India will work, a world in which there is the free co-operation of free peoples, and no class or group exploits another.

Again, we hope that an independent India will have friendly and co-operative relations with England and the countries of the British Commonwealth.... We send our greetings to the people of the United States of America to whom destiny has given a major role in international affairs. We trust that this tremendous responsibility will be utilized for the furtherance of peace and human freedom everywhere.

To that other great nation of the modern world, the Soviet Union, which also carries a vast responsibility for shaping world events, we send greetings. They are our neighbours in Asia and inevitably we shall have to undertake many common tasks and have much to do with each other.

We are of Asia and the peoples of Asia are nearer and closer to us than others. India is so situated that she is the pivot of Western, Southern and South-East Asia. In the past her culture flowed to all these countries, and they came to her in many ways. Those contacts are being renewed and the future is bound to see a closer union between India and South-East Asia on the one side and Afghanistan, Iran, and the Arab world on the other. To the furtherance of that close association of free countries we must devote ourselves. India has followed with anxious interest struggle of the Indonesians for freedom and to them we send our good wishes. China, that mighty country with a mighty past, our neighbour, has been our friend through the ages and that friendship will endure and grow. We earnestly hope that her present troubles will end soon and a united and democratic China will emerge, playing a great part in the furtherance of world peace and progress.

After the independence of India on 15 August, 1947 Pandit Jawaharlal Nehru was not only the Prime Minister, but also the Foreign Minister of India. He was given a free hand to formulate his foreign policy in any way he pleased. The remarkable thing is that no departure has been made from the policy statement made by him on 7th September, 1946. Some sort of consistency is apparent in the foreign policy of the country. In the course of time, there has been emphasis on certain aspects but on the whole the policy remains the same. It is a matter of great joy that this foreign policy has been endorsed year after year by the Parliament of India. It is true that at the beginning it led to a lot of misunderstanding and we were dubbed as hypocrites and opportunists, but that time has passed by and there is a general appreciation of the role that is being played by India in world politics.

FOREIGN POLICY IN GENERAL

A general idea of the foreign policy of India can be had from some of the statements made by Jawaharlal Nehru and other Indian leaders on various occasions. According to Nehru, "India does not seek domination over others and our sole object is to be left in peace to ourselves to solve our own problems and where possible, to help and cooperate with others. In doing so, we try not to be swept by passion and anger and so maintain that temper of peaceful approach.

The basic object of India's foreign policy has been the maintenance of friendly relations with all nations of the world. Our policy is not to commit ourselves beforehand to follow a certain line. Our policy is independence of action. If we say we are permanently neutral, it has no meaning except permanent retirement from public affairs, in the national sense 'sannyas'. No country can do that and certainly we have no desire to retire from world affairs.

In the sphere of foreign affairs, India will follow an independent policy; keeping away from the power politics of groups aligned one against another. She will uphold the principle of freedom for dependent peoples and will oppose racial discrimination, wherever, it may occur. She will work with the other peace-loving nations for international co-operation and goodwill without exploitation of one nation by another.

India's policy in regard to any matter is determined by India and is, it may be said, pro-India with friendship towards others.

The use of the word 'neutral' to describe India's foreign policy is wrong except in terms of war. If you say there is a war on to-day, we are neutral. If you say there is a Cold War, we are certainly neutral. The Cold War is in some ways worse than a shooting war, worse not in disaster but in the sense that it is more degrading and it lowers the standards all the time. We do not propose to join that war. It does not matter who is wrong. We will not join in this exhibition of mutual abuse, because we do not serve anybody that way, certainly not the cause of peace. We want to befriend every country so that our circle of friendship may grow and become wide and co-operation and peace may thrive. What kind of friendship is that which envisages enmity with others? We should befriend all and stretch out our hands to all. For this reason our coming closer to the great country, the Soviet Union, is very important. But this does not mean that we have drifted away from any other country. This is neither the position now nor will it be at any time in the future. We have always wanted and we still want co-operation among the countries of the world to increase, and world peace to be strengthened."

Addressing a meeting of the Foreign Policy Association, Morarji Desai, India's Finance Minister, stated that India's alleged neutralism was not an attitude of indifference or unpreparedness to judge between right and wrong. Nor did that rest on any assumed role of being outside the fray and therefore, somehow above it. All that India was seeking was to establish for herself a record of fair play and openmindedness, a freedom to assess — subject to all the limitations of human judgment in these matters — each case on its merits, of readiness to see the strong and weak points on either side. The issues which confronted India were too complex to be settled in terms of 'yes' or 'no' or of 'for' or 'against'. There were differences of degree, differences of emphasizing in particular contexts as well as those in basic approaches which all had to be reckoned with. Friendship for all and readiness to absorb the best from all peoples of the world was at the root of India's foreign policy.

Jawaharlal Nehru rightly pointed out that the foreign policy of India has been partly determined on account of her geographical location on the globe. According to him:

> India is curiously situated from the geographical point of view as well as from many other points of view. It belongs to South-East Asia, it belongs to South Asia, it also belongs to West Asia. It just depends on which way you look at it, because it happens to be the centre of all these. And whether you think in terms of East Asian travel or South Asian travel, India is there in the middle of the picture. All international routes or routes round that would have almost inevitably to pass over India. When you look at it from other points of view like trade and commerce, or when you think of it in terms of defence, India becomes the pivotal centre of South, South-East and Western Asia. Geography has given her that position, and because geography gave India that position, and also no doubt because of other factors, the course of history has shown how India has influenced all the countries around her and has been influenced by them.

Ernest Bevin, former British Foreign Secretary referred to the importance of the geographical position of India in these words:

> India is the key to the situation. If that key can be held in security, then the peace of the world can be held for hundreds of years.

According to Guy Wint:

> Indian Ministers will probably differ little in practice from the former British regime in what they regard as the essential interests of India in foreign policy. The interests are determined chiefly by geography and technical science and will be much the same in the next decade or two as in the past few years.

MAIN CHARACTERISTICS

1. The main characteristic of India's foreign policy are discussed below:

The first characteristic of India's foreign policy is non-alignment. This means that India is not prepared to join either the Anglo-American bloc or the Soviet bloc. The country is determined to keep aloof from them. Its contention is that it can serve the cause of world peace only if it retains the independence of judgement and is prepared to call a spade a spade. If India becomes a camp follower of any bloc, it cannot do so. The attitude of India is determined by a balancing of three considerations, viz. whether it is on the side of justice or truth, whether it furthers the cause of universal peace or freedom and whether it is favourable to India's national interests. Alignments possess some significance in the context of war. One tries to side with another to safeguard one's own interest and also to cling on to something which enables one to tide over the crisis. In times of relative peace the talk of alignments is wholly irrelevant. It can have only one result and that result is to create a feeling of scare among the peoples of the world, to create a war-time psychology which in itself might prove a potent factor in accelerating the breaking out of a war. A period of tension or one of open conflict is not conducive to the best interests of India either domestically or internationally. Even in view of the self-interest of India, a policy of non-alignment is best suited to its requirements. According to Nehru: "About 150 years ago, the Western world was breaking up on account of all kinds of imperial and revolutionary wars. Having achieved independence by breaking off from the British Empire, the United States was naturally affected by these upheavals; nevertheless it avoided being involved in the chaotic situation of Europe — although doubtless it had its particular sympathies — because that was the natural thing for a nation in that state of affairs to do. Now this analogy, although it may not be a particularly good one in the circumstances of today, has a bearing and I wish to point out that for a country that has newly attained freedom and independence, this is the natural policy to pursue."

The foreign policy of India is not a passive or negative policy. It is a positive policy of helping those forces which India considers to be right and disproving of those which we consider to be wrong. While doing so, India has to keep itself away from alignments of power which normally lead to wars.

The foreign policy of India is aimed primarily at preventing world conflict and to retain a position for India from which it can stop the same. India does not join the power politics so that it is in a position, when the time comes, to throw in its weight in the interest of peace. According to Appadorai: "This independent foreign policy is not the same thing as neutrality; it may demand, if and when war comes, that India should join the free nations to realise its objectives of freedom and peace. It is not a negative policy, it is a positive one, designed to realise the objectives of peace, freedom, friendliness with like-minded nations and the economic development of her and other underdeveloped nations. This independent foreign policy only means that India refuses to commit itself in advance to either bloc by means of a pact or otherwise to surrender her freedom to judge each issue as it arises on its merits."

According to V.K. Krishna Menon: "India has not aligned herself with any Power bloc in the world and therefore, wishes no enemies and perhaps no friends. India has done so because she is anxious that she should not give cause for enmity to any Power. Alignment with one of the Power blocs will eventually make our country a stepping ground, arsenal or the target of attack by the other bloc."

Pandit Jawaharlal Nehru defended his policy of non-alignment in many of his statements made from time to time some of which are given below: "In any event, speaking for India, whatever happens, I am not prepared merely to say ditto to any country in the wide world. I think it is degrading for a country as it is for an individual just to be an automation, just to be a puppet and to repeat what others say. I do not think that anything could be more injurious to us from any point of view—certainly from an idealistic and high moral point of view but equally so from the point of view of opportunism and national interest in the narrowest sense of the world—than for us to give up those policies that we have pursued, namely of standing up for certain ideals in regard to oppressed nations, and trying to align ourselves with this great Power or that and becoming its camp follower in the hope that some crumbs might fall from their tables. I realise—I frankly admit that there are always certain risks involved, not risks on paper but risks in the same sense that certain obligations might be felt which might affect our policy without our knowing it. Those risks are there. All I can say is that we should be wide awake to avoid our committing mistakes because of those risks. If any country imagines that we are going to change our policies and sell ourselves for a mess of poltage from any other country, she, I submit, is completely mistaken. I am quite sure in my mind that if at any time any help from abroad depends upon the slightest variation of our policy, we shall give up that help, the whole of it, and prefer starvation and everything to it. So it is this way that we accept help and I think the world knows it well enough."

It is pointed out that it is on account of our policy of non-alignment that we have been able to serve the cause of peace in the world. We have been in a position to examine a problem dispassionately and point out a solution for the same.

The Government of India played an important part in bringing the Korean War to a close. While India joined the Anglo-American bloc in branding North Korea as the aggressor, she refused to do so when a resolution was passed declaring Red China as the aggressor. Likewise, India had no hesitation in telling the American government that the armies of the United Nations must not cross the 48th Parallel. There was very likelihood of the war spreading rather than coming down. The advice of India was not palatable to the American Government but it was on account of our special position that we could point out the consequences of such an action. It was on account of our non-alignment policy that we could afford not to sign the peace treaty between the United Nations and Japan at San Francisco in 1951. We signed a separate treaty with Japan in 1952. It is for the same reason that we recognised Red China even when the United States did not.

Likewise, we have been trying to bring Red China into the United Nations although that move is opposed by the American government.

Walter Lippman has given a comparison of the foreign policy of India and the United States in their early years in these words: "Despite all the obvious and enormous differences in position, history, outlook between the America then and India today, the fundamental pattern of Indian foreign policy is extraordinarily like the original American foreign policy.

The present foreign policy of the Indian Government is not one of the mysteries.... Like our own during the epoch of the founding fathers it is in all its essentials — in its aspirations limitations and reserves — the natural expression of the vital interests of a new state.

India must struggle to survive before it can take the risks of wider and more adventurous commitments. For some time to come India must regard herself not as a world power but a regional power (together with Pakistan) — the natural orbit of Indian interest and influence is in the countries around the Indian Ocean, with a moderate extension to Indonesia and the South Pacific. This region is to India what the Western Hemisphere was for so long to the United States. Beyond it they cannot hope or be expected to act effectively, though no doubt like America since the beginning they will be issuing declarations on all sorts of contentious issues that they cannot and will not do anything more about.

In the Indian Ocean region their main concern will be like that of the founding fathers in the Western Hemisphere — to consolidate their own position in relation to their nearest neighbours, and to create in the whole area a zone of security designed to insulate them against the rivalries of world powers, to protect them against the rise of new empires — Chinese, Soviet or Western — and to develop good neighbours for themselves by helping the native peoples to liquidate peaceably what remains of the old empires."

2. Another feature of India's foreign policy is that we are opposed to imperialism and colonialism. The Government of India has consistently championed the cause of the exploited nations against the colonial powers. Even when India was not free the Indian National Congress expressed its sympathy against all those countries which were struggling for their liberation from the yoke of the imperialist Powers. We had suffered terribly under the foreigners and we were in a position to understand and appreciate the sufferings of those who were in a similar position. No wonder, when Jawaharlal Nehru formed the interim Government, he declared that his Government was particularly interested in the emancipation of colonial and dependent countries and their peoples.

India has not merely raised slogans of anti-colonialism, it has actually helped nations struggling to be free. When after the end of the World War II, the Dutch Government tried to re-establish her strangle hold over Indonesia, the Government of India resisted it. A meeting of the Foreign Ministers was called in New Delhi and an appeal was made to the Security Council. The result was that ultimately the independence of Indonesia was recognised. The part played by India in the independence of Indonesia was recognised by A.H. Sastroamidjojo, the then Prime Minister of Indonesia, in these words: "The assistance which India has given so fully and wholeheartedly to my people will be written in letters of shining gold in the pages of history of free Indonesia."

Libya owes her independence almost entirely to the Indian initiative. India has continued to resist the policies of the Union of South Africa to incorporate the territories of South West Africa into the Union. The Government of India played an important part in bringing about an end to the war in Indo-China. India has also advocated the cause of the independence of Tunisia and Algeria. There has been a lot of resentment in India over the virtual annexation of Tibet by the Government of Red China. India has opposed the efforts of the great powers to exploit the people of the Middle East. It has stood for a policy of nonintervention in the affairs of those peoples. She has neither liked the Cominform nor the Eisenhover Doctrine. It hates the bossing over of the weak by the strong nations. The late President Nasser of Egypt also appreciated India's role in this regard: "The records of the cases of Palestine, Libya, Tunisia and Morocco, not to mention other cases, bear witness to the invaluable support which India is generously ready to extend to the cause of freedom."

3. Another characteristic of India's foreign policy is its opposition to racial discrimination. According to Nehru: "We repudiate utterly the Nazi doctrine of racialism whosesoever and in whatever form it may be practised. We seek no domination over others and we claim no privileged position over other peoples. But we do claim equal and honourable treatment for our people wherever they may go and we cannot accept any discrimination against them." No wonder, we have condemned

in strongest possible terms the policy of apartheid followed by the Union of South Africa. We have supported morally the fight of the coloured people in South Africa against the White Supremacy. In July 1954, the office of the Indian High Commissioner in the Union of South Africa was closed. India has been instrumental in the passing of resolutions by the United Nations against the policy of discrimination followed by the Government of South Africa. We have also sympathized with the fight of the Negroes of the United States against the Whites.

4. It is true that India follows a policy of friendship towards all the nations of the world. However, her definite bias in favour of Asia cannot be denied. In March 1947 was held the Asian Relations Conference in Delhi. Addressing the meeting Jawaharlal Nehru observed thus: "In this crisis in the world history, Asia will necessarily play a vital role. The countries of Asia can no longer be used as pawns by others; they are bound to have their own role to play in world affairs. Europe and America have contributed very greatly to human progress and for that we must yield them praise and honour and learn from them the many, lessons they have to teach. But the West has also driven us into wars and conflicts without number and even now, the day after a terrible war, there is talk of further wars in the atomic age that is upon us. In this atomic age, Asia will have to function effectively in the maintenance of peace. Indeed, there can be no peace unless Asia plays her part. There is today conflict in many countries and all of us in Asia are full of our own troubles. Nonetheless, the whole spirit and outlook of Asia are peaceful, and the emergence of Asia in the world affairs will be a powerful influence for world peace."

In order to assure those countries which might think that India was going to create a separate Asian bloc with a view to opposing others, Pandit Nehru observed thus: "I give this assurance to Europe and America that we have no designs against anybody; ours is a great design of promoting peace and progress all over the world. We propose to stand on our own feet and co-operate with all others who are prepared to co-operate with us."

Whenever there has been any difficulty in any part of Asia, the Government of India has tried to solve it. It has already been pointed out that the Government of India decided to take effective measures against the Dutch Government when the latter tried to re-establish her authority over Indonesia. At the instance of India, many Asian countries took steps to ban Dutch Airlines from plying across Asia in retaliation. Seventeen member states of the United Nations met in January 1949 in New Delhi and on that occasion Nehru observed thus: "We meet today because the freedom of a sister country of ours has been imperiled and the dying colonialism of a past age has raised its head again and challenged all the forces that are struggling to build up new structure of the world. That challenge has a deeper significance than might appear on the surface, for it is a challenge to newly awakened Asia which had so long suffered under various forms of colonialism. It is also a challenge to the spirit of man and to all the progressive forces of a divided and distracted world.... Any person who is acquainted with the spirit of the Indonesian people today knows that this attempt to suppress Indonesian people will fail. But if open and unabated aggression is not checked and is condoned by other Powers, then hope will vanish and people will resort to other ways and other means even though these might involve the utmost catastrophe. One thing is certain. There can be and will be no surrender to aggression and no acceptance or re-imposition of colonial control." The Delhi Conference had the desired effect and through the good offices of the United States, the independence of Indonesia was recognised.

In April 1955, another Asian Conference was held in New Delhi. It was presided over by Remeshwari-Nehru and was attended by about 200 delegates from various countries of Asia.

However, the most important was the Bandung Conference where the representatives of both Asia and Africa met to vindicate their united stand against racialism and colonialism. The Government of India played the most important part in making that conference a success. On the occasion of the Bandung Conference, Pandit Nehru observed thus: "Apart from the problem of new countries in Asia and Africa — and these problems are important — there is the basic problem of Asia and Africa, if I may use the words, pulling their weight regarding their own problems in world affairs. It is important that the

Asian-African Conference should help to put Asia and Africa in proper perspective in the world because old perspectives no longer apply. It is not our purpose to form blocs and the like. We meet for mutual co-operation among ourselves as well as with others."

According to the *Times of London:* "In part, no doubt, India's prominence as the spokesman of the Asian point of view is due to the vigour with which she has taken up the claims of the new Asian national movements in their dealings with the Western World. But it is significant that the Asian countries which are most closely associated with her are precisely those which owe the foundation of their civilization to the culture which they learnt from her."

5. Another aspect of India's foreign policy is her sympathy for divided countries. This is due to the fact that on account of the partition of India, we had ourselves to suffer a lot. Most of the problems between India and Pakistan are the creation of the partition of India. That is the reason why the Government of India opposed the partitioning of Palestine and suggested the establishment of a federation of the Arabs and Jews. That is the reason why India was opposed to the division of Korea and the divisions in Indo-China. We also did not like the perpetuation of the division of Germany into Eastern and Western Germany.

6. India stands for the maintenance of peace in the world through the United Nations. She has taken a very active part in the work of the United Nations. For that very reason, the Government of India took the question of Kashmir to the United Nations. India has co-operated with the United Nations to solve many international problems. However, it is true that we have refused to align ourselves even in the United Nations either with the Soviet bloc or with the Anglo-American bloc. The Indian stand has always been determined by the interests of the world. When a conference was summoned in New Delhi in January 1949 to tackle the question of Indonesia and India was accused of ignoring the United Nations, Jawaharlal Nehru gave the reply in these words: "We meet to supplement the efforts of the Security Council, not to supplant that body. We meet in no spirit of hostility to any nation or group of nations, but in an endeavour to promote peace through the extension of freedom."

5

Panch-Sila (Panchsheel)

MEANING AND NATURE

Panch-Sila is the foremost basis of India's Foreign Policy. The expression Panch-Sila has a history which goes back to at least 2500 years. Though it has undergone some changes in the modern times. It consists of two Sanskrit words 'Pancha' meaning 'Five' and 'Sila' or 'Sheela' meaning "Rule of Conduct". The Sanskrit word is properly transcribed in Roman script as Panch-Sila or Pancha-Sila. The word has had an interesting evolution in Indonesia where it is written as Panja-Sila. In India, it is frequently written in the English journals as Panch-Sila. This transcription sometimes leads to an inaccurate re-transliteration in the Nagari and other Indian dialects and has brought about a total misunderstanding of the word because Sila means stone or rock or a slab of stone.[1]

The ideas behind the expression Panch-Sila have been changed or expanded in recent times during the last 10 years from its original meaning in Buddhism. Buddhism has the following five rules of conduct:

1. Not to destroy any life.
2. Not to take what was given to one.
3. To lead a life of contentment and chastity.
4. Not to tell a lie.
5. Not to take any intoxicant.

The above five principles are the Buddhist Pancha-Sila.

On 1st June 1945, Sukarno made a very important speech before a gathering of Indonesian patriots and fighters who had pledged to win their independence and in that speech announced to the world the ideals which the free Republic of Indonesia had placed before herself. Those five ideals known as Panch-Sila are as follows:

1. Faith in one's people — nationalism — without which no nation can achieve anything and which alone can be the basis of national endeavour.
2. Faith in humanity which must be the basis of all international relations. Considering the case of one's own people against the broad background of the universal brotherhood of man.
3. Faith in freedom which is the basis of democracy, freedom of mind, body and spirit.
4. Faith in social justice or equal opportunity for all citizens of a democratic society without any special privileges for any one.
5. Faith in God as the people of Indonesia, whether Muslims or Christians or Hindus or Buddhists, all believed in the existence of an ultimate reality behind life.

The Panch-Sila of Nehru was first embodied in a treaty signed by India and China on the issue of Tibet on May 29, 1954. The five principles mentioned therein are as follows:

1. Mutual respect for each other's territorial integrity and sovereignty.
2. Non-aggression.
3. Non-intervention in another's domestic affairs.
4. Mutual benefit and equality.
5. Peaceful co-existence.

The first principle implies that India and China both agreed to recognise the territorial, sovereign and independent status of each. The second implies that neither would go to war against the other. The third principle implies that China would not persuade or abet the Indian Communists to move against the

Indian state and the Government of India also would not interfere in anything dealing with the internal policy of China. The fourth principle implies that the two countries would recognise each other's equal status and would follow those paths which would prove to be beneficial to both. The fifth principle implies that the two countries should be existing side by side without undermining the social, economic and political system of each other.

The above-mentioned five principles were also embodied in a joint statement issued on June 28, 1954 by the Prime Ministers of India and China. The two Prime Ministers declared that the five principles mentioned above should be applied in their relations with other countries in Asia and in other parts of the world. It was contended that if those principles were applied, not only between various countries but also in international relations generally, those were bound to form a solid foundation for peace and security and the fears and apprehensions that then existed, would yield place to a feeling of confidence. The Prime Ministers recognised that different social and political systems existed in various parts of Asia and the world. However, if the above-mentioned principles were accepted and acted upon and there was no interference by any country in the affairs of another, those differences should not come in the way of peace or create conflicts. With the assurance of territorial integrity and sovereignty of each country and of non-aggression, there, would be peaceful co-existence and friendly relations between the countries concerned. That would lessen the tensions that existed in the world and help in creating a climate of peace.

On the occasion of the Bandung Conference held in 1955, the following new items were added to the Panch-Sila:

1. Respect for fundamental human rights.
2. Right to defend singly as well as collectively.
3. Joining of the pacts without any external pressure.
4. Participation in secret pacts only for the sake of benefit.
5. Settlement of disputes peacefully.
6. Respect for justice.

The other four principles were those which were given in the Panch-Sila except peaceful co-existence. In this way, the Panch-Sila was transformed into Dus-Sila at the Bandung Conference.

According to Jawaharlal Nehru "Two systems — one democratic and other totalitarian — are facing each other with panoplied strength. There is so much of war-preparedness that no war is possible. Each bloc has to save each other and goes on piling up armaments for peace. To this perfectly Gilbertian situation, India has made a positive contribution — Panch-Sila."

It cannot be denied that the policy of Panch-Sila is gathering strength in the world and many countries have commended it as worthy of universal respect. The names of some of these countries are the Soviet Union, China, Indonesia, Burma, Afghanistan, Yugoslavia, Poland, Saudi Arabia, Laos, Viet Nam, Liberia, etc. There is a demand that these principles should be applied in international relations. Marshall Tito of Yugoslavia expressed the importance of the philosophy of Panch-Sila thus: "It is clear that the world can be saved from a new war catastrophe only if peaceful co-operation between states and peoples with different social systems is established and if co-existence becomes stable and in the present time the only possible form of international relations. Accordingly, we fully share the fate of the leading men and peoples of India in the correctness and efficacy of such an international policy."

Panch-Sila has been criticised on many grounds. Critics point out that there is nothing new in it. The Covenant of the League of Nations affirmed the Panch-Sila by prohibiting the members not to resort to war. According to Stalin, Lenin was the first to give this idea. The Atlantic Charter while prohibiting colonial aggrandizement confirmed Panch-Sila. At the end of the World War II, President Truman observed thus: "If we don't agree to die in war, we should agree to live in peace." The Charter of the United Nations also stated that the member states agreed to save the succeeding generations from the scourge of war.

Panch-Sila has been described as the Magna Carta only for the Reds. According to the *New York Times,* Panch-Sila enormously added to the position of Communist China as an aggressor in the Far East. It alienated Delhi from Washington and put it near Moscow.

According to Pibul Songram, the then Prime Minister of Thailand, the Panch-Sila undermines the United Nations. However, it is pointed out that there is no inconsistency between the principles of Panch-Sila and the Charter of the United Nations. The acceptance of Panch-Sila principles does not lead to the formation of a parallel organisation.

Some of the critics brand Panch-Sila principles as simple appeasement. However, it is contended that it is wrong to maintain that India sold Tibet to China as Tibet never belonged to India. Chinese sovereignty over Tibet had a historical background of centuries and was recognised by even some foreign powers.

It is pointed out that the principles of Panch-Sila can never be put into practice. However, it has rightly been pointed out by Adlai Stevenson, that in spite of conflicts in the past, the conflicting parties have survived. The object of the crusades was to destroy Islam but in spite of that Islam and Christianity even today exist side by side. The object of the Thirty Years' War was to destroy Protestantism but in spite of that even today Protestantism and Catholicism exist side by side. Likewise, it can be said that both Communism and Capitalism can exist side by side.

Panch-Sila is at best an abstract conception like equality, freedom, discipline, respect for law, etc. It is a negative concept, the mere acceptance of two state systems. Its mere enunciation does not solve our problems. A tremendous effort has to be made in order to create the conditions which should facilitate its practice. Peaceful co-existence can be possible only when certain essential conditions are present. Otherwise it will only be a pious wish to which nations may pay lip service.

NOTE

1. N. Jayapalan (2001). *Foreign Policy of India,* Atlantic Publishers and Distributors Pvt. Ltd., New Delhi , pp. 33-53.

6

Changing Political Scenario

Policy-making is quite a complex matter. A foreign policy is never uniquely determined by any one factor, or a set of factors but is the result of the interplay of a large number of factors that affect the formulation of policy in different ways in different circumstances. The end of 20th century embarked upon new values, new thinking, new culture, new technology, and new institutions. With the great revolution in Information Technology, everything has changed. New developments, new trends and new forces have emerged. What was experienced in India though, was the part of worldwide phenomenon of change, like the victory of democratic institutions and prevalence of market economy, coalition culture and nuclear technology.

Since independence, Indian political scenario has been full of surprises of both positive and negative kinds. There is a slow but gradual evolution of political consciousness from election to election. The operationization of rational and irrational forces in the electoral process from one stage to another affects the health of democracy. Violence, caste conflict and terrorism persist in India. But in the face of all these hurdles, Indian democracy has matured and has come of age and its future seems secure. Democracy in India is a way of life and can never be changed. According to Henry Kissinger, "India has matured into a fine making democracy."[1] Prof. Chia Nakana of the Tokyo University opined that, "In Asia and in the world, there is no parallel to the Indian democracy. Democracy is innately and inherently strong in India and can withstand all shocks and surprises."[2]

Foreign policy is expected to be dynamic—making constant adjustments with changing circumstances, internal as well as external. The framework of Indian foreign policy began to change in a subtle but definite way in the 1990s. A combination of domestic and external factors shaped these changes.

The foreign policy of every country is a mirror reflection of domestic co-relationship of social forces. During the 1990s, Indian foreign policy became reactive, defensive and obliging, because political parties have fractured the Indian society on the basis of caste versus caste, community versus community, region versus region, and language versus language. The consequence of this highly fragmented political process is that political parties have multiplied to promote their sectional and sectarian group interests. The Indian foreign policy has lost its initiatives of the 1950s, 1960s, 1970s and 1980s, because regionalists, casteists, communalists along with propertied classes have created social conditions for the weakening of the Indian state. An internally fragile, unstable, fragmented coalitional political process cannot face the new challenges of the emerging global capitalism of the 21st century. Likewise, the Prime Minister of a hung parliament cannot provide leadership while dealing with powerful Western countries and global institutions.

There have been five general elections between 1989 and 1999, all of which have produced a fractured mandate. With no single party able to muster a clear majority on its own, India entered the period of coalition politics in the last decade of the twentieth century. This has had effects on the foreign policy. Besides, in order to overcome the domestic economic crisis, India opted for aid from the International Monetary Fund and the World Bank in the early nineties. As a result, the process of liberalisation and privatisation got underway, which in turn brought various pressures on India's foreign policy. The other domestic factors, which made influence on India's foreign policy in this period, range from—caste-class conflict, religious extremism, insurgencies, terrorism, decline in Parliamentary culture, fragmentation in party system, crisis of governance, to—globalisation, nuclearisation and women, empowerment.

CULTURE OF COALITION POLITICS

Six decades after independence, coalition politics has become a fact of life in Indian politics because no single political party on its own seems to be in a position to muster majority in the Lok Sabha elections. Since the first general elections in 1952 the Congress managed to walk away with a majority of Lok Sabha seats without even getting fifty per cent of total votes polled, except once in 1984. In fact it is an irony of electoral system of India that the seats won by a political party in an election at both the union and the state levels are disproportionate to the share of votes polled by it. With less than fifty per cent votes, the Congress party managed to win two-third seats in Lok Sabha. At the state level, there are examples where the party has won the majority seats with mere thirty per cent of vote share.

After independence, Gandhi's advice to disband the Congress and convert it into a social organisation went unheeded by ambitious and power-hungry leaders of the party. But the Congress operated, mostly, as a coalition itself. It worked as a centrist party (except in 1977-80). In 1989 came the end of the Congress hegemony. The non-Congress political parties discovered the joy of putting together a post-election alliance. V.P. Singh was Prime Minister for 11 months, Chandrashekhar for 4 months, Narasimha Rao for five years by purchasing loyalties of MPs, Deve Gowda for 10 months, Inder Kumar Gujral for six months and Atal Behari Vajpayee for 13 months. Not only this, even during their short, temporary and tension ridden regimes all the Prime Ministers were on tenderhooks because of their quarrelsome coalitional partners. Also the weak and unstable coalition governments at the Centre are finding it difficult to face the new international order based on the hegemony of the Western capitalist countries and to formulate the foreign policy of India in accordance with the same.

In 1996, it was the turn of non-BJP parties to come together to keep the BJP out of power. However, BJP joined hands with the other like-minded parties to form the National Democratic Alliance (NDA) and fought the 1998 elections and after the early dissolution of the Lok Sabha 1999 elections secured majority in the house. With this started the era of coalition politics in India. The present Congress Government is also an alliance of several political parties.

A widespread concern is discernible in the public discourse over the coalitions in the country. And the concern is almost recent while the phenomenon is not new and is in fact very much inherent in the parliamentary form of government itself. Coalitions have been in existence in many of the European democracies and elsewhere. In India too the formation of coalitions precede independence and the first coalition government in a state came in existence as early as in 1937 in PEPSU and in many of the states the process was institutionalized much before the phenomenon surfaced at the Union level. The phenomenon till it was limited to the states was perhaps not a matter of great concern; it was only after the 'menace' spread to the center, it became the cause of concern. The stability is the biggest cause of concern. There is another dimension of the perceived crisis, its moral aspect. It is said that minuscule parties bereft of public mandate form immoral alliances in order to get into governance, particularly post-poll alliances are seen with much disdain in this regard and the biggest cause of concern being computational alliances formed to topple a sitting government and to form a new one.

The situation today reveals that no single party would gain majority and excessive worry over a so-called hung Parliament suggests an innate distaste for coalitions. This is unwarranted.[3] Coalitions are legitimate and can be purposeful and long lasting. There seems to be an irrational prejudice in India against the coalition pattern.[4] Superficially the argument against coalition appears convincing but the facts speak differently. It is very easy to access and know the reality but the general prejudices prevent people to reach the right conclusions. First is the issue of national development, which is the first exhortation of every Indian. The basic fact about coalition is that it leads to instability and an unstable government hinders the process of development. As has been stated earlier that coalitions have existed in the developed countries of Europe and that did not push those countries towards poverty. Coalitions did not adversely affect their developed status. On the other hand in many Third World countries, stability, which in many place was jealously ensured by the military juntas, hardly helped them to overcome their wretched existence. India is not a different case. It was the minority government of P.V. Narsimha Rao, which initiated reforms in the country, and which have been sustained by the coalition government thereafter. India achieved the status of the second fastest growing economy of the world only in this era of coalition governance. In short, coalition government is in no way a factor adversely affecting the economic development of the country.

Besides, the given political scenario underlines the dire need that a coalition government at the center as inevitability in the existing equation of political parties in the Lok Sabha and it is the only alternative to the traditional one-party rule mode in the multi-party situation obtaining in our country. It is wrong to hold the opinion that the coalition model cannot work successfully at the centre.[5] For the success of this model, there should be mutual respect, tolerance and approval of time-bound common action plan between different constituents. India has witnessed disastrous experiences of coalition governments[6] at the center because of the heterogeneous character of such governments and outside support by some parties which keep on threatening to withdraw their support on various issues.

At the same time to believe that India is ripe and ready for coalition governments is to give too much credit to political actors and to their many *ad hoc* justifications for seeking power. It undermines the urgency to articulate developmental issues and overvalues, instead, the preservation and protection of specific interests. Given the vast disparities in living conditions in India, coalitions have the dangerous potential of exaggerating these painful diversities even further. Sometimes, of course and electoral verdict leaves no option other than a coalition government, but there is no need to make a virtue of necessity.[7]

While in many Western democracies, coalition government neither are hardly exceptional nor do they signal something abnormal or disagreeable. But, in contrast to the developing world, western societies possess one exceptional feature that allows them to function effectively with coalition governments: these countries have a large middle class and an overwhelmingly uniform pattern of consumption and lifestyles. This not only accounts for the similarities between parties in Europe and North America, but also marginalises the significance of developmental issues in their politics. In fact, many western scholars have commented on the post-modern exhaustion of experience where nothing new can be added in substantive terms. What is left is but to play with commodities. As planning for the future has no allure in such societies, Western democracies provide congenial settings for coalition governments.[8] The situation is vastly different in an old-new, rich-poor, multi-cultural country like India. Masses of poverty and a fragile middle class make development programmes a primary concern here. As Indian public is far from being homogenous and uniformly prosperous, it is only through developmental programmes that the existing heterogeneity of groups and interests can be realistically addressed. The Indian electorate still regards social development as a desirable goal. This is probably why there has been a social issue every time a coalition has fallen.[9]

Two other issues related to coalition, which cause consternation, are immorality and disregard for ideology. Crass opportunism is said to be the bottom line of coalition politics and which ironically is the reality. But the end result is positive. The coalition politics has a moderating effect on extremist party lines. There has evolved and has got institutionalised a system of checks and balances which takes care of several ills that many of our political parties suffer from. The situation has changed considerably from earlier times. The ideology as it is, stands negated in today's world. With the disintegration of the erstwhile Soviet Union in early 1990s, no one talks of ideology anymore. In an era of liberalisation and globalisation ideology has taken a back seat and fierce economic competition is the bottom line today.

In fact the above arguments which are only illustrative, not exhaustive, are only meant to show that the coalition politics does not reflect any crisis or decline in the political order. Problems are there but they have been there even during the earlier times of stability. It's only a new edition of the earlier system but with positive features as its character is nearer to the spirit of the cabinet system, as the members of the cabinet have among themselves a relationship of relative equality. Moreover, the coalition politics is essentially reflective of the ongoing democratisation of public life in India. D mocracy essentially relates to the political order but in order to be vibrant it must permeate the public psyche and the social fabric. The Indian society is witnessing such permeation. And this process is bringing in different sections hitherto marginalised to the mainstream of politics. This is the democratic federalisation of the country rather horizontally. The 'littles' not only want their voice heard but also want to be there, at the hubs of activities, at the center of decision-making processes, in the limelight of attention and above all want the share in the spoils of the governance. On the other plane the mega nationalist unified party-system had left little scope for dignified representation of regional identities. Democratisation process led to the demand for further federalisation both vertical and horizontal even by these regional identities. The vertical federalisation was reflected in demands for creation of smaller states, autonomy and devolution of more powers to the states. The term horizontal federalisation has been used in the sense of the demands of these regional identities for equal participation in the federal power structure. The emergence of the coalition politics at the union level is in fact the federalisation of the union executive. The coalitional cabinet as such resembles a federation of social groups and regional identities. The diversity of India has discarded the umbrella of hegemony in the name of unity and moved into a federation of equal identities. Therefore, the process itself reaffirms something very positive, i.e. the democratisation of the national social order.

If there is nothing new or anything actually bad about coalition politics and if it is essentially a reflection of the democratisation of the polity, why is there a concern over coalition politics among a large section of Indian intelligentsia? Reasons are obvious:

1. The era of stability ensured uninterrupted appropriation of national resources by the incumbents of governance for their personal gains and their unquestioned mastery over people. The confusion regarding a political power in a coalition government and frequent changes in the government do not allow

them to build up sure and stable arrangements for themselves.

2. The other reason is related to factors like caste and class or simply the status. The erstwhile dominant status groups are not comfortable with the rise of the underprivileged class, particularly of the lowest categories to the political power. Scheduled castes and lower castes people have risen from their ascriptive status of servitude to political prominence.
3. The people of the middle class feel morally deprived with the entry of the underclass in the power circles and are harassed by these lowly upstarts. Nonetheless, there is a darker side of coalition politics.

However, this remains a positive phenomenon as it is the extension of the democratisation of society but it has its negative side because it is an outgrowth of the distorted democratisation. The most obvious distortion is the decline of the party system in India. Coalition politics in a way is based on the decline of a role of the parties. In India the emergence of the coalition is the result of the fragmentation of the party system, which started with the end of the predominance of the Indian National Congress. This decline of the party can be attributed to a number of factors:

1. The parties now appear more as political arms of various ethnic or economic groups rather than championing national cause. More accurately, many of these smaller parties hardly champion the cause of any group. Their leaders mobilise the vote banks by exhorting the parochial identities of the voters for personal gains, any public good if that is at all served by their actions is by and large incidental. The parties thus decline in organisation, function and their social base and above all, in political role.
2. The party earlier could sustain its mega presence by using things like charisma, tradition, parochialism or utopianism. The charisma and the system of personal patronage and loyalties were good for the bygone time but are no longer viable these days. People are now

> more informed, more politicized and more exposed. They cannot be mesmerised by charisma or bullied by local bigwigs, swayed by parochial and Utopian appeals.

As the national parties on their own are not in a position to get 30-35 per cent votes to win a Lok Sabha seat, they have to enter into some kind of an electoral alliance with small players at their terms and conditions. No section is too small to be overlooked in the present scenario.

Running the government with several coalition partners is uncomfortable and at times embarrassing, but our politicians have now willy-nilly accepted the idea of coalitions.[10] They are, however, choosing their partners not on the basis of an identity of views but purely out of a desire to acquire power.[11] Ideally, the three major contenders for power should have worked out coalitional arrangements before the polls and presented clear choices to the voter, but the disinclination to do so shows that they wanted to be guided by post-poll arithmetic which, incidentally, has not turned out to be helpful to any major player. The fall of one coalition can lead to that of another and with the attendant risk of horse-trading, the situation can become messier and precipitate an early dissolution of the new Lok Sabha and fresh elections. A search for new ways might help to end the impasse. One such idea is to induct a wider coalition — a national government — consisting of all-important national and regional parties. A national government would require a new mindset, the taming of conflicting ambitions and the replacement of competitive politics with a collaborative, consensual approach for steering the nation. [12] However, the formation of a national government is not going to be easy. Beside, favouring the presidential form of government has tempered their case by suggesting a remarkable variation: Let Parliament elects the Prime Minister; in other words if not a national government, let us have a "national" Prime Minister! If no party has a majority, a Prime Minister elected by a majority in Parliament, obviously with the help of MPs (Members of Parliament) from other parties, will not be troubled by the specter of instability and will therefore concentrate on governing rather than on horse-trading.[13] A little reflection will show the vacuity in this reasoning. If MPs from some other parties support the leader of a particular party, presumably for good reasons, then why not take this to its logical end and form an open and honest coalition?[14] While the common feature of various experiments at coalition at the power center is that they have been forged without reference to the electorate in other words, the political parties have not faced the voter on the strength of their combined election commitments. Rather, they reflect only the fractured nature of party-system in India today.[15]

POLITICAL PROCESS, ROLE OF ELITES AND PARTY SYSTEM

The political set-up of India is undergoing rapid transition where the old power centers are collapsing and the new alignments are emerging. Near disappearance of public priority, growing coercive power of the state over the citizens, corruption, debasement and criminalisation of political process have characterised the political system.

Over the decades, there has been some significant change in the voting pattern for the electorate, while all the elections held between 1971 and 1984 were 'plebiscitary', marked by overriding national issues, to which the electorate responded in a broadly uniform pattern — either almost all over the country — or at least in the Sutlej-Ganga-Brahmaputra valleys, the elections since 1989 have become much more regionalised. Since the 1989 polls, the electoral map has become dotted with an ever-increasing number of political parties resulting from the fragmentation of existing national and regional parties as well as formation of myriad new regional parties.[16] During the 1990s, beginning with the Ninth Lok Sabha elections of 1989 to the Fourteenth Lok Sabha elections of April/May 2004, the Indian voters have not decisively voted for any one party to rule over the country. Its consequence has been that the Central Government of India has become weak, unstable and fragmented. Contrary to shibboleths, India is not evolving towards a two-party system, but towards a more complex structure to which regional parties are crucial. The BJP-Congress collective vote is just about half the total — and not rising. Indeed, their political strength has decreased. BJP remains estranged from and irrelevant to the concerns of the underprivileged. It has not reached out to the poor. The verdict confirms many trends in Indian politics. Among these are growing regionalism, declining importance of charisma-based politics, identity-related issues and rising demand for accountability. The results reinforce long-term tendencies of self-assertion of Dalits and OBCs and increasing tendency of Muslims to vote secular-political candidates.

Political process of the 1990s has much specificity, but one fact which deserves mentioning is that the role of money power is increasing because of frequent elections and the emergence of more than 50 parties and groups which are competing for the Lok Sabha elections. Every political party and group has a fund-collector for contesting an election.[17] The fund-givers play a critical role in political process before and after the elections. During the 1990s, four Lok Sabha elections were held and the new economic policy, which was a break with the past, was never brought before the voters. Political parties opposed to the New Economic Policy (NEP) contested the elections by criticizing the NEP, but while in power, every political party implemented very enthusiastically the NEP. The new economic policy does not enjoy the voters verdict. The NEP is based on a very narrow political consensus among political classes, bureaucrats, upwardly mobile parasitical middle classes, big industrialists and capitalist farmers. Thus, the foreign policy of India in the 1990s, irrespective of party/parties in power in the Central Government, had been pursuing the goals of new economic policy which did not have democratic approval but which had the support of powerful sections of the ruling classes, urban and agrarian and functionaries of the Indian state.[18]

C. Wright Mills had stated that the 'ruling elite' rule on the basis of elections. Hence, it is absolutely wrong to maintain that India had evolved a national consensus in the 1990s on foreign policy irrespective of serious differences among political parties. On the contrary, political process had been hijacked by very powerful and narrow-based social elite, which was promoting its own interests through foreign policy of India. Thus, the foreign policy of India has become a tool in the hands of very limited powerful elite, who are using electoral and political democracy for their own group benefits.[19]

In brief, if on the one hand political class is involved in serious internal conflict, competition and politics of confrontation on the other, domestic powerful groups are able to determine national priorities in their own interest and collaborate with foreign centers of capital. The mediating role of the state *vis-à-vis* domestic powerful groups and external powerful nations has become weak because of the multiplicity of parties and the emergence of farcical coalitional governments at the centre.[20]

In the recent years, the party system in India has suffered severe setbacks. Some of these pertain to an overall sink of the social system, which is evident in almost every walk of life. Some of these ailments, which affect the party system include absence of inner party democracy, negligible number of female representatives, disappearance of ideology from politics, declining ethical values and prevalence of opportunism and expediency and lack of transparency in funding of party organisations, casteism, communalism, regionalisation of parties.[21] The growing violence and criminalisation of politics, fractionalisation and coalitional tensions compound these problems in varied ways.

Lack of Ideology and Moral Values in Politics

There has been very sharp erosion in the ideological orientation of Indian political parties. The democratic norms and institutions and the inspirational values have been destroyed systematically over the last about sixty years of the working of our Constitution. There also is a crisis of character amongst the politicians, as the system does not encourage honest leaders. Due to these facts, there exists a drop of morals in public life. The criminalisation of politics and politicisation of criminals have become the norms. The major principle, which is conveniently followed and widely practised by politicians, is opportunism and expediency which they call pragmatism. Besides, huge sums of tainted money have been poured to play a decisive role in pre-and post-election situations. These criminals rise to the positions of ministers in politics and political parties, which cover their misdeeds. In this way the lawbreakers transform themselves into the lawmakers.

Absence of Inner Party Democracy

The leadership in most political parties in India may be democratic in appearance but is highly oligarchic in reality. Leaders refuse to understand that a political party is a public institution and cannot be treated like a personal fief. Without intra-party elections, without regional support and encouragement of a variety of opinions, the ministers and the political parties are likely to wither away. It is obvious that parties based on oligarchic principles cannot play a positive role in a democratic country.

Party Funds

To perform its functions and contest elections every political party needs funds. But this financial aspect of party budgets is kept secret while other organisational details are kept open for public. The parties and candidates use dubious methods in raising funds like kickbacks, funds from foreign sources and even donations from Mafia gangs and other criminal elements. To let the parties get honest funding from legitimate sources for their political activities has emerged as one of the most crucial and contemporary concerns of the reform agenda of political parties in India.

Representation of Women

Representation constitutes a major issue of concern in the reform agenda regarding political parties in India. How can women who constitute half of the population be denied a legitimate share? All parties have attempted to create women wings in their organisations but no political party has exhibited courage of fielding a satisfactory number of women candidates in national and state elections. The parties do not even want to reserve thirty-three per cent seats in the legislatures as provided in the amendment to the Constitution, leave aside the fifty per cent share.

Leadership Quality

The older leadership in Indian political parties used to rise from the ranks. They respected party discipline. As a contrast, the present-day political leadership seems to be in a tremendous hurry to reach up to the top and is not averse to use short cuts, dubious methods, money or muscle power to achieve their self-seeking objective. The entry of criminals to responsible positions is a serious consequence of these trends. As a result, important issues facing the nation do not get attention and policy-making and good governance suffer in the process.

Campaign Methods

The film and T.V. idols have taken away the element of serenity and the spirit of public service from political leadership. The election campaigns at the regional and national levels have become some kind of stage shows. The matinee idols are being paraded to attract voters in support of their candidates without seriously educating the electorates about the issues at stake in the elections.

Casteism

In place of ideological polarisation, the policies, programmes and electoral candidates are being finalised on the caste considerations. Castes also in turn influence the parties by voting en bloc for candidate of their castes without considering merits or demerits of the candidate.

Regionalisation

The regionalisation has compelled political parties to mould their policies to suit to interests of their regional units. They adopt different policies in different states according to the prevailing conditions there. Regionalism has made 'ethnicity' respectable. These regional parties form coalitions with national parties and pressurise the Central Government to make more allocation of funds and grants to their states. This implies their regional aspirations. Moreover, the Central Government, which is a coalition government, has to cope with these pulls and pressures of plurality of regimes in the states.

Communalism

Communal polarisation posed a threat to political ethos of pluralism, parliamentarianism and federalism in India. Despite the adoption of the principle of "secularism" as a constitutional creed, the trend towards communalism has grown day by day. The spirit of tolerance, which is essential for a secular society, seems to be vanishing from the country. The covert communalism practised by political parties, in pursuit of electoral gains through vote banks has earned the epithets of "pseudo-secularism" and "minorityism". The dynamics of politics of the last decade is a mute witness of the clashes and conflicts between the so-called "secularist" and "communalist", more particularly in Kashmir, Uttar Pradesh and Gujarat. Further, caste and religion have recently gained much momentum as formulas or equations that give parties a winning edge over their counterparts.

Criminalisation

The persons in politics today are not only helped by the criminals but also by the professional outlaws who have discovered a new and safe heaven in politics. Formerly, they had to plead and take help from the politician for saving them from the clutches of law but today they are discovering themselves in a new role of the members of legislatures and even ministers (lawmakers), to cover their misdeeds. Earlier, the criminals were playing the role of a second fiddle to help the politician win elections but now the roles stand reversed and politicians are seeking protection from these criminals. The Election Commission and the People's Representation Act are toothless in preventing criminals from contesting elections.

Fractionalisation and Coalitions

Efforts were made by the coalition partners to set up institutional mechanisms to evolve consensus on the common minimum programmes for action and coordination, vertically and horizontally. They tried to institute multi-layered coalitional structures and created steering and coordination committees for inner-party and party-government consultations to resolve differences through emissaries of the Prime Minister. But then all these efforts remained ad hoc in nature and could not institutionalise devices for effective action.

Political Parties and Governance

Four major factors have influenced the nature of political change in India:

1. The de-institutionalizing role of national and regional leaders.
2. The impact of weak political parties.

3. The undisciplined political mobilisation of various castes, ethnic, religious and other types of groups.
4. The increasing conflicts between the haves and have-nots in the civil society.

If these trends continue unchecked, India's political crisis is likely to become worse.

Jumbo Council of Ministers

The experience of minority and coalition governments resulted in the practice of creating abnormally large or what is known as jumbo size council of ministers to accommodate the coalition partners in government. It has given rise to serious impediments in the process of governance. Besides, the inherent problem of conflicting jurisdictions of the various ministers' personality clashes and egos and the woefully inadequate physical facilities and assistance for their effective and efficient function. Inefficiency, delays and slackness increased because of the inflated governmental machinery, which caused malpractices and corruption. The recent amendment limiting this size to fifteen per cent of the strength of the legislature is a welcome change that promises discipline and stability.

Conclusively it can be said that although political parties in India suffer with many problems, these must be remedied either through legislations or by creating awareness among the people, including the politicians.

RISING COMMUNALISM AND REGIONALISM

The most vital role which independence of India played is the construction of a modern national identity and a new civilisation around the values of liberty, equality, justice, dignity of the individual and unity of the nation and within the framework of a political system committed to a union-type of federal democracy, secularism, rule of law, open society and an egalitarian polity. In this gigantic endeavour, two sets of factors — one of diversity and the other of dissension — impede the process of preferred and intended change. The factors of dissension congregate around plurality of regions and sub-regions marked by distinct languages/dialects, social transformations and culture-forms, set patterns of economy and level of material development, a specific background of local history, particular psychological make-up and overall impress of sub-national identity and homogeneity. The factors of diversity manifest in an undue attachment to one's own religious community, caste, *jati* or tribe, that tends to weaken national solidarity and disrupt the process of national integration, so essential for the unity of any plural society and federal system.[22] Therefore, the terms regionalism and communalism should be treated differently. The real task is to reconcile legitimate regionalism with valid nationalism.

As far as communalism is concerned, as a political phenomenon, it seeks to destroy the four pillars of India's modern identity, namely, nationalism, secularism, democracy and fraternal unity.[23] In this sense, communalism is the most disastrous factor of national dissension and decay. Adherence to religion and religious system is not communalism. Exploitation of religion is communalism. Attachment to a religious community or religiosity is not communalism. Using a religious community against other communities and against the nation is communalism. Communalism is perversion of religion from a moral order to a temporal arrangement of contemporary convenience, from a faith into an electoral constituency, from a strategy of living into a tactics of politics; in brief, from an end into a means. Communalism exploits both religion and politics. It is promoted by a real or an imaginary fear of other communities and of the process of modernised transformation and secular change, which is wrongly perceived as detrimental to religious community's welfare. It is conversion of religiosity into political bellicosity. Communalism is the enemy of progress, revolution, democracy and of federal nation-building on rational, scientific lines. In this sense, communalism is not a phenomenon of conservative reaction, but of modernised reaction and therefore more subtle and complex. It is a sectarian, restrictive and negative response to the process of modernisation and modern nation-building.

Ruling classes and strata have used communalism and communal cleavages to remain in power by obtaining electoral support, by creating electoral pockets and vote-banks. Of the eight religious communities, the main problem of reconciliation and accommodation in India arises mainly in the case of the Hindus, the Muslims, the Christians and the Sikhs. Likewise, politicians misuse casteism for their own benefit — to get electoral support and divided Indian society. Politicians instigated the sentiments of Hindu and Muslim communities, when some people demolished the Babri mosque and tried to construct the Ram temple in Ayodhya. Likewise, Gujarat carnage is a burning instance of political selfishness, inhumanity, immorality and cruelty. Even within one community, there are several rival groups on the basis of caste. In the name of social justice, each group wants to make its own political identity. By unjust means, they are hoping to get so-called justice — thanks to the politicians, who interpolated the mind of masses. By and large, the whole society gets divided along caste lines and political parties are using one caste against the other.

DECLINE IN PARLIAMENTARY CULTURE

In place of the intellectuals, it is the professional politician that is firmly rooted in Parliament. One of the most animated discussions that have taken place in Parliament in recent years during which the vote is unanimous and boisterous, concerns granting of privileges to the MPs. No national issues ever attract either that level of debate or interest. Also the educated people of India and the industrialists, on whom the country depends for development, have been delivered into the hands of the professional politician.

Unfortunately, most politicians of today are more concerned with sharing the spoils of power than doing anything for the country. This is evident from their day-to-day antics, which show a callous disregard for national concerns. There may be some truth in Mani Shankar Aiyar's view that there has been deterioration in public life as those who are unemployable are now in politics. The major difference appears to be that while earlier, serving the nation was seen as a privilege and attracted many well-meaning people, now it is the privilege that attracts the politician.

The politicians have subverted all systems. The scandals just grow in size. As scandals break out with alarming regularity, it seems that nothing has been spared: whether it be buying stamp papers, medicines or even fodder for animals, leaders have been making money. The people of India are tired of the parties, which have no morals left. Since the fifties, the Congress commanded an absolute majority in Parliament; the number of seats it won has declined. It is not just the Congress, which has lost the faith of the people, other political parties are also losing the trust of common people. No other political party has been able to fill the gap, and all over the country, electorates are delivering hung verdicts. The politician is not trusted anymore. Today, party leaders face serious charges of cheating, corruption, communalism and terrorism. The people today are fed up of corrupt politicians. They want morality in public life. If the Congress — or for that matter any other party — can offer this, the confidence of the people can be won. For that, three things are required: honesty, morals and concern for the common man. Unfortunately, these are the three things that are almost extinct in India's public life.

SECESSIONIST INSURGENCIES

The roots of insurgencies in India lie in the post-independence process of nation-building and uneven economic development of the economy. These two processes were not entirely independent of each other, but converged and their effects led to the marginalisation and alienation of certain ethnic groups. Fallout of this process has been the increasing use of violence in the articulation of demands of the deprived sections and where the conflicts have become protracted, they have transformed into insurgencies.

The political arrangement envisaged in the Indian Union constituted several provincial states organised on the principle of quasi-federalism. Subsequently, the reorganisation of states on the basis of language accommodated the ethno-linguistic aspirations of a number of groups.

The demands for autonomy or a separate sovereign state do not only arise out of ethnic consciousness, but are also linked to the process of economic development. In developing societies, the economic disparities often coincide with the ethnic divisions and ethnic groups have assumed political identities to seek redressal. The demands for political autonomy to fulfil developmental aspirations are, therefore, being articulated in the language of ethnicity.[24]

The roots of most insurgencies, with the exception of Kashmir and Punjab, therefore, maybe traced to socio-economic factors. The basic causes of separatist movements may be located in deprivation and discrimination *vis-à-vis* an equal share of political, administrative and economic power. Most ethnic conflicts have originated with a demand by minority ethnic groups to be accommodated and given a share in the power structure. Mobilisation is on the basis of various demands like "affirmative discrimination, autonomy and secession."[25] Since the 1970s most of these groups have developed separatist tendencies, which earlier used to be mainly autonomist.[26] These conflicts have taken a violent turn as the majority group shows no willingness to concede to the demands of the minorities and insurgency has become the basic mode of confrontation. A major factor that has given sustenance to these conflicts is the involvement of external powers, which exploits these situations either for strategic or economic reasons.[27]

Thus, secessionist or separatist movements, also known as extra-systemic movements, are by ethnic, religious or ethno-religious minorities, which question the sovereignty and territorial integrity of the state and affirm their right of self-determination.

Most secessionist insurgencies in India rely predominantly on guerilla warfare and use this method both in jungles and urban areas depending upon the terrain they are operating from. The hilly terrain in Kashmir and the jungles in North-eastern India provide ideal conditions for waging guerilla warfare. However, the Kashmiri militants predominantly use urban guerilla warfare because of the support they enjoy among the local population. Generally, their strategy includes hit and run tactics with the intention of weakening the resolve of the administration.[28] This is carried out by attacking security personnel and assassinating political leaders and high level government officials opposed to the movement. The Sikh insurgency has been the weakest in terms of strategy. All insurrectionary movements seek external support whether it is moral support, material aid or sanctuary for their effectiveness and sustenance. This may be covert or overt in its nature and also varies in intensity, particularly over a period of time.

Apart from seeking support from sympathetic neighboring states, insurgent groups in India have also tried to forge links with each other and with groups in the neighboring countries, irrespective of their ideology and goals. Perhaps the necessity for these linkages arises from their difficulties in procuring weapons to sustain the insurgency. In some cases, these linkages could be due to purely mercenary reasons. For instance, some reports indicate that Afghans and Tamils have been involved in training Kashmiri militants in camps located in the PoK.[29] Besides, the JKLF is believed to have established links with the Sikh militants[30] and the Hizbul Mujahideen has been more successful in establishing contacts with the Khalistan Commando Force (KCF), the ULFA and the People's War Group (PWG).[31] Other reports point to links between the LITE and the ULFA militants. Earlier, ULFA had established contacts with the KIA in Burma in 1986, which agreed to train ULFA militants in the Burmese jungle hideouts, but at a very high price.[32] In 1988, Munim Nobis, an ULFA leader had gone to Pakistan via Bangladesh to ask the ISI to facilitate a meeting with the Afghan Mujahideen. Apparently, the ISI arranged a meeting of five ULFA leaders with Gulbuddin Hekmatyar, the chief of the Hizb-e-Islami in Peshawar in 1990. The Hizb started training them, but the ULFA leaders felt that it was too elementary as they had already mastered the same and thus left after a week or so.[33]

The geographical location of the North-east helped the insurgents find a safe haven in the un-administered regions of Myanmar and Chittagong Hill tracts in Bangladesh. In the 1960s, it was much easier for them to operate from the then East Pakistan due to adversarial relations between India and Pakistan. But the emergence of Bangladesh in 1971 adversely affected the strategy of the insurgents. However, reports point to the possible involvement of the Bangladesh government in training the National Socialist Council of Nagaland (NSCN).[34]

The North-eastern region of India has been plagued by insurgencies since the early years of independence. Various factors such as ethnic heterogeneity, linguistic diversity, demographic changes, historical and geo-political developments, lack of economic growth and infrastructural development, gave sustenance to insurgencies in this region.

The Nagas were the first to initiate an armed insurgency in 1956 to be followed by the Mizos in 1966, the Tripuris in 1978, and in Assam in 1979. The Naga insurgency is the oldest in India. The Nagas, led by the Naga Nationalist Council (NNC), had declared independence a day before India got its independence.[35] They boycotted the general elections in 1952 and the NNC, under the leadership of A.Z. Phizo, started a violent and organised insurgency in 1956. Laldenga formed the Mizo National Front (MNF) out of the Mizo Famine Front (MFF) in 1959 with independence as its goal. The MNF formed a Mizo National Army (MNA) to fight the Indian forces. In 1966, Laldenga launched "Operation Jericho". The 20 year long insurgency in Mizoram ended as a result of Rajiv Gandhi's accord with the MNF leader, Laldenga. Laldenga agreed to the conditions of recognizing the Indian Constitution, laying down arms and joining the mainstream. Elections were held on February 16, 1987 and Laldenga became the Chief Minister of Mizoram. On February 21, Mizoram became a full-fledged state of the Indian Union.

The genesis of insurgency in Tripura lies in the massive influx of settlers from Bangladesh and other parts of India, thus, upsetting the socio-economic pattern in the state and increasing pressure on land. The insurgency in Tripura has been primarily led by the Tripura National Volunteers (TNV) formed in December 1978 to fight for an independent tribal Tripura state.

The United Liberation Front of Assam (ULFA), formed in April 1970, has led the violent insurgency in Assam. It was essentially an offshoot of the Assam agitation led by the All Assam Students Union (AASU), and was against migrants and Indian rule. Till 1985, ULFA was dormant. By 1990, the ULFA was at the peak of its power and had a highly effective system of levying taxes, and also organised community work, at times by coercing people.[36] The Indian government's military action was able to immobilise ULFA by early 1992. Simultaneously, a section of the leadership decided to hold talks with the government. This resulted in a split in the organisation and while some of its cadres have been rehabilitated, its hardcore members have managed to take shelter in Bangladesh.

The Akali Dal spearheaded a movement for more autonomy under the Anandpur Sahib resolution of 1973. Violence against Hindus on a large scale had started around September-October 1983. The Dal Khalsa along with the All India Sikh Students Federation (AISSF) was believed to be behind this violence. By this time, the Sikhs demand for autonomy had taken separatist overtones and a violent form. Due to antagonistic relations between India and Pakistan, the latter readily provided armed support to the Sikh militants for destabilizing India. Jagjit Singh Chohan, leader of the National Council of Khalistan, had claimed that Z.A. Bhutto whom he met in 1972 (before the signing of the Simla Accord) in New York had offered to help to start a movement for Khalistan from Pakistan's territory.

Finally, in June 1984, the Central Government launched an assault on the Golden Temple where Sikh extremists had sought sanctuary. Anti-Sikh riots in different parts of the country following Indira Gandhi's revenge killing by her Sikh bodyguards in October 1984, further fuelled violence in Punjab. Prime Minister Rajiv Gandhi signed an accord with Sant Longowal in 1985 to resolve some of the outstanding issues, but it failed to end violence in the state. The government managed to restore the political process in March 1992 and thereafter by strong counter-insurgency measures was able to contain violence by early 1993. During the course of Operation Rakshak-II in December 1991, the Army only played a supportive role in cordoning areas while the police and paramilitary forces carried out search and sanitizing operations to flush out the insurgents.[37] But before this operation, K.P.S. Gill, the Director-General of Police in Punjab, had already weakened the Sikh insurgents considerably by using very unconventional methods, at times, exceeding the limits of law.[38]

Pakistan's support for the subversive activities in Kashmir may be traced even to the period before its accession to India in 1948. However, it is important to note that both in 1947 and 1965, the local Kashmiri population did not respond to Pakistan's support to the tribal incursions and infiltration. But, by late

1980s, the situation had reversed and now various militant groups sought support from across the border.

At the time of independence, Kashmir had been given a special status under Article 370 of the Indian Constitution. Over the past five decades, New Delhi has progressively curtailed the powers and scope of Article 370 by extending most of the provisions of the Indian Constitution to that state. Often, the center adopted both fair and foul methods, including the rigging of elections, dismissal of duly elected governments and appointing state Governors of its own choice, even against the wishes of the state government. These lapses on the part of the central leadership, along with corruption and dismal employment prospects for the Kashmiri youth, led to their growing alienation and disenchantment with the policies of New Delhi. It was against this background, that Rajiv Gandhi and Farooq Abdullah had arrived at an electoral agreement in 1986, whereby an alliance of the National conference and Congress-I was formed to fight the 1987 elections. Having lost faith in the democratic political process, the disgruntled elements soon took to the path of militancy. Following the installation of the National Conference government, violent protests over the issue of unemployment and power shortages took place throughout 1988-1989. The state bureaucrats and political leaders had misappropriated central government assistance for the development of the state. Due to lack of satisfactory life chances and political opportunities, the Kashmiri youth took up arms[39] to express their dissatisfactions, coupled with the corrupt behaviour of the state politicians. There is little doubt that Pakistan has sponsored the insurgency in the valley by exploiting the alienation of the people.[40] Apparently, the JKLF was approached by the ISI in 1984 for initiating an insurgency in Kashmir, and after 1988, a significant spurt in their activities was discernible. While Pakistan has been covertly providing arms and military training to the Kashmiri militants,[41] in some instances, they have also provided covering artillery fire to help them cross into the Indian Kashmir. This strategy was adopted after intensive deployment of Indian security forces on the Line of Control had made the task of infiltration much more difficult and at times even hazardous.[42] By the end of 1989 and early 1990, the militants were holding sway in the valley and the politicians were getting marginalised.

There have been reports of mercenaries, especially Afghan Mujahideen joining hands with the Kashmiris to fight a *jihad* in the Valley.[43] The last decade has witnessed the resurgence of Islamic fundamentalism, and Muslims from various countries have been to Bosnia, Central Asia, Kashmir and other Muslim trouble spots to fight a *jihad*.[44] Besides, some fundamentalist Muslims from Sudan are also believed to have infiltrated into Kashmir.[45] While for many Muslims, it is *jihad*, for Pakistan it is a proxy war against India.

State responses to insurgencies in India have been varied. The first approach is cooperation or accommodation. This approach is applicable mostly in the case of insurgencies based on ethno-nationalism. For instance, it was used against MNF and TNV, whereby they were weaned back to the parliamentary process by giving substantial concessions in terms of political power. The dialogue between government and NSCN is on the progress. Both NSCN and government are trying hard to get some permanent solution of the problem. Central Government's mediator K. Padmanabhaiya told that Naga leaders are now ready for decisive talks. In fact, UPA government indicated that State Reconstruction Commission may consider the merger of Naga speaking areas of Manipur, Assam and Arunachal Pradesh into Nagaland. But, its decision will not be obligatory for Central Government to accept the demand of NSCN for Greater Nagaland. The Commission will also give importance to the views of other states in this regard, which are going to be affected. There is demand for social, religious and traditional unification of Naga speaking areas. However, NSCN is itself aware of the complexities and reality that political merger of Naga speaking areas will take a long time.

Indo-Bangladesh talks over the problem of insurgents have been going on intermittently for some years now. All these developments are significant. The other approach is coercive by adopting strong counter-insurgency measures. This is the approach to most insurgencies inspired by revolutionary ideologies. Thus, the Naxalite insurgency came under severe repression. In the case of separatist insurgencies, a dual process of captive and coercive methods is used. Such coercive methods used by the two Army operations — Operation Bajrang, and Operation Rhino were instrumental in immobilizing the ULFA insurgents.

The failure to accommodate ethnic minorities in the process of nation-building has been the basic cause of insurgencies in India. The uneven process of development, which has economically marginalised some ethnic minorities, has further compounded this. Swarna Rajagopalan in his book *State and Nation in South Asia*, talked about the incompatible visions and has beautifully summarised the contradiction between the vision of state (about itself and its constituent units) and vision of its constituent units (about itself and the state). He has insisted upon building political communities out of states through twin principles of reconciliation and accommodation.

The ethno-nationalist insurgencies are continuing due to popular as well as external support. In North-east India, the change in the Chinese attitude towards the insurgent groups has helped the government in controlling the situation to some extent. In contrast, Pakistan's moral and material support to Kashmiri insurgents has intensified the level of conflict there.

LACK OF COHERENT POLICY AND CRISIS OF GOVERNANCE

In India, the compartmentalization in the planning of defence and development exists. This is because it does not have an integrated national security policy-making process that seeks to harmonise defence policy, economic policy, foreign policy and internal security policy with one another and with an overall national strategy. Indeed, an integrated approach is essential, for, no matter how potent the military or economic power of a country might be, it will remain inchoate and diffused unless it is welded together through coherent policy formulation.

Like NSC (National Security Council) in the United States, where it is composed of a dedicated group of professionals, who are often drawn from outside with a lifetime of specialisation in their subjects, as for instance even an intellectual giant like Samuel P. Huntington found it attractive to serve in a middle-level capacity in the Carter NSC, in India too we can have an efficient NSC, provided it is empowered by law and not by an executive order and which can, outside the routine bureaucracy, attract the best talent available in the country.

With the passage of time, the people are protesting sometimes violently and more often by keeping away from electoral processes. It may be worth asking: Why the incumbency factor has acquired importance during the elections? Why is the electorate expressing anger by voting out the incumbent governments whom they had favoured earlier? Is it not time that the polity moves from governing to governance that assigns primacy to the people's participation? To a system that enables the people to govern themselves?[46] In the prevailing milieu it is difficult to offer good governance and engineer relevant people-oriented social change in the absence of an active participation by the civil society.[47]

The 1999 Human Development Report on South Asia, authored by the late Mahbub-ul-Haq, points out that "South Asia (including India) is facing a crisis of governance, which, if left unchecked, could undermine the region's democratic progress, and the economic and social well-being of its teeming masses. Home to nearly one-fourth of humanity, the region is characterised by government that represents the poor, but aids the rich; taxation that is insufficient and regressive; and expenditures that are misdirected, and ineffective. The report provides an in-depth analysis of the phenomenon of corruption and advocates a concrete and realistic reform agenda for promoting 'humane governance'. The concept of humane governance puts people at the center of all governance policies, strategies and actions. The basic precepts of the human development model are to improve the capabilities and expand the opportunities of all people, irrespective of class, caste, gender and ethnicity. The concept of humane governance takes this model forward by asserting that governance, if it is to promote human development, has to be not just pro-people or people centered, it has to be owned by people.... Humane governance has three interlinked dimensions: economic, political and civic. Economic governance consists of those factors required to sustain economic development. Political governance is defined as the use of institutions by the government to govern and civic governance as the right and responsibility of the governed to participate in, and promote good governance. It is to be expected that a country with high economic, political and civic governance would also have high human development. Humane governance can only be achieved through a combination of all the three dimensions of economic, political and civic governance. One dimension does rot come before another. They must occur in unison for the concept of humane governance to be realised."[48]

The Human Development Report may be viewed as a part of the worldwide debate on the needed modifications in styles and expanse of governance. The Japanese believe that for "deciding the public good" radical changes are called for. Such changes should accord centrality to the civic society.

Liberalisation demands changes. Since India is now soaked in the process of globalisation, we have to take notice of the worldwide trend that is seeking to ensure that the changes would place the people at the center and enthrone the civil societies.[49]

Governments alone cannot and need not run human societies nor build nations without a great deal of active and conscious help from the citizens. There are some basic requirements for the creation of the civil society:[50]

1. To build a legal foundation of the state from the top to the bottom and to ensure that the laws of the land are universally and impartially enforced.
2. An independent, efficient judiciary, that speedily hands out justice.
3. The government has to be vastly decentralised, with the people given opportunities to govern themselves and take charge of their own affairs.
4. The concept that the government is the giver of everything and is the sole provider is inimical to the building of such a society.
5. The citizen must be empowered and enabled to appreciate that in many ways he or she is, his or her own master and responsible for the sustenance of a peaceful social order based on co-operative co-existence of different interests in society.

An enlightened civil society alone can assist in ensuring that every child goes to school, that teachers actually teach and doctors attend regularly on patients at rural health centers. The Directive Principles of State Policy — Part (iv) of the Constitution from Article 38 onwards are fundamental for the welfare of Indian Republic. But unlike Fundamental Rights, the Directive Principles of State, though equally important — did not get similar treatment for their judicial enforcement. The Directive Principles provide the fundamentals of good governance, and for this the state is duty bound to implement them by legislation. Unless the Directive Principles are accorded the needed legal resonance, the roadway to people's participation will continue to be full of potholes and speed-breakers; and without making governance people-centric, the promise of the Constitution that was framed by "We, the people" will get fossilised.

ECONOMIC REINTEGRATION

The main threat to India's future is not political, but economic.[51] The Indian economy has been semi-closed for most of the post-World War II period. Since independence in 1947, the Indian government has pursued a strategy of self-reliance with autonomous industrialisation at its core. The state has attempted to transform the material basis of Indian society through detailed intervention in the economy.

But, beginning in the 1980s and in 1991, the government decisively moved away from an interventionist posture by drastically altering its industrial and trade policies in favour of an 'open' economy. To understand the shift in economic policies India's post-independence capitalist development trajectory is divided into two phases. The first phase (roughly from 1950 to 1980) is called the phase of resistance, a process by which the Indian state along with the Indian bourgeoisie attempted to resist the forces of global capitalism and foster self-reliance. The second phase (1980 onward) is called the process of reintegration with the world economy, whereby previous attempts to fend off external economic forces are substituted by a desire to participate in the world economy.[52] Resistance denotes a national response to colonial experience, while reintegration indicates an ongoing accommodation of global economic and other forces. With the emergence of the middle class, global reintegration is perceived as an economic necessity, but the process is mediated by the structures and politics of Indian society. The process of resistance sowed the seeds of reintegration. The self-reliant model, in the Indian socio-institutional context, cultivated an economy of shortages, lethargic technological development, inefficiency and corruption and 'rising expectations' of the middle class. Over time, it became difficult for the national productive structure to meet the changing demands of an increasingly differentiated Indian society. Moreover, international pressures to liberalise the Indian economy and the collapse of the Soviet Union have called for a thorough re-evaluation of the model of Indian resistance to global capitalism.[53]

GLOBALISATION

Between 1980 and 1990 the amount of capital directly invested in foreign lands nearly tripled. It is needless to underline that capital has assumed global character and its upsurge and diversification has been leading to changes in economies and polities of all countries of the world. Thus, globalisation, though not a novel concept, has assumed new significance since the turn of the 1990s mainly because of the changed international balance of forces resulting from the collapse of the Soviet Union, the disintegration of the world socialist system and the end of the Cold War.[54] Globalisation means the attempt to bring the world under single domination or one system.[55]

Marx and Engels in *The Communist Manifesto*[56] had clearly presented their vision of capitalism's triumphant globalisation.[57] They had written:

> Modern industry has established the world market, for which the discovery of America paved the way...the bourgeoisie has through its exploitation of the world market given a cosmopolitan character to production and consumption in every country. In place of the old local and national seclusion and self-sufficiency, we have...universal interdependence of nations, and as in material, so also in intellectual production.

Further, in the course of his unique address to the nation on the eve of Republic Day 2000, K.R. Narayanan, the then President of India, came forward with a scathing criticism of what was going on in the country particularly on the economic front. It is simply unprecedented. On the issue of globalisation and excessive focus on advertisement-driven consumerism he said:[58]

> The unabashed vulgar indulgence in conspicuous consumption by the *nouveau-rich* society has left the underclass seething in frustration. One half of our society guzzles aerated beverages while the other has to make do with palmful of muddied water. Our three way fast-lane of liberalisation, privatisation, globalisation must provide self-pedestrian crossing for the underpowered India also so that it too can move towards equality of status and opportunity.

Another most severe indictment on the issue of globalisation has emanated from no less a person than the Director General of the International Labonr Organisation, Juan Somavia. He has characterised the process of globalisation as the glorification of "casino capitalism."[59]

GLOBALISATION AND INDIA

The origin of the process of globalisation in India can be traced, when, during Indira Gandhi's Prime Ministership, she organised the Asian Games in New Delhi way back in 1982. She indulged in this extravaganza and spent crores of rupees to project her son, Rajiv Gandhi, as her future successor. She for the first time decided to import luxury goods like color TVs, etc. to cater to conspicuous consumption of the upper middle class section of our country at the expense of the common taxpayer. As a matter of fact these color TVs had no takers then, as those were very expensive. Gandhi's government had to give subsidy so as to enable the affluent section of Indian society to purchase these American goods. Rajiv Gandhi tried to pursue these policies once he assumed the office of the Prime Minister after the cruel assassination of Mrs. Gandhi.[60] He initiated a process of liberalisation and decided to integrate the Indian economy with the global economy.[61]

But it was Narasimha Rao, who became the chief architect of the process of globalisation after he assumed the office of the Prime Minister in 1991 in the Tenth Lok Sabha. He appointed Manmohan Singh as his Finance Minister. It was left to him to usher in fundamental changes in the Indian economic structure at the instance of the International Monetary Fund and the World Bank. The IMF/WB Group suggested that India should adopt a programme of structural adjustment, which they had recommended to other countries, particularly those in Latin America, in similar situations. They promised India that if their conditionalities are strictly observed, India could get adequate financial support in the form of structural adjustment loans (SAL) to implement the structural adjustment programme (SAP). India seems to have agreed to all the conditionalities.[62] This was revealed in the letters of Union Finance Minister Manmohan Singh written to the President of the WB on November 11, 1991 and to the Managing Director of the IMF on June 2, 1992 besides the Union Budget for 1992-93 and the Memorandum for Economic Policies for 1992-93 covering the Performance Criteria for Domestic and Financial Policies in 1992-93. The World Bank Confidential Report No. 8998 of November 30, 1991 considered as the "Mother Document" on the SAP relating to India, reviewed how much India had done since July 1991, and spelt out how much more India should do in 1992-93, 1993-94 and 1994-95.[63]

Manmohan Singh repeatedly asserted that his government inherited an economy on the verge of collapse. He also pointed out that lenders always imposed conditionalities and India in the present context of its history had no other alternative.[64] Manmohan Singh has taken a U-turn in his approach when he straightway went against all those principal recommendations contained in South-South Report, at the South Commission in Geneva, of which he was the Secretary. This South-South Report was prepared under the chairmanship of the late Julius Nyerere, the former President of Tanzania and a senior world statesman. The report categorically and forcefully stated that the economics of the Third World countries would be devastated in case those countries take recourse to structural adjustments in their economies as a sequel to the globalisation of the economy.[65] In the report, he stated:

> Developed countries were able to use the international financial institutions to impose their view on Third World countries and at the same time demand that the latter should adjust their economies through contradictory polities. This was a form of neo-colonialism. The debt crisis was used by the North as an opportunity to influence their domestic choices and to impose on them externally determined values, policies, concessions and patterns of development. The social and political costs of inappropriate measures were then paid by the victim countries and their people...and any resulting instability was used by the North as a further opportunity for external intervention.... The establishment of a system of international and economic relations in which the South's second class status would be institutionalized is an imminent danger.[66]

Furthermore, it is one of the greatest tragedies of our times that neither the Parliament of India was taken into confidence nor the then ruling Congress party under the leadership of Narasimha Rao debated the issues of globalisation prior to its announcement in the Lok Sabha as a *fait accompli*. The country's economic sovereignty was bartered away without the consent of the people and Parliament.[67] Many State Governments like those of Bihar, West Bengal, Tamil Nadu, and Orissa approached the Supreme Court in 1993 and complained that they had not been consulted before the Government of India committed the country to the concept of structural adjustment, particularly in the context of agriculture being a state subject as per the provisions of the Constitution. Besides, a people's commission was constituted under the chairmanship of the former Supreme Court Justice, V.R. Krishna Iyer, the other members were the former Supreme Court Justice Chennappa Reddy and a former Chief Justice of the Delhi High Court, Justice Rajindar Sachar. They submitted a unanimous report and recommended that globalisation is completely antithetical to the Preamble of the Constitution of India and it is also ultra vires of the Fundamental Principles of the Constitution. Another people's commission was constituted under the chairmanship of Justice Krishna Iyer with members like noted economist Prabhat Patnaik and famous scientist and former UGC Chairman Yashpal to report to the nation as to whether the 1970 Patent Act should be changed or not. The nation is grateful to the members of this commission for their unequivocal declaration, that the 1970 Patent Act has not only served the best interests of the nation, but has helped the growth of indigenous pharmaceutical industries in a big way. The modern medicines (allopathic medicines) are sold to consumers in India at the cheapest rate, which is unique in the world due to the provisions of the 1970 Patent Act. They have also specifically recommended that any dilution in the 1970 Patent Act would impinge on the right to life enshrined in the Fundamental Rights of our Constitution.[68]

During Narasimha Rao's regime, the mainstream political parties, up to the dictates of the IMF, World Bank and World Trade Organisation, okayed the provisions of the Marrakkesh agreement, and got a resolution passed in this regard in 1994 in Parliament. All the provisions of this agreement militate against our national interest. It is on record that the BJP, which was then functioning as an opposition party, opposed this on the floor of Parliament. But when Atal Behari Vajpayee became the Prime Minister of the country in the thirteenth Lok Sabha he okayed this infamous Patent Bill thereby abrogating the 1970 Patent Act.[69]

REFORMS AND THE NEW ECONOMIC POLICY

In a review of India's New Economic Policy (NEP), the IMF/World Bank have expressed happiness though they are not satisfied with the pace of reforms. India's economy, which had lumbered along at 3.5 per cent growth per year from 1950 to 1980, picked up to 5.5 per cent in the 1980s and averaged 7 per cent growth in fiscal years 1995 to 1997. Some claimed that India had joined the ranks of Asia's tiger economies. However, India looked more like an elephant again, as the industrial growth in the first three quarters of fiscal year 1998 slipped from its peak between 1994 and 1996.[70]

The Indian economy has been progressively globalizing since the initiation of reforms. Trade, an important dimension of global integration, has risen steadily as a proportion of GDP. Inward FDI has taken off and there is a surge in outward investment from a very low base, with net FDI continuing to grow at a good pace. The surge of capital flows in 2007-08 is a third indicator that testifies to the growing influence of global developments on the Indian economy. Capital flows, as a proportion of GDP, have been on a clear uptrend during this decade. They reached a high of 5.1 per cent of GDP in 2006-07 after a below trend attainment of 3.1 per cent in 2005-06. This is a natural outcome of the improved investment climate and recognition of robust macroeconomic fundamentals like high growth, relative price stability, healthy financial sector and high returns on investment.

Indian economy has moved to a higher growth plane during the last decade, with growth in GDP at market prices exceeding 8 per cent consistently since 2003-04. Macroeconomic fundamentals continue to infuse confidence, which is reflected in the pouring inflows of foreign direct investment. Though during 2007 there appeared some reversing trend as a result of global slowdown and some fiscal measures taken by the government to check soaring inflation.

However, India's annual GDP has been showing a high growth of above 8 per cent on a consistent basis since the financial year 2004-2005. The industrial output also showed a robust growth during these years. It was felt that, in order to maintain this growth, the pace of economic reforms needs to be accelerated.

A slower pace of reform and lower growth rates will not only cause economic pain but also endanger India's social and political progress. One reason for the slow progress of reforms is the fear of the Indian government on the possible risks involved. Mainly three risk factors are identified:[71]

1. The failure of the government to implement the package of structural adjustment programme due to social and political reaction to cuts in subsidies, retrenchment of labour on account of exit policy and high inflation.
2. The failure to generate strong supply response from the domestic private sector, NRIs, and foreign investors.

3. Related to the external sector developments and political developments unfavourable to India.

The experiences of countries, which have already implemented SAP, have suggested that structural reforms do not automatically lead to high growth. Like Mexico and others, India faces the quandary of a half baked reform process. Even so, further reform is critical for several reasons:[72]

1. India's financial sector still cannot effectively mobilise and mediate capital to respond to economic changes. The resulting high cost of capital makes Indian industry and exports less competitive.
2. India's abysmal infrastructure is a major constraint in growth.
3. Indian trade has been opened enough to expose many companies to greater competition, but not enough to provide a strong, sustained impetus for growth.
4. Uncertainty about Indian macro-economic policy worries investors and managers.
5. India needs greater labor market flexibility to make its companies more competitive and its economy more productive.
6. Political instability and gridlock in Delhi may frustrate restructuring, as they have in Japan. A government dependent on many parties for its political survival will find it hard to enact even those reforms it favours.
7. The political base for reform remains narrow. The only significant constituency for reform is the urban middle class, which is at most a quarter of the electorate.

The international environment for reform may be worsening. True, India has been spared the worst of the East Asian troubles, because of its lower dependence on exports, healthier current account balance, modest short-term debt and the limited convertibility of the rupee.[73] Besides, India has a powerful and experienced regulator in the form of the Reserve Bank of India. It keeps a watchful eye on commercial banks and other financial institutions and has prescribed guidelines and framed rules and regulations, which they have to follow. They have to report their dealings to the RBI. There is a system of disclosure whereby the banks have to make public their assets, liabilities and lendings and it is not easy for them to fudge their operations and conceal bad debts. Further, India has a vibrant parliamentary democracy. The government is responsible and answerable to Parliament. The media world too is vibrant and never hesitates from bringing to light suspected shady deals. In this situation, it is not easy for the Indian financial and banking sector to behave as its counterpart did in East Asian countries. But, nobody can say the same thing about the years to come if the government goes in for full-scale liberalisation in order to become a part of the globalised world economy because it will lead to three things, namely freeing the prices including the exchange rate of the rupee, i.e. making the rupee fully convertible; retreat of the state, i.e. state giving up most of its role including that as a regulator of the economy, and selling public enterprises to the private sector to bring in a greater measure of competition.[74] All these steps are fraught with dangerous implications. In the present age of revolution in the sphere of information technology and electronic banking, financial capital can take flight from one economy to the other without much difficulty. In this situation, it will be difficult for a nation-state to regulate its activities, not to speak of controlling it.[75]

Globalisation—Dangerous Implications

Obviously, India has to be very cautious in deciding to globalise its economy. MNCs have been eyeing India's vast market and resources for a long time and they will not like India to have its own independent economy. We do not totally oppose the idea of India becoming internationally competitive.[76] But what India should do first is to open up its economy to domestic competition and thereby improve its efficiency and prepare indigenous producers for facing global competition. If this is not done and instead, India just jump for globalisation on a full scale, it might result in the collapse of domestic industry, which was surviving under the insulated/protected environment for a period four decades after India's independence.

Furthermore, the other factors, related to the very survival of India, should be seriously taken into account.

The national movement and the governments after independence have been committed to the removal of regional disparities in economic development. To recall, the policy of the British government as well as its discriminatory attitudes to various regions and their inhabitants led to the rise and growth in regional economic disparities. Bihar and most parts of UP after 1857, and Bengal after 1905 were knowingly neglected while Punjab was favoured in various ways. In order to reduce regional disparities, governments, prior to 1991, gave special attention to hitherto backward areas and formulated special packages. Backward area development schemes were incorporated in almost every plan. Now, with focus shifting from state-directed to market-propelled economic development and the reliance being placed on private, both Indian and foreign investments, only those areas will be receiving investments which are already ahead in development and have infrastructural facilities besides a better law and order situation. This means, the regions east of Delhi will be neglected and further go down the ladder of development. If this happens, it will have serious political repercussions for the survival of India as one nation.[77]

Added to this is the formulation of the World Bank,[78] which talks of localisation and globalisation. In other words, a unified national market is thought to be irrelevant. It means that no region or part of India needs the unified national market. It can develop its own local market and link it with the global market to reap all the benefits, and with the revolution in the field of Information Technology, it will not be in any disadvantageous position. One may recall that the entire struggle against imperialism before and after independence has been for building and protecting our national market and reserving it for our goods.[79] Now, with this formulation being nullified by the World Bank thesis, the very basis of India as one nation will disappear and the way will be paved for disintegration. "Politically, globalisation is helping to spawn the atomisation of countries. When international barriers to trade and financial flows crumble, nations lose one of their main weapons against separatist sentiment. If the world market is open, the threat of being cut-off from the national market isn't much of a threat at all."[80]

"Yet another idiosyncrasy of contemporary globalization is that it goes hand in hand with degeneration. Even as economies integrate, entire companies and industries are disintegrating. It is possible that one day soon a major manufacturer will own no factories of its own. In fact, some technology companies are already at this stage."[81]

With globalisation, unemployment is bound to increase. "We have already lost two crore jobs when almost twenty-five crores of our people are below the poverty line. Lakhs of our indigenous and small scale industries have been closed down as a result of such government policies that categorically and specifically favour importing such consumer goods like women's *bindi* which were exclusively reserved for the small and tiny sector industries in our country. This import policy of the Government of India runs counter to the basic philosophy of *swadeshi* and self-reliance as propounded by Mahatma Gandhi."[82] The American multinational companies like Coca Cola and Pepsi have the dubious record of destabilizing national governments in many countries,[83] which refuse to serve their commercial interests.

Further, new industries and activities will require new kinds of skills. Mostly the upper segments of the society, which can afford to pay for them, can acquire new kinds of skills. Obviously, inequalities in the society will increase and this coupled with demonstration effect and consumerism, fueled by the modern electronic media will lead to crimes, anarchy and chaos. With the governmental activities and public sector shrinking, the total number of jobs is getting fast reduced and in this situation reservation for SCs, STs, and OBCs has lost all significance. Thus, globalisation is going to nullify another national objective, namely socio-economic homogenisation.[84]

Moreover, it is worth recalling the fact that the first Finance Minister of the Indian Republic, the illustrious and late lamented C.D. Deshmukh, did a yeoman service to India's financial sector when he, in 1950, nationalised the insurance sector, which was in the private sector at that time. On the other hand, Yashwant Sinha would share the ignominy of handing over a portion of

Indian nationalised insurance industry to the private and multinational companies, when Indian insurance companies are making profits and America's are on the decline. Hence, it is bound to result in the outflow of India's capital to America and other countries rather than the inflow of their capital to India. In this regard, who loses? America or we? It is we who are bound to lose in this unequal bargain.

Opportunities and Challenges

Despite these severe implications of globalisation, what is important, now, is to take urgent and effective steps to explore, harness and use available resources and opportunities for the furtherance of national economy and development.

It is estimated that there are approximately 15 million Persons of Indian Origin (PIOs) and Non-Resident Indians (NRIs) outside India. When one considers the growing strength and potential of overseas Indians, it is evident that they can be a formidable asset to India, both in political and economic terms. While in countries like Mauritius, Surinam, Fiji and Trinidad and Tobago, they enjoy power and influence, in countries like South Africa, the US, Canada, the UK, Singapore and Malaysia, they occupy an important position in the power structure of these countries because of their relative economic strength.[85] It took Indian government an unduly long time to understand, appreciate and use this enormous asset India has. Even now very little organised efforts are there to inform and involve the Indian communities in overall national efforts — potential, economic or even cultural. For most of these overseas Indians, their links with their motherland continue to remain strong, abiding and deep and many of them would not only be prepared but would consider it a privilege to remain associated with India and be of assistance to the country of their origin. The growing financial strength and success of NRIs and PIOs now, more than ever before, is available for furthering India's national interest and developmental needs. Apart from financial resources which could be tapped, the considerable technological and scientific skills and talents of Indians are recognised and acknowledged the world over and can, under certain conditions, become a major impulse for India's own scientific and technological advancement.[86]

Unfortunately, so far India has paid very little focused attention to this aspect. Apart from the need to have a full-fledged and separate department or ministry to handle this, Indian diplomatic missions must now play a more proactive and meaningful role in mobilizing and harnessing this resource for India's national advantage, be it in science and technology, culture, investments, tourism or for using their growing and now considerable political clout and influence to further national objectives. For this to happen, overseas Indians should be looked at as an extension and an inseparable part of India and given national treatment in all matters thus involving them fully and incrementally in India's national efforts. Overseas Indians are now poised to play a significant role in India's economic development and in creating a more propitious international environment conducive to India's national interest. This is a major opportunity and a challenge to India's diplomacy and missions abroad. While the conduct of India's external economic diplomacy should primarily be the responsibility of the Ministry of External Affairs (MEA) and its diplomatic missions abroad, that in practice is simply not the case. The direction of India's external economic diplomacy is neither coherent nor the overall responsibility of any one single government ministry or department. Economic work, broadly speaking, is currently distributed between the ministries of Finance, Commerce, Industry, Agriculture, Petroleum, and External Affairs. However, international and multilateral economic diplomacy in the coming century is likely to be a serious and specialised job profoundly affecting the vital national interests of countries. In the changed and emerging situation, it cannot be the responsibility of five or six ministries/departments who at times do not even keep each other informed, much less involved, while taking decisions affecting overall economic interests.[87]

Development and Human Freedom

Another area, which requires an immediate attention, is to tackle the basic problems of the people. The reforms must be seen to benefit India's huge rural population. Without their support, agricultural subsidies cannot be reduced or eventually eliminated. In the end, the most important constituency for the reforms is the rural poor, whose increasing political participation and rising economic expectations must be accommodated to maintain political stability.[88] In this regard, Robert A. Dahl (1971-74) suggests 'a very general hypothesis' that:

"The chances that a country will develop and maintain a competitive political regime (and, even more so, a polyarchy) depend upon the extent to which the country's society and economy: (a) provide literacy, education and communication, (b) create a pluralistic rather than a centrally dominated social order, and (c) prevent extreme inequalities among the politically relevant strata of the country."[89]

In a similar vein, John D. Aram (1997) also finds 'strong evidence' supportive of the hypothesis that 'growth leads to democracy' and that increasing affluence and democratisation go together.[90] Likewise, going a step further, Amartya Sen, in his book *Development as Freedom* (1999) argues that growth is not enough. While not denying the importance of raising output and per capita income, especially in very poor countries, he argues for a broader goal for development: increasing the capability of all human beings to achieve those things that they most value. Higher income, of course, increases such capabilities in important ways, so it is a significant component of development. But it is not the only part. It does not assure good health, adequate education, greater longevity, the ability to influence the political decisions that affect one's life, or the freedom to choose alternative lifestyles — or even goods and services beyond those that are immediately on offer. Therefore, higher income is not sufficient to assure development — only necessary. Development is not merely an economic process but a political one as well. It therefore ultimately requires a "democratisation" of political communities to give citizens a voice in important decisions made for the community. To fail in this regard, Sen argues, is to limit human freedom and, by extension, the possibility for full human development.[91]

NUCLEARISATION

Investments in defence, however affordable, but which do not establish a credible capability in relation to the likely challenges and tasks, become totally infructuous and, because they might provide a false sense of security, counterproductive.

The reverse can be to allocate so much in defence in order to make it highly credible and capable, but development would suffer heavily.[92] The full story of India's path to nuclear capability acquisition is bumpy but absolutely absorbing and spread over sixty years.

Indian scientists, particularly Homi J. Bhabha, foresaw the coming in of the atomic age even before the Americans conducted their first nuclear test at Alamogordo in New Mexico on July 16, 1945. In 1944, Bhabha wrote to the Tata Trust urging them to establish a training and research institution for fundamental research in Nuclear Physics so that when the nuclear era was ushered in, India would have trained people already in place.[93] Bhabha was able to enlist the support of Pt. Jawaharlal Nehru from the beginning. An Atomic Energy Commission was established in the forties through a Government resolution with Bhabha as the Chairman, and the Prime Minister always held the portfolio. Subsequently, the commission was made statutory through an enactment. Nehru's strong tilt towards science-technology development in India provided the sinews, and Bhabha transformed this dream into a glowing reality.[94]

The horrors of Hiroshima and Nagasaki were followed by a new vista of atoms for peace, of nuclear power generation, transformations in agriculture with nuclear technology and medical diagnostics and therapy using atomic science and technology. Bhabha was elected to preside over the first international conference on Atoms for Peace in 1956. He predicted that fusion energy was not far away and once energy at very cheap cost was available, countries like India should be able to advance rapidly.[95] But the ultimate horror of nuclear weapons still loomed large in the backdrop.

India's path to acquisition of nuclear capability has been distinct, with several features which mark it out from all other countries opting for nuclear technology — whether for weapons or power generation. India's was the middle path — prioritizing atomic power generation and other peaceful uses of nuclear technology, but at the same time keeping the weapon option open. In the early sixties, Bhabha told a special gathering of MPs in the central hall of Parliament: "Give me 18 months' notice and you can have the atom bomb. But focusing on weapons would be too costly for India; a country like ours should invest on nuclear science to combat poverty — for power generation, medicine, agriculture and other spin-off benefits."[96] However, many people, both in India and abroad, charge that Bhabha intended to build a bomb from the beginning and he was misleading the Prime Minister. The real truth is that in the initial years Bhabha was opposed to India exercising nuclear option. According to Gopal, who has studied Bhabha's papers, at one time Bhabha even suggested to Pt. Nehru that India should unilaterally give up the nuclear option. Jawaharlal Nehru, who knew international relations better, told Bhabha that India should keep its nuclear capability as a bargaining chip.[97]

Thus, for both areas — peaceful applications and the weapon option — Bhabha had a clear strategic vision and priorities. A poor country like India cannot afford to give priority to atomic weapons. And uranium enrichment based on the diffusion method, then the prevalent route to weapon making, was ruled out absolutely for the massive input of electricity and other resources that it involves. Bhabha's vision tied Indian weapon option to envisaged breakthrough in plutonium technology, the cheapest route and one most suited to Indian need of a nuclear watchdog. The Indian weapon option then was to be a by-product of India's nuclear power generation development plans.[98] Bhabha was able to chart this path for India — realised after his sudden death — because of a breakthrough in the advanced technology of reprocessing spent fuel for extracting plutonium.

The path to nuclear capability charted out by Bhabha had two basic features. One, that Indian nuclear technology acquisition gives primacy to a long-term strategy for power generation, along with all-round growth in allied scientific knowledge, a spin-off for industry in metallurgy, and nuclear applications for agriculture and medicine. Weaponisation takes a low priority in this scheme of things."[99]

The second basic feature of the Bhabha route to nuclear capability is stress on indigenous, self-reliant growth by laying a sound foundation. This meant building an extensive infrastructure of research and development to achieve what in scientific parlance is called capability along the entire nuclear fuel cycle.[100] Build-up of nuclear and related industrial capability all along the line ranges from uranium mining and refinement, fuel fabrication for diverse reactors, designing and construction of reactors, building heavy water plants and nuclear industrial units, to running atomic power stations. Safety and the problem of nuclear wastes management were of course given primacy right from the start.[101]

Bhabha's fifty year plan for Indian Atomic Energy Development had three phases. In the first phase, India will construct natural-uranium-heavy-water reactor using indigenous uranium and heavy water. These reactors will produce plutonium. The plutonium will be separated and used as fuel for the fast-breeder reactor in the second phase. Fast-breeder reactors produce more fissile materials than they consume. By using India's abundant thorium in the fast-breeders as blankets, the thorium will be converted into Uranium 233, which is a fissile material. In turn, that will be used to fuel the enriched-uranium-light-water reactor in the third phase. With this long-term plan in view he contracted to set up the Canada-India experimental reactor at Trombay, which was a natural-uranium-heavy-water reactor. As this reactor was established, he also took steps to develop indigenously the technology to separate plutonium from the irradiated uranium rods of Canada-India reactor. No nation was prepared to transfer this technology and India developed this on its own.[102]

A landmark in the build-up of infrastructure for India's nuclear capability was the construction in 1964-65 of a nuclear spent fuel reprocessing test plant at the Bhabha Atomic Research Center (BARC) by a team of scientists and engineers headed by Homi Sethna. It is this breakthrough that provided the link between nuclear power production and the weapon option based on the plutonium route. Over the years, as Indian scientists acquired a grip over spent fuel reprocessing, the plutonium route to atomic weapons opened up, bypassing the enormously costly uranium enrichment method. India now has four reprocessing plants — while the pioneering BARC unit has become a full-fledged plant, at Tarapur a spent fuel reprocessing plant was built and has been operating for the last two decades and the most modern and advanced reprocessing plant has come up at

Kalpakkam. The fourth unit, a specialised reprocessing plant, has recently been commissioned at Kalpakkam itself. The acquisition and rapid development of spent fuel reprocessing technology justifies the Indian claim that this country's route to the nuclear weapon option is a spin-off from the power programme and the cheapest weapon programme anywhere in the world.[103]

Prime Minister Jawaharlal Nehru tirelessly denounced the trend towards nuclear arms race. It became a passion for him to plead for disarmament.[104] As early as 1940, Nehru had said: "We believe that complete disarmament by all nation states should be aimed at, as in fact an urgent necessity if the world is not to be reduced to barbarism." In 1948, at the time of consideration of the report of the newly created UN Atomic Energy Commission, India had proposed limiting the use of atomic energy to peaceful purposes and elimination of nuclear weapons from national arsenals.[105] It was on India's initiative that the UN undertook a study of the economic consequences of disarmament, which debunked the thesis, so fashionable those days, that propagated that disarmament would lead to large-scale unemployment and the disruption of the economy of the developed countries.[106]

Following the Chinese nuclear test on October 16, 1964, Bhabha became a fervent advocate of India exercising its nuclear option. However, there were strong West-oriented lobbies that had great faith in West supporting India against China. Under the influence of that lobby, the then Prime Minister Lal Bahadur Shastri approached Britain for a nuclear umbrella. Britain was not willing to provide any security guarantees. By 1965, it was also becoming clear that the West had no intention of assisting India in its defence preparedness programme against Pakistan and China and India had to rely increasingly on the USSR for its defence equipment and technology. Thus, as early as, in 1965, Bhabha was able to persuade the then Prime Minister to sanction the subterranean nuclear explosive project (SNEP). That would have made India a recognised nuclear power in the international community at that stage.[107] The work on the project unfortunately came to an end when Bhabha was killed in the Mont Blanc air crash on January 24, 1966 (the very day Smt. Indira Gandhi was sworn in as the Prime Minister). Bhabha's successor, Vikram Sarabhai, did not subscribe to the idea of India going nuclear. Indira Gandhi sent her envoys, Vikram Sarabhai and L.K. Jha, to Moscow, Paris, London and Washington to seek security guarantees from these four powers. Their quest for security guarantees failed and they came back empty-handed.[108] At that stage the two superpowers came out with their draft Non-Proliferation Treaty and brought to bear on India an enormous amount of pressure to accede to it. India rejected the NPT and decided not to accede to it. Further, in 1971 India faced a Pakistan-China-US line-up when General Yahya Khan cracked down on the Awami League and population of East Bengal. Faced with this hostile combination of powers, Mrs. Gandhi was compelled to sign a Peace and Friendship Treaty with the Soviet Union to generate adequate deterrence against Chinese adventurism. US President Nixon dispatched the nuclear-powered and nuclear-armed aircraft carrier US Enterprise into the Bay of Bengal on an intimidatory mission. The Soviet navy sent its task force behind it and the Soviet Naval Headquarters generated a lot of signals to their submarine fleet at sea in a deterrent exercise. Obviously, all these incidents persuaded Mrs. Gandhi to order the scientists to go ahead with the Pokhran-1 test.[109] Thus, India exploded her first nuclear device in Pokhran in 1974, within four years of the NPT coming into force. R. Venkatraman, former President of India, argued that in 1974 there was no threat perception to India's security as India's defence capabilities and reputation stood high after the 1971 Bangladesh war. According to him, the first Pokhran test was a protest against the arbitrary and unequal Non-Proliferation Treaty. It was undertaken to demonstrate India's nuclear capability to the rest of the world.[110] India has more convincingly broken China's nuclear monopoly in Asia.[111] No doubt Mrs. Gandhi got cold feet after the tests and suspended further testing. The UN charter recognises that a country can take measures for its own self-defence. India has faced aggression from both Pakistan and China and has also noticed the clandestine acquisition of nuclear weapon technology by Pakistan from the West and nuclear and missile technology from China,[112] while the nuclear weapon states stood idly by. There is no evidence of India proliferating nuclear or missile technology to any other country. There is also no evidence of India obtaining any such technology clandestinely. However, the 'nuclear option', which had been implicit for non-signatories to the NPT, had been repeatedly hinted at by successive Indian governments. India felt it had gained nothing by abstaining from further testing since 1974, while the nuclear weapon states continued to test after that time. The principles and objectives for Nuclear Non-Proliferation and Disarmament stated, "pending the entry into force of a Comprehensive Test Ban Treaty, the nuclear weapon states should exercise utmost restraint in carrying out further tests." Notwithstanding the solemn declaration, China conducted on 15 May 1995, its 42nd test and on 17 August 1995, its 43rd nuclear test. France declared its intention to carry out a series of eight tests starting from September 1995 and ending in May 1996. These are two interesting examples of the "utmost restraint" that the nuclear powers had undertaken to observe before the CTBT came into force.[113] No wonder, India declined to join the Comprehensive Test Ban Treaty. In fact, the nuclear powers had no interest in genuine disarmament or elimination of nuclear weapons.

Despite India's efforts to this end during the negotiations of the NPT and CTBT and in bilateral discussions with the nuclear weapon states, there was no evidence of movement towards elimination of nuclear weapons within a certain time frame, although the USA and the former Soviet Union did move through the INF, START-I and START-II agreements towards elimination of intermediate range nuclear forces in Europe and deep cuts in tactical nuclear weapons and in the total number of nuclear warheads possessed by both sides.[114] Thus, the West, instead of marching towards the goal of elimination of nuclear weapons and general and complete disarmament, began to talk of arms control and arms control negotiations. Having irrationally built nuclear arsenals which are excessive and a significant portion of which is unusable, they are now rationalizing their arsenals and cutting them down to sizes which are still several times what is required to destroy even the whole human civilisation. At the same time they are doing research in new generation weapons. They insist on sustaining the legality of the use of nuclear weapons.[115]

About a decade later, in 1983, India made preparations for a second nuclear test at Pokhran. It was undertaken to demonstrate again India's nuclear capability to the rest of the world. "The preparations for the test", said former President of India, R. Venkatraman, "were completed and as Defence Minister, I had gone down the shaft and seen all the arrangements. We did not, however, conduct the test at that time for several reasons including pressures from international sources."[116] Again, in 1988, faced with the challenge of China-Pakistan nuclear collaboration, Prime Minister Rajiv Gandhi ordered a programme of Indian nuclear weaponisation. As V.P. Singh disclosed in the BBC "Hard Talk" interview, India was ready for testing during his tenure of office and he did not do it because India was economically weak and would not have been able to withstand sanctions.[117] However, the programme has been sustained and developed by his successors Chandrashekhar, Narasimha Rao, Deve Gowda and I.K. Gujral. Further, following the legitimisation of the nuclear weapons by the international community through the unconditional and indefinite extension of the NPT in 1995, Narasimha Rao ordered testing of the weapons. Again they were called off because of US pressure. But the shafts made were available for fresh tests at short notice, as most of the preparations for the tests were completed.[118]

Furthermore, in 1996 the CTBT was adopted and the Chinese acted in an unfriendly manner by bringing in at the last moment the force clause. China persuaded other permanent members of the Security Council to introduce article XIV in the CTBT which insisted that India should sign the treaty to bring it into force, after India had declared that it would not sign the treaty, since it would be against its national security interests. It was a clear attempt by China to curb India's independence and assign India's security a standard lower than China's. That made India's nuclear tests inevitable. Moreover, the kind of pressure built against India following the Shakti tests would have been built to compel India to sign the CTBT. It was better for India to face the sanctions after inducting the tests and declaring itself a nuclear weapon state instead of facing them without having conducting the tests.[119]

On May 11 and 13, 1998 India detonated five nuclear devices at Pokhran, with yields ranging from 15 KT to 45 KT, one device with a yield of 45 KT was a hydrogen or H-bomb. Between Pokhran-I and Pokhran-II a vast scientific and nuclear technology acquisition by Indian scientific institutions is revealed; a striking advance on all sectors of nuclear capability made possible by the linkage between Indian nuclear capability for peaceful applications and the weapon option.[120] Simultaneous testing of a weaponised fission device, a low yield fission device and a thermonuclear device is an unprecedented event in nuclear history. The two subsequent sub-kiloton tests have yielded additional data; and our capability in computer simulation of new designs has been enhanced. Atomic Energy Commission Chairman, R. Chidambaram and Director of the Bhabha Atomic Research Center, Anil Kakodkar played crucial role in this effort; they also provided a link with Pokhran-I. Defense Research and Development Organisation gave necessary support to BARC in fabricating and testing the nuclear explosives. Indian scientists and engineers can now fabricate nuclear weapons of different configurations and for various delivery systems. Bharat Ratna Abdul Kalam, therefore, announced: "Nuclear weaponisation is now complete." He added, that the Agni and Prithvi missiles could now be armed with nuclear warheads. A new vision of Agni being developed with a range much higher than 2500 kilometers would be able to carry nuclear warheads weighing 1000 kilograms. The data generated by the tests should be used for developing a modest missile-borne nuclear deterrent capability. We should not repeat the nuclear follies of others by stockpiling redundant nuclear weapons.[121] Those protesting against Indian tests are themselves beneficiaries of nuclear peace. Their urgent pleas to adhere to 'nonproliferation norms' are designed to deny the status India deserves as happened after Pokhran-I. Derogatory remarks of Madeleine Albright notwithstanding, India is a nuclear weapon state. Former Prime Minister Atal Behari Vajpayee has rightly observed:

> It is not a conferment that we seek; nor is it a status for others to grant. It is an endowment to the nation by our scientists and engineers. It is India's due, the right of one-sixth of humankind."[122] He emphasised: "I would, therefore,

say that the greatest meaning of the tests is that they have given India Shakti, they have given strength, they have given India self-confidence.[123]

However Richard Grenier, a columnist for *The Washington Times,* analysed that the nuclear tests have given India what its Prime Minister calls 'Shakti' a kind of power possessed by Hinduism's gods. And the vegetarian Hindus have also begun to eat meat.[124]

Implications of Pokhran-II

India has broken the monopoly of the Nuclear Five. The question is asked whether India should join the Nuclear Club and enjoy its privileges. Having pleaded for a total elimination of nuclear weapons, it would be immoral for India to join any group, which would have the privilege of increasing the nuclear arsenal. On the contrary, India should strive through the United Nations to bring about a Treaty on "no first use" of nuclear weapons by any of the Member-States.[125]

After a gap of twenty-four years, India has demonstrated its scientific and technological prowess to test a variety of warheads ranging from thermo-nuclear to sub-kiloton devices.

The tests conducted on May 11and 13, 1998 proved beyond any shadow of doubt, India's superiority over Pakistan in nuclear capability. In contrast, Pakistan's nuclear and missile capabilities are limited by what China can provide for Pakistan. While China has decided to arm Pakistan with nuclear weapons and missiles to countervail India, it cannot be in its own interest to permit Pakistan to become an autonomous nuclear weapon power.

India and Pakistan have forced their way into the nuclear club. The tests have increased tension, made nuclear war very likely in the subcontinent and have unleashed an arms race. India was aware of Pakistani nuclear weapon capability as Pakistan has been making nuclear weapons since 1987. Pakistan has not behaved with restraint in spite of losing the fourth war in Kashmir — the covert war. The tests have brought only one new element to the India-Pakistan equation. Pakistan can now feel more secure *vis-à-vis* the larger India. That in fact is a contribution to stability.[126] Thus, the emerging symmetry with declared capability by both countries is less dangerous than an undeclared 'covert' nuclear situation, which lent to greater insecurity, unpredictability and furtive acts.[127]

India's claim to the status of a nuclear weapon state has been vehemently opposed by the United States. Thus, the chance of India's getting a Security Council membership has also been ruined by her nuclear tests. The United States and China will veto, if necessary to prevent India's membership in the Security Council. However, a large number of countries are supporting India's candidature for permanent membership of Security Council. These countries include Russia, France, Germany, Sweden, Australia, New Zealand, Poland, Japan, Singapore, Thailand, Malaysia, South Africa, Egypt, etc. which cover all the regions of the world.

Challenges after Pokhran-II

Nuclear weapons are destructive, they degenerate security and create more insecurity. Henry Kissinger in 1957 reminded the Americans in his book *Nuclear Weapons and Foreign Policy* that if the enormous US nuclear weapon capability was not related to a doctrine framework, it could lead to a nuclear disaster. The same is true of India as well. A nuclear doctrine is necessary that could define the role of nuclear weapons and their use or non-use in a crisis situation as nuclear strategy aims at escalation and can lead to a nuclear war.[128]

Among the eight nuclear and undeclared nuclear weapon powers India stands alone in agonizing over its nuclearisation and confounded by its ignorance. There is no attempt among political parties, many of whose leaders nurtured the nuclear weapons programme to come together to evolve a consensus. In almost all nuclear weapon powers, when the weapons were acquired large sections of population were not adequately informed about them. The depth of ignorance can be gauged from the fact that it took forty years from the dawn of the nuclear era for the strategists and political-military leaderships of the nuclear weapon powers to develop some understanding about the fight ability of nuclear war. Even now if the people of those countries understood the true nature of nuclear weapons and their limitations they would not be paying their taxes to maintain such monstrous stockpiles. In that sense, the lack of knowledge in India is not worse than that it is in the US, UK, France, Russia and China. But, in those countries there is a consensus, however misguided it may have been, to support the nuclear weapon policy of their respective governments. In India, in spite of the policy being more rational there is no consensus, nor even a concerted attempt at building a consensus. The initiative to build the consensus must come from the government since it took this historic decision to make India a declared nuclear weapon state. The government needs to organise discussions and seminars for the parliamentarians, including ministers. It will be very helpful if politicians of the ruling party discipline themselves not to talk about the nuclear issue and leave it to one or two better equipped leaders alone to deal with.[129]

In democracies, government white papers are pre-eminent. The absence of any white paper on foreign and defence policies in India over sixty years is a shameful record and an indication of the clandestine and furtive manner in which both the defence and external affairs ministries function. Economic liberalisation is not the only liberalisation we need. If defence and foreign policies are to be receptive to world changes, they must be made more in the open.[130]

Nuclear Doctrine

A draft nuclear doctrine of the National Security Advisory Board (NSAB) headed by K. Subrahmanyam was released on August 17, 1999. It provides a broad framework for the development, deployment and employment of India's nuclear forces. It has proposed a credible minimum nuclear deterrent-retaliatory capability, consisting of sufficient, survivable and operationally prepared nuclear forces with the necessary support of an effective intelligence and early warning system.[131]

It has called for a triad — bombers, land-based ballistic missiles and ballistic missiles launched from submarines. Such a triad is expected to constitute a "minimum and credible" deterrence against nuclear attack on Indian cities by the two main adversaries — Pakistan and China. But, since the present Indian capabilities are limited, the triad will take many years to materialise.[132] Inherent in the doctrine is the advocacy of a 'no first use' policy. This suggests that retaliation against a nuclear attack will be the preferred policy and not an offensive posture of the kind presently favored by the US, Russia, France and the UK as also Pakistan.

Since 1964 when China detonated its first atomic bomb, it has declared a 'no first use' policy. It has reiterated, however, that such a declaration does not apply to territories that are its own. This suggests that in so far as Taiwan and Arunachal Pradesh are concerned, China could contemplate first use of nuclear weapons of low yield (sub-kilotons) tactical weapons. The Indian doctrine of a 'no first use' rejects the development of tactical weapons. Hence in a second strike retaliatory mode the use of the weapons would be against cities and population centres. This is classified as a "counter value" as against a "counterforce" doctrine. Counterforce pertains to nuclear attacks against military targets.[133]

What distinguishes the proposed doctrine from all other nuclear doctrines is that it is anchored in India's continued commitment to global, verifiable and non-discriminating nuclear disarmament, describing it as India's national security objective. The Preamble categorically states that any use of nuclear weapons would constitute "the gravest threat to humanity and to peace and stability in the international system."[134]

Another distinctive feature of the proposed nuclear doctrine is the rejection of war fighting. Although often presented as complementary, there is a fundamental difference between strategies of nuclear deterrence and nuclear war fighting. For nuclear deterrence, it is not necessary that warheads should be matched with warheads and missiles with missiles. A modest sufficiency is enough. For nuclear war fighting, however, there is always a quest for nuclear superiority: more accurate delivery systems are also needed to destroy a large number of military targets. Nuclear deterrence threatens only punishment while the objective of nuclear war fighting is victory.[135]

Both the United States and the former Soviet Union invested billions of dollars and roubles in early warning installations, blast-proof bunkers, redundant communication networks, and airborne command posts like the so-called Looking Glass aircraft and Take Charge and Move Out (TACAMO) planes. The proposed doctrine rejects such nuclear follies. Operational Indian nuclear forces are going to be very modest.

R. Chidambaram, former Chairman of the Atomic Energy Commission (AEC), has claimed that the five nuclear weapons tests at Pokhran in May 1998 have provided enough data to his scientists and engineers to be able to conduct computer simulated sub-critical experiments (SCEs) at the laboratory not in the field.[136] Such a view has not been shared by many of his own former compatriots, such as P.K. Iyengar who has favored conducting further nuclear tests. Addressing a group of scientists, including those who participated in Pokhran-I and II, Iyengar said that from the scientific point of view "a survivable nuclear deterrent" envisaged in the proposed nuclear doctrine could not be achieved without further testing. He said that Indian nuclear weaponisation should include the development and testing of a neutron bomb because it is "more efficient in weight and total energy produce." In any case, it has taken the United States and Russia thousands of nuclear tests to arrive at SCEs. In any case, laboratory tests and computer simulations cannot provide complete reliability. India has to conduct many more tests to improve the warhead designs and maximise the yield to weight (Y/W) ratio as to reduce the payload on the missile.[137]

Further, commitment to 'no first use' necessitated a robust command and control system that can survive a nuclear first strike and then deliver a devastating blow. "If command and control fails, nothing else matters."[138] However, an 'elaborate' command and control apparatus is not necessary.[139] It is implied, that the present system of the higher direction of war would fulfill the requirements with minimum modifications. The aim appears to be to find a low cost solution to an obviously complex challenge.

Besides, what is needed after Pokhran-II is a clear go-ahead irrespective of the costs involved to develop 10-15 long range Agni missiles and the same number of Prithvi missiles and emplace on them plutonium and hydrogen bombs. Only then can there be credibility to the Indian "minimum" nuclear deterrence.[140]

Missile Programme

Indira Gandhi took the first step in the development of indigenous missile capability and for this she instituted the Integrated Guided Missiles Development Programme (IGMDP) in 1983. This was accelerated during the Rajiv Gandhi administration. India's 'Missile Man' Abdul Kalam provided dynamic leadership to this programme. The IGMDP draws its physical, technical and human resources from a wide range of DRDO agencies and beyond. Besides IGMDP as the country's chief technology generator, the DRDO is the overarching agency tasked to develop the Indian missile programme. As a result, India has one of the most advanced and ambitious space programs among the developing countries:[141]

(i) Prithvi

Prithvi is a single-stage, short-range, surface-to-surface missile (SSM). Transportable by road and equipped with two liquid-fuel engines, the Prithvi is reported to have the highest ratio of warhead-weight to overall-weight of any missile in its class.[142] The Prithvi comes in three variants. The SS-150 is a battlefield support system for the army (range 150 km., 1000 kg. payload) and the SS-250 is dedicated to the Indian Air Force (range-250 km., 500-750 kg. payload). Between 1988-98, 18 field trials of the SS-150 and SS-250 designs were conducted. In 1994, the SS-150 version was inducted into the army and 20 SS-150s now form the 333rd Missile Regiment of the XI corps based in Hyderabad. The SS-250 is expected to enter service soon. The third variant is the naval version — the SS-350 (range-350 km., 500 Kg. payload). Currently in the advanced stages of testing and field trials, the SS-350 is designed to be launched from both the ocean's surface, as well as underwater.

(ii) Agni

Agni is a two-stage intermediate range ballistic missile (IRBM) fitted with a re-entry vehicle that employs a carbon-composite ablative shield that heats up to 3500 degrees Celsius during flight while keeping the interior cooled to 40 degrees. Agni-1 (1500 km./1000 kg. or 2500 km./500 kg. combination), employing liquid/solid fuel combination, was derived from India's first civilian satellite launch vehicle (SLV-3). It was tested thrice during 1989-94 and then recalled in December 1996 with the government classifying it as a "technology demonstrator (TD)". The Agni TD was revived following the 1998 nuclear tests and an extended-range Agni (ER-Agni or Agni-II, 3700 km. 1000 kg.) was successfully flight-tested on April 11, 1999.[143] This missile used solid fuel in both stages and was tested up to a range of 2000 plus km.

(iii) Surya

Although the government will not confirm the status or even the existence of this intercontinental ballistic missile (ICBM) believed to have a 8000-12000 km. range and 1000 plus kg. payload, it is thought to be in the advanced stages of design and is undergoing simulated testing of components.

(iv) Sagarika

The Sagarika (Oceanic) is a single-stage, solid-fueled system being developed as a cruise as well as a sea-launched ballistic missile (330 km., 500-750 kg.). Configured to carry nuclear warheads, the ballistic missile variant (and perhaps also the cruise missile version) is designed to be launched from either the surface of the sea or from a submarine. The naval version of Prithvi is the same as Sagarika. The cruise missile variant of Sagarika was tested under the name Dhanush Bow.

In addition to the above nuclear-capable missiles, DRDO has produced a number of other units that strengthen Indian combat capability. A few prominent systems are:

(v) Nag

Nag (Cobra) is a third-generation ant-itank guided missile that is hardened against electronic counter measures (ECMs) and employs an advanced tiny seeker head that can identify and lock onto targets (range 4 km.). Two types of guidance systems are being developed for Nag — one based on an imaging infrared seeker (successively tested on January 22, 2000) and another on a millimetric wave seeker.[144] Its tandem warhead can defeat explosive reactor armor. The land version of Nag has been tested from a tracked vehicle commonly known as the MICA (missile carrier). It is also configured for use aboard the indigenous advanced light helicopter (ALH). Nag is in advanced stages of user trials.

(vi) Pinaka

Pinaka (range 38 km.), a 214-mm. multi-barrel rocket launcher, has been inducted into the army.[145]

Remotely Piloted Vehicles (RPVs)

Two RPVs called Nishant (end of darkness) and Lakshya (target) are notable here. Nishant is undergoing field tests while Lakshya performed crucial surveillance functions for India during the later stages of the Kargil conflict in July 1999.

Hyperplane

The most ambitious project of DRDO is the hypersonic platform for Air-Breathing Ascent to Near Earth Orbit project, or Hyper plane. Still in its conceptual stages and likely to cost at least US$ 2 billion, this hybrid between jet aircraft and rocket will be a hydrogen-fueled, fully reusable (over 20 times) single-stage hypersonic (Mach 5-7) vehicle that can take off from a conventional airfield. Its unique feature will be its abilities to use high specific impulse air-breathing propulsion in the atmospheric phase of the trajectory and collect, liquefy and store atmospheric oxygen in the cruise phase for fueling the rocket engine during the terminal phase.

Hypersonic Test Vehicle (HTV)

Although the Government of India has not yet approved the Hyper plane project, a miniature reusable version called the HTV is likely to be approved shortly. Costing only about US$ 9.6 million, the 3-metric ton HTV will carry out surveillance, reconnaissance and intelligence functions but, unlike the rocket-powered Hyper plane, will not launch satellites. According to one of the designers of HTV, Air Commodore (Retd.) R. Gopalaswami: "cruising at a speed of Mach 7 at a height of 30 kilometers gives the hypersonic test vehicle a surveillance, reconnaissance and intelligence capability unmatched by satellites."[146] Also capable of dropping a 500 kg. warhead up to 2000 km. away, the HTV can be built in three to five years, according to the project proposal.

In addition to missile development, Indian security planners are also engaged in developing significant anti-missile capabilities as well as a rudimentary defensive shield comprising the following:

(i) Akash

Akash is a multi-target, command-guided, medium-range surface-to-air missile (SAM). It has a range of 25 km. but can also detect and destroy aircraft at treetop height. It has a quick reaction time (from detection to launch) of fifteen seconds. Its fire control radar is a multi-target, multi-function phased array system called 'Rajendra'.

DRDO is working to extend the range of Akash to 40-60 km. and plans to modify it to also engage ballistic missiles.[147] In this context, the DRDO negotiated with Russia for the purchase of S-300 PMU-1 systems for the Indian army and S-300V for the air force.[148] In June 1998, India agreed to purchase six batteries of S-300 anti-tactical ballistic missile systems from Russia at a cost of about US$ 1 billion.[149] In addition, Indian scientists might be involved in testing and evaluation of the design parameters before receiving delivery of the system.

The modified Akash, a medium-range theater defence SAM, is expected to be integrated with the S-300 V to provide an effective air defense against incoming short-range ballistic missile (SRBM) or IRBM threats, and is to be deployed along the Pakistani and Chinese borders.[150] The army version of Akash is to be integrated with the S-300 PMU-1.

(ii) Trishul

Trishul (Trident), a short-range all-weather SAM with an effective range of nine kilometers, is fitted with a high explosive fragmented warhead. Highly maneuverable, this missile is powered by a two-stage solid propellant system akin to the one used by the US Patriot anti-missile array. The Trishul's detection-of-target to missile launch time is six seconds, making it a quick-reaction system. Trishul is available in army, air force and navy versions. The army and air force versions fly between 300-500 meters per second and can engage aircraft and helicopters using their radar command-to-line-of-sight guidance. The naval version will give the Indian navy its first anti-missile missile capability.

(iii) Astra

Astra (weapon) is described as a beyond-visual-range air-to-air missile with a 100 km. head-on range and a tail range of 15 km. With a maximum speed of Mach 4 plus and altitude of 20 km., it can also undertake 40-g turns close to sea level when attacking a maneuvering target. It is widely believed that Astra will be mounted on the indigenous Light Combat Aircraft (LCA).

WOMEN'S POLITICAL EMPOWERMENT

In the contemporary feminist literature, the word 'women' has been replaced with the term 'gender' as a new category of analysis to assert that much of sexual differentiation is a social and political construct, related to but not determined by biological sex difference. It is seen as the process by which individuals who are born into biological categories of male and female become the social categories of men and women through the acquisition of locally defined attributes of masculinity and femininity. It has been a long battle to show that a woman is not a mere composite of female anatomy, and physiology, sex and gender are not identical. In fact the invention of this word 'gender' is the result of two decades of intensive thought and research. In its most recent usage, gender seems to have first appeared among American feminists. It is through the application of the concept of gender that the feminist scholars challenged the structure of current socio-economic, political and cultural processes.

The brief, of gender explains the division of spheres of action into private and public. The private sphere belongs to women while the male is assigned the public spheres. It is argued that the public-private divide has been used to legitimise women's exclusion from public politics (J.B. Elshtain: *Public Man, Private Woman*). Firestone argues against this separation of spheres of activity. However, the public-private dichotomy has resulted in women being marginalised in all spheres of activity — social, economic and more specifically, political. Joan W. Scott, therefore, emphasises the need to expose the social construction of gender by deconstructing it.

In brief the socio-political environment determines the participation and involvement of women in politics. Right from the Mexico conference in 1975 through Copenhagen, Nairobi and Beijing, there has been a global awareness and realisation that political participation does not only mean the right to vote, yet women's presence in legislative bodies is scarce despite the absence of legal constraints. Thus, women have been accepted as voters but not as policy formulators and decision-makers. Anne Philips is in favour of politics of presence. In her book, *The Politics of Presence* (1995), she speaks about gender parity and accounts that a significant number of political parties (in South Africa and European countries like UK, Germany, and the Nordic countries) have adopted the measures to raise the proportion of women elected. It can ensure that there is a possibility of gender parity, as politics of presence can provide separate recommendation for the excluded group.

Women in Pre-independence Politics

In 19th century, for the first time, women's question came to the forefront, when the women's issues such as *sati,* child marriage, female infanticide, widowhood, *purdah,* polygamy, *devdasi* and education were raised. It was mainly because of the efforts of social reformers and the cooperation of some of the colonial rulers that some progressive legislation such as banning *sati* (1829), permitting widow remarriage (1856), and determining age of consent (1891) were passed. Gradually, women realised they needed their own forum, and some organisations came into existence. From the first two decades of the 20th century, the articulation of women's issues was based on liberal principles of equality. In this context, three major women's organisations, the Women's Indian Association (WIA-1917), the National Council for Women in India (NCWI-1925) and the All India Women's Conference (AIWC- 1927) played a major role in articulating women's issues. WIA was one of the earliest women's organisations to ask for women's right to vote.

Demand for franchise was made as early as in 1917 by the elite women, but ignored by the British government. However, the Government of India Act, 1919, lays down that the provinces could settle the question of franchise. And thus, Bombay and Madras were the first provinces to grant franchise to women in 1921, the United Provinces followed in 1923, Punjab and Bengal in 1926, and Assam, Bihar, Orissa in 1930. Yet the number of enfranchised women remained very small. Women were also voicing their demand to be elected to the legislatures. Muthulakshmi Reddy became the first woman legislator when she was appointed to the Madras Legislative Council in 1927. With the continuous efforts of Women's organizations for women's rights, two important acts — the Child Marriage Restraint Act (1929), and the Hindu Women's Right to Property Act (1937) were passed.

Most of the women who attended the sessions of the Indian National Congress, worked mostly as volunteers, very few participated in the deliberations or rose to high positions, like Annie Besant, who became the first woman president of the Congress in 1917, followed by Sarojini Naidu in 1925 and Nellie Sengupta in 1933. This, however, does not mean that women had no political sensitivity. Women's participation in the nationalist struggle was intense and they actively took part in the Civil Disobedience movement of 1930-32 and the Quit India movement of 1942. While the nationalist struggle provided women with an opportunity to enter the public sphere and bring about changes in their lives, it could not totally transform the reality. The basic issue of women's inequality and the traditional role of woman were not challenged. Women's issues and movement were submerged in the tidal wave of the nationalist struggle.

Women in Post-independence Politics

Planning was high on the agenda of Independent India. Nehru emphasised the need for a special policy towards women. The Planning Commission of India defined three areas of women's development: education, social welfare and health. The period from the seventies onwards witnessed new awareness and sensitivity towards women's issues. In 1971, the Government of India appointed the Committee on the Status of Women in India. The committee submitted its historic report entitled "Towards Equality", which proved to be an eye-opener for the government and concerned citizens. The women's movement, which was very visible during the seventies and mid-eighties, was confronted by certain serious challenges in the late eighties and thereafter. The major controversial issues during this phase were the Shah Bano case, the Roop Kunwar *sati* incident, the reservation policy and the growing phenomena of communalism and fundamentalism.

Women and the Constitution

The Fundamental Rights as guaranteed by the Constitution try to remove the inequalities, which Indian women had suffered. It seemed in 1950, that India had ushered in a new era of liberty and equality where women were equal to men. Some of the provisions in the Constitution are incorporated in Article 14 (equality before the law and equal protection by the law), Article 15 (prohibition of discrimination on grounds of religion, race, caste, sex or place of birth), Article 16 (equality of opportunity in employment) and Article 23 under Fundamental Rights. Besides, some provisions are under the heading Directive Principles of State Policy, such as Article 39 (equal pay for equal work for both men and women), Article 42 (just and humane conditions of work and maternity relief), Article 44 (uniform civil code) and Article 51 (fundamental duty of every citizen to renounce practices derogatory to the dignity of women), which provides equality, safety and dignity to women.

The Constitution has accepted the principle of affirmative action favouring women and children. Such principle has activated the state to make provisions for reservation for women in elected bodies of local government and other selected bodies. The 73rd and 74th Constitutional Amendments have provided for reservation of seats for women at the local level in the elected bodies in rural and urban areas. The sad reality remains that such provisions have not laid solid foundations for legal equality between men and women.

Women and the Law

The discrimination felt by the women in India is sanctified by tradition and is seldom challenged by the law. In fact, women have a very feeble voice in the formation, implementation and interpretation of laws. The Fundamental Rights as guaranteed by the Constitution have not been able to ensure equality for women in all spheres, and the Directive Principles of State Policy have remained mere pious words. Personal laws based on religion and at present continuing under the cover of freedom of religion hold women's lives in their octopus-like grip, controlling issues of marriage, divorce, guardianship, adoption, maintenance and property. In spite of the shortcomings of the legal system in India, it is the law, which has been and is still expected to be effective as an instrument of social change, a strategy to free women from the shackles of inequality and subjugation.

Secularisation of law has always been a formidable struggle in India because of the pluralities and diversities found among various communities and the ineffectiveness of the rulers in dealing with them. Most of the laws enacted before independence indicate this reality (the situation after independence has its own problems). The Hindu Women's Right to Property Act of 1937, the Muslim Personal Law (Shariat) Application Act, 1937 and the Dissolution of Muslim Marriages Act, 1939 granted limited rights to women but did not question the fundamental gender inequality experienced by both Hindu and Muslim women. Unfortunately, the two important legislations (The Special Marriage Act of 1872 and 1923 and the Indian Succession Act of 1925) could not be further developed to evolve into a uniform civil code.

The Hindu Code Bill created a furore in Indian society to such an extent that it had to be taken up later by piecemeal legislations: the Hindu Marriage Act, 1955, the Hindu Adoption and Maintenance Act, 1956, the Hindu Minority and Guardianship Act, 1956 and Hindu Succession Act, 1956. But the provision for maintenace to the Muslim divorced women has been a concern for progressive elements not only among Muslims but also among all segments of society. Provisions of maintenance to the divorced wife are limited to the period of *iddat,* which is usually three months and if the wife is pregnant it continues until delivery. The Shah Bano case, in this context, deserves a mention. The judgment of Mohd. Ahmed Khan *vs.* Shah Bano and others attracted the attention of the nation and had an impact on national politics. It was held here that a divorced Muslim woman, so long as she has not remarried, could claim maintenance under Section 125 of the Criminal Procedure Code. There have been previous judgements along this line; still this judgement is a landmark. The judgement recognised the right of the divorced woman for maintenance and pointed out the need for a common civil code. This stirred the conservative elements among the Muslim society. And the then government bowed down to the pressure and the Muslim women (Protection of Rights of Divorce) Act was passed in 1986. This law has provided for maintenance of the wife during the *iddat* period. This legislation was a rude shock to the progressive elements. The courts have, however, taken a progressive stand in a few cases pertaining to maintenance even after this Act was passed.

The situation today is that personal laws of the minorities continue to be operative and the state does not want to touch them lest such efforts should invoke unrest and upset the political balance. In the case of Hindu women, the state has managed to get increased rights for Hindu women, but in the case of personal laws of Muslim, Parsi and Christian women, the state has not intervened. This issue demands attention. However, the dynamics of personal laws and the Constitution have been complex. All personal laws are discriminatory against women. They have been challenged time and again on the contention that they amount to discrimination on grounds of sex. The courts have generally adopted a hands-off attitude regarding personal laws. On the one hand they have been exhorting the state to enact a uniform civil code, and on the other hand they persistently refuse to apply the Constitutional mandate of non-discrimination in matters pertaining to personal laws.

Women and Political Parties

The Women's Movement and the declaration of 1975 as the women's year and later 1975-1985 as the women's decade brought some change in the perspective of political parties towards women. It is important to note that although all the parties give some place to women in their manifestos, the promises remain on paper. Most of them mobilise women for rallies and demonstrations. Women rarely find place in decision-making committees of political parties. So far, only a few women leaders have been able to reach the position of party president or leader in the legislative parties, as did Indira Gandhi and Sonia Gandhi (Congress), Mrinal Gore (Janata Party), Gita Mukherjee (CPI), Vijaya Raje Scindia and Sushama Swaraj (BJP), Mamata Banerjee (Trinmool Congress), Jayalalitha

(AIADMK), Mayawati (Bahujan Samaj Party) and Jaya Jaitly (Samata Party).

In the 1999 election, it was observed that parties, which promised reservation of seats for women, did not encourage women to fight elections. There were only 277 women contestants for the thirteenth Lok Sabha, only 47 won. Out of the 50 candidates fielded by the Congress, just 14 won. The BJP fielded 54 women candidates, but only 15 won. The Telugu Desam Party sent three women to the Lok Sabha, and the Shiv Sena sent only one woman.

Political parties and leaders have not considered women's vote to be of much consequence. Besides, women also have not crystallised themselves into voters' bloc.

Women and the Legislature

The women members of Parliament perform a double role as representatives of the people and as representatives of the oppressed section of society, that is, women. Many important laws regarding women are a result of women's pressures and demands inside and outside the House.

However, getting a ticket is in fact very difficult for women aspiring for political power. There are considerations of the strategies of the party leader, party politics, money power, caste affiliation, regional politics and individual capacity of the candidate. Parties are not willing to invest their energy in the election of women contestants, they are doubtful about their success. Often, women candidates are dropped to make political compromises, or are given tickets for constituencies where there is little chance of their winning.

So far, very few women have captured seats of power as ministers. Though the number of women elected is very small, the performance of elected women members in the deliberations of the legislature has been noteworthy. Women have been vocal on the floor of the house. They do not only concentrate their attention on 'womanly' and 'soft' subjects, but also express their views on sensitive political matters.

The statistics of the Lok Sabha reveal the fact that the percentage of women members in Lok Sabha never went beyond 8.8 per cent. It presents a zigzag trend. At the time of emergency in 1977, it touched upon the lowest 3.4 per cent. The pattern of representation of women in the Rajya Sabha is not very different from that in the Lok Sabha. The pattern of representation of women in the legislative assemblies of the states is puzzling. Kerala, with its high literacy rate and a matrilineal tradition, has only a few women legislators. Similarly, Manipur, where women play a dominant role in both the family and the community, did not produce a woman legislator until 1990. In contrast, Uttar Pradesh, Bihar and Madhya Pradesh, with their low education levels and repressive cultural norms for women, have sent a relatively larger proportion of women to the Lok Sabha and legislative assemblies.

There have been women Chief Ministers, too, such as Sucheta Kripalani (Uttar Pradesh), Nandini Satpathy (Orissa), Shashikala Kakodkar (Goa), Mayawati (Uttar Pradesh), Rabari Devi (Bihar), Jayalalitha (Tamil Nadu), Sheila Dixit (Delhi) Uma Bharti (Madhya Pradersh) and Vijaya Raje Scindia (Rajasthan). It has to be noted that most of them were pushed to the top position by the forces of party politics and contemporary state politics.

Besides, there are multiple barriers to the participation and involvement of women in politics. These range from illiteracy, backwardness, caste, and culture to criminalisation of politics, communalism and corruption.

Women and the Reservation Policy

The 1995 UN Conference on Women in Beijing was a landmark, where the focus was on political empowerment of women and consequently, on the issue of women's reservation. This received an international recognition. The final consensus was that establishment of quota for women's political participation was legitimate and practical. In India, during Rajiv Gandhi's regime, efforts were made to amend the Constitution so as to provide for 33 per cent reservation to women in local grassroots level Panchayat bodies. The amendments — 73rd and 74th were made in 1992 providing for one-third reservation to women in the Panchayats and quietly ratified in 1993. Between 1993 and 1996, women's organisations united for a joint demand for reservation in State Assemblies and the Parliament. The demand was accepted and featured in the manifestos of the major parties. The response to the demand was the bill for the 84th and 85th Amendment to the Constitution, to allow one-third of the total number of seats in the Lok Sabha and State Assemblies to be reserved for women including for those from Scheduled Castes and Scheduled Tribes. The bill was tabled on September 12, 1996. It evoked spontaneous support as well as fierce opposition. Since then, on a number of occasions government tried to introduce the bill, but nothing could be achieved.

Political parties have no unanimous stand on the bill. Against all theoretical assurances, the major political parties are taking vague positions on the issue of caste-based and religion-based women's reservation regarding four sub-categories within the women quota — backward caste, Muslims, Christians and Sikhs. In fact caste and communal card was used to confuse the whole issue and divide the women. Nevertheless, most women members of Parliament, cutting across party lines, have been vocal in their support for the bill.

The policy of reservation has certainly brought power within reach of rural women. Karnataka and West Bengal had already reserved seats for women in elected bodies in rural areas even before the 73rd Amendment. Their experiences and now those of other states have been largely positive. As women in rural India are getting absorbed into formal politics at the local level, they are shattering the myths regarding their inefficiency and inability to govern. Developmental activities are high on their agenda. There are many instances in Karnataka, Rajasthan, Haryana, Madhya Pradesh and other states where women have fought bravely against corruption, alcoholism and other social evils and have worked for the development of the community.

The reservation policy is not an end in itself; it is a means to achieve gender equality. It is important that women enter in decision-making bodies in sizeable numbers, this 'critical mass' is important if women's voices are to be heard in politics. The risk is uphill, not impossible. Women's empowerment has to be seen in the larger context of the democratic system. It demands the percolation of the values of equality and justice in daily life, the support of citizen's groups in protest against oppression and acceptance of the feminist perspective in the public sphere.

Women have to recognise, collectively and politically, the forces that limit them and to work collectively and continuously to change the unequal power structure. In other words they have to experience the process of empowerment.

NOTES

1. R. Saxena, *Indian Politics in Transition,* Deep & Deep Publications, New Delhi, 1994.
2. *Ibid.*
3. *Ibid.*
4. *Ibid.*
5. *Ibid.*
6. In 1977-79 and almost all governments of 1990s.
7. D. Gupta, 'Coalition Politics Making a Virtue of Necessity', *Times of India,* 26 June 1998.
8. *Ibid.*
9. *Ibid.*
10. H.K. Dua, 'Hung Parliament', May 27, 1998. *Times of India.*
11. *Ibid.*
12. *Ibid.*
13. S. Kaul, 'Stability and the Poll', *The Hindustan Times,* January 10, 1997.
14. *Ibid.*
15. M.P. Singh and R. Saxena , *Ideologies and Institutions in Indian Politics,* Deep & Deep Publications Pvt. Ltd., 1998.
16. *Ibid.*
17. C.P. Bhambhri, 'Political Process and Foreign Policy', *World Focus,* Oct.-Nov.-Dec., 1999.
18. *Ibid.*
19. *World Focus,* Oct.-Nov.-Dec., 1999.
20. *Ibid.*
21. The well known idioms used by Morris Jones in his study of *Indian Politics.*
22. R. Khan, 'Challenges of Communalism in India', *World Focus,* August, 1988.
23. *Strategic Analysis,* January, 1996.
24. D.L. Sheth, 'State, Nation and Ethnicity', *Economic and Political Weekly,* Vol. 25, No. 12, March 25, 1989, p. 624.
25. See Urmila Phadnis: 'Ethnic Conflict in South Asian States', in Phadnis and Others, No. 5, pp. 100-107.

26. *Ibid.*, pp. 100-101.
27. S.D. Muni, 'Dimensions of Domestic Conflicts in South Asia', in Urmila Phadnis and others (Eds.): *Domestic Conflicts in South Asia*, Vol. 1, New Delhi, 1986, p. 61.
28. A.D. Bahera, 'An Analysis of Separatist Insurgencies in India', *Strategic Analysis*, January 1996.
29. Although it is not clear who these Tamils are, one can presume that they are from the LTTE and could be doing it for some favours in return. See Chris Smith, n. 25, p. 31.
30. See 'JKLF: Diminishing Sway', *India Today*, October 31, 1991, p. 102.
31. See *Frontline*, October 12-25, 1991, p. 12.
32. *Hazarika*, No. 15, p. 179.
33. *Ibid.*, pp. 170-74.
34. According to intelligence reports, NSCN has a training camp in Tarishdaba where Bangladesh Rifles and ISI of Pakistan are providing training. See, Soutik Biswas: 'Living on the Razor's Edge', *India Today*, October 15, 1993, p. 85.
35. The Naga leadership has maintained that the Nagas were not an Indian or subcontinental community. They were probably of Mongoloid origin and have been demanding self-determination. See N.K. Das: *Ethnic Identity, Ethnicity and Social Stratification in North-East India*, New Delhi, 1989, pp. 243-45.
36. The ULFA was successful in carrying out these activities because of its widespread support among villagers, the urban middle class and Assamese students. *Hazarika*, n. 15, p. 175.
37. K.P.S. Gill, "The Dangers Within: Internal Security Threats", in Bharat Karnad (Ed.): *Future Imperilled: India's Security in the 1990s and Beyond*, New Delhi, 1994, pp. 130-31.
38. Some of these methods included summary executions, arming of civilians by employing special police officers who were paid Rs. 35 per day and pitting Jat Sikhs against Jat Sikhs. For details see, Tarun Tejpal and Ramesh Vinayak: 'Punjab: New Signs of Independence', *India Today*, September 15, 1992, pp. 56-59; Kanwar Sandhu: 'Official Excesses', *India Today*, October 15, 1992; and Shekhar Gupta and Kanwar Sandhu: 'True Grit', *India Today*, April 15, 1993, p. 64.
39. The former Governor of Kashmir, Jagmohan believes that it was due to these factors that "fundamentalists, pro-Pakistan elements and terrorists", aided and abetted by Pakistan came to hold sway over the minds of Kashmiris. See Jagmohan: *My Frozen Turbulence in Kashmir*, New Delhi, 1991, pp. 13, 112.
40. According to Noorani, the present uprising is a result of carefully laid out plans. The foundations of the insurgency were laid by the late President Zia-ul-Haq and furthered by Nawaz Sharif. See A.G. Noorani: 'The

Betrayal of Kashmir: Pakistan's Duplicity and India's Complicity', in Raju G.C. Thomas, n. 21, pp. 257-62.

41. Media reports about the ISI-sponsored camps or private training camps in Pakistan are a fairly consistent feature in both Indian and Pakistani Media. See 'Kashmir: Training the Fighters', *Viewpoint,* October 10, 1991, pp. 23-24; 'Kashmiris Urged to Help Liberate Valley', *The Pakistan Times,* October 31; 'Sponsoring Terrorism', *Sunday,* August 21-27, 1994, pp. 26-27; and 'ISI Training Camps in Kashmir Now', *Asian Age,* No. 94, September 26, 1994.

42. For instance, in May 1991, Assam Rifles personnel killed 73 militants trying to cross over to India. See Rajesh Kadian, n. 37, p. 32.

43. This Development is linked to the Afghan Mujahideen's liberation struggle against the erstwhile Soviet-backed Marxist government in Kabul. During that struggle, a lot of Kashmiris had joined the Afghan Mujahideen. Thus, linkages were established with groups like the Hizb-e-Islami led by Gulbudin Hikmatyar, which have been providing training and arms to the Kashmiris. See *Strategic Analysis,* Jan. 1996.

44. S. Gupta, and P. Pathak, 'Pan-Islamic Fundamentalism — Exporting Terror', *India Today,* May 15, 1994, pp. 31-32.

45. C. Smith, 'The Diffusion of Small Arms and Light Weapons in Pakistan and Northern India', London, 1993, pp. 31-32.

46. Excerpts from the lecture delivered by I.K. Gujral at the India International Center, New Delhi, Feb 16, 2000; *Mainstream,* April 22, 2000.

47. *Ibid.*

48. *Mainstream,* April 22, 2000.

49. Excerpts from the lecture delivered by I.K. Gujral at the India International Centre, New Delhi, Feb. 16, 2000; *Mainstream,* April 22, 2000.

50. *Ibid.*

51. M.M. Bouton, 'India's Problem is not Polities', *Foreign Affairs,* May-June, 1998.

52. P. Anthony D'costa, 'The Long March to Capitalism: India's Resistance to, and Reintegration with the World Economy', *Contemporary South Asia,* 1995.

53. *Ibid.*

54. G. Mishra, 'Globalisation and India', *World Focus,* Oct.-Nov.-Dec., 1999.

55. History tells of a number of attempts in this direction. From Alexander to Chenghis Khan and Napoleon Bonaparte, efforts were made to bring all the world under one supreme ruler and the center of decision making was to be located in the capital of the conqueror's country. It needs to be noted that none of these conquerors (with the exception of Napoleon Bonaparte) disturbed and altered the prevailing mode of production in the conquered countries or areas.

56. Termed by *New York Times* as 'Masterpiece' on the occasion of its 150th anniversary.
57. *New York Times,* 26 April, 1998.
58. R. Ray, 'Quo Vadis Globalisation?', *Mainstream,* April 1, 2000.
59. *Ibid.*
60. *Ibid.*
61. K.R. Nair, 'India and the New Economic Policy', in K. Raman Pillai (Ed.): *Indian Foreign Policy in the 1990s,* Radiant Publishers, New Delhi, 1997.
62. *Ibid.*
63. *Ibid.*
64. *Ibid.*
65. R. Ray, 'Quo Vadis Globalisation?', *Mainstream,* April 1, 2000.
66. K.R. Nair, 'India and the New Economic Policy', in K. Raman Pillai (Ed.): *Indian Foreign Policy in the 1990s,* Radiant Publishers, New Delhi, 1997.
67. R. Ray, 'Quo Vadis Globalisation?', *Mainstream,* April 1, 2000.
68. *Ibid.*
69. *Ibid.*
70. M.M. Bouton, 'India's Problem is not Polities', *Foreign Affairs,* May-June, 1998.
71. K.R. Nair, 'India and the New Economic Policy', in K. Raman Pillai (Ed.): *Indian Foreign Policy in the 1990s,* Radiant Publishers, New Delhi, 1997.
72. M.M. Bouton, 'India's Problem is not Polities', *Foreign Affairs,* Vol. 77, No. 3, May-June, 1998.
73. *Ibid.*
74. G. Mishra, 'East Asian Crisis and India', *World Focus,* September, 1998.
75. *Ibid.*
76. K.R. Nair, 'India and the New Economic Policy', in K. Raman Pillai (Ed.): *Indian Foreign Policy in the 1990s,* Radiant Publishers, New Delhi, 1997.
77. G. Mishra, 'Globalisation and India', *World Focus,* Oct.-Nov.-Dec., 1999.
78. Given in the *World Development Report,* 1999-2000.
79. G. Mishra, 'Globalisation and India', *World Focus* (Indian Foreign Policy), Oct.-Nov.- Dec., 1999.
80. Far Eastern Economic Review, while reviewing the *World Bank Formulation,,* 14 October, 1999.
81. *Ibid.*

82. R. Ray, 'Quo Vadis Globalisation'?, *Mainstream,* April-1, 2000.
83. Like the democratically elected Marxist Government under the leadership of Salvador Allende in Chile in the seventies. When American companies engineered a general strike in Chile and indulged in large scale violence throughout Chile.
84. G. Mishra, 'Globalisation and India', *World Focus* (Indian Foreign Policy), Oct.-Nov.-Dec., 1999
85. A.N. Ram, 'India's Economic Diplomacy', *World Focus,* Oct.-Nov.-Dec., 1999.
86. *Ibid.*
87. *Ibid.*
88. M.M. Bouton, 'India's Problem is not Polities', *Foreign Affairs,* May-June 1998.
89. See Rekha Saxena, 'Democracy-Development Interface', in M.P. Singh & Rekha Saxena (Ed.): *Ideologies and Institutions in Indian Politics,* Deep & Deep Publication Pvt. Ltd., 1998.
90. *Ibid.*
91. R.N. Cooper, 'The Road From Serfdom', while reviewing *Development as Freedom* by Amartya Sen, *Foreign Affairs,* Jan.-Feb., 2000.
92. Jasjit Singh, 'Indian Defence Planning', *World Focus,* Oct.-Nov.-Dec., 1996.
93. K. Subrahmanyam, 'Indian Nuclear Policy Perspective', *World Focus,* August, 1988.
94. O.P. Sabharwal, 'Nehru-Bhabha Legacy', *World Focus,* June-July, 1998.
95. K. Subrahmanyam, 'Indian Nuclear Policy', *World Focus,* August, 1988.
96. O.P. Sabharwal, 'Nehru-Bhabha Legacy', *World Focus,* June-July, 1998.
97. 'It is only after the Chinese attack and Chinese nuclear test that Dr. Bhabha became an advocate of Indian nuclear option', *World Focus,* August, 1988.
98. O.P. Sabharwal, 'India's Nuclear Strategy', *World Focus,* April, 2000.
99. 'Had this priority for weapon-making not been low, India's first Pokhran test might well have taken place in 1966 or 1967 rather than in 1974. India could then have been within the NPT's burra sahib's club. The terse reality is that the Indian breakthrough in spent fuel reprocessing in 1965 hastened the advent of the NPT, aimed specifically to keep India debarred from weapon status under the non-proliferation treaty's rules', *World Focus,* June-July 1998.
100. *Ibid.*
101. O.P. Sabharwal, 'India's Nuclear Strategy', *World Focus,* April, 2000.
102. Subrahmanyam, K., 'Indian Nuclear Policy Perspective', *World Focus,* August, 1988.

103. *Ibid.*
104. N. Chakravarty, 'Evolution of Foreign Policy', *World Focus,* Nov.-Dec., 1987.
105. S. Pande, 'India and Disarmament', *World Focus,* April, 2000.
106. N. Chakravarty, 'Evolution of Foreign Policy', *World Focus,* Nov.-Dec., 1987.
107. K. Subrahmanyam, 'Indian Nuclear Policy', *World Focus,* August, 1988.
108. *Ibid.*
109. K. Subrahmanyam, 'Nuclear India', *Indian Defence Review,* April-June, 1998.
110. R. Venkatraman, 'Nuclear Explosion and its Aftermath', *U.S.I. Journal,* July-September, 1998.
111. T.T. Poulose, 'The Bomb and National Security', *Journal of Peace Studies,* Vol. 6, Issue 4, July-August, 1998.
112. By 1987 Pakistan achieved nuclear weaponisation with China's help. The weapon was of Chinese design tested in 1967 as a missile warhead.
113. R. Venkatraman, 'Nuclear Explosion and its Aftermath', *U.S.I. Journal,* July-September, 1998.
114. A. Chakrapani, 'Plain Speaking About Indian Nuclear Testing', *The Round Table,* 1998.
115. K. Subrahmanyam, 'Nuclear India', *Indian Defence Review,* April-June, 1998.
116. R. Venkatraman, 'Nuclear Explosion and its Aftermath', *U.S.I. Journal,* July-September 1998.
117. K. Subrahmanyam, 'Nuclear India', *Indian Defence Review,* April-June, 1998.
118. *Ibid.*
119. *Ibid.*
120. Indian Nuclear Doctrine, *World Focus,* April, 2000.
121. M. Zuberi, 'Pokharan-II and Chagni', *World Focus,* June-July, 1998.
122. *Ibid.*
123. *Sunday Times,* May 24, 1998.
124. *Ibid.*
125. R. Venkatraman, 'Nuclear Explosion and its Aftermath', *U.S.I. Journal,* July-September, 1998.
126. K. Subrahmanyam, 'Nuclear India', *Indian Defence Review,* April-June, 1998.
127. Lt. Gen R. Sharma, 'The National Security Environment and Nuclearisation', *U.S.I. Journal,* July-September, 1998.

128. T.T. Poulose, 'The Bomb and National Security', *Journal of Peace Studies,* July-August, 1998.
129. M. Zuberi, 'Nuclear India', *Indian Defence Review.* April-June, 1998.
130. *Ibid.*
131. M. Zuberi, 'The Proposed Nuclear Doctrine', April, 2000, *World Focus.*
132. To develop such a triad would require 10-15 years with an expenditure of the 15000 crore annually. The most comprehensive study, on the costing of an Indian nuclear deterrence, was performed by the former MP and Economist Subramanian Swamy for the Bhartiya Jan Sangh in 1969. At that time his system analysis envisioned an expenditure of Rs. 500 crore annually for 100 nuclear tipped ballistic missiles. In the 21st century, that figure has to be inflated at least by a figure of 10-20 times to provide a mere 10 missiles on land and at sea.
133. R.R. Subramanian, 'A Minimum and Credible Deterrence for India', *World Focus,* April, 2000.
134. *World Focus: Indian Nuclear Doctrine,* April, 2000.
135. *Ibid.*
136. *Ibid.*
137. *Ibid.*
138. B. Blair, *Strategic Command and Control,* Washington D.C., Brookings, 1985.
139. K. Subrahmanyam, 'Nuclear Force Design and Minimum Deterrence Strategy', in Bharat Karnad (Ed.) *Future Imperilled: Indian Security in 1990s and Beyond,* New Delhi, Viking Penguin India, 1994, pp. 191-92.
140. R.R. Subramanian, 'A Minimum and Credible Deterrence for India', *World Focus,* April, 2000.
141. A. Srivastava, 'India's Growing Missile Ambitions', *Asian Survey,* Vol. XL, No. 2, March-April, 2000.
142. The DRDO has decided to increase the payload of SS-250 to 1000 kg by using boosted liquid propellant to generate higher thrust-to-weight ratio.
143. 'Agni-II Successfully Test Fired', *The Hindu,* April 11, 1999.
144. 'Fire-and-Forget System for Nag Tested', *Times of India,* Feb. 22, 2000.
145. P. Sawhney, 'A Force in Waiting: India's Defense Organisation Sets Its Sights on the Future.' *Jane's International Defence Review,* May 21, 1998.
146. 'Next Indian Satellite Will Have Surveillance Capability,' *Deccan Herald,* August 2, 1999.
147. P. Sawhney, 'Anti-missile Role Planned for Akash,' *Jane's International Defence Review,* January 1, 1997.
148. V. Raghuvanshi, 'India Mulls Russian Air Defence Deal', *Defence News,* February 24, 1997.

149. V. Raghuvanshi, 'India Plans to Acquire Russian S-300 System, Pair Renew Trade Pact', *Ibid;* June 29, 1998; and Dadan Upadhyay: 'Indo-Russian Deal on Air Defence System,' *Indian Express,* June 19, 1998.

150. 'India Should Develop Anti-ballistic Missile System, Say Experts', *Times of India,* June 30, 1998.

7

India's Nuclear Policy

BACKGROUND

With the end of World War II, a revolution had started in world affairs — the recasting of nations and relations between nations, and the emergence of a new technology which fundamentally changed the role of warfare.[1]

In June 26, 1946 Jawaharlal Nehru, soon to be India's first Prime Minister said: "As long as the world is constituted as it is, every country will have to devise and use the latest devices for its protection. I have no doubt India will develop her scientific researches and I hope Indian scientists will use the atomic force for constructive purposes. But if India is threatened, she will inevitably try to defend herself by all means at her disposal."[2]

In 1947, when India emerged as a free country to take its rightful place in the comity of nations, the nuclear age had already dawned. Our leaders then took the crucial decision to opt for self-reliance, and freedom of thought and action. We rejected the Cold War paradigm whose shadows were already appearing on the horizon and instead of aligning ourselves with either bloc, chose the more difficult path of non-alignment. This has required the building lip of national strength through our own resources, our skills and creativity and the dedication of the people.

Among the earliest initiatives taken by the first Indian Prime Minister Jawaharlal Nehru, was the development of science and inculcation of the scientific spirit.[3] He was the architect of modern India that did a wonderful service in the field of nuclear policy.

As early as in 1948, the Atomic Energy Act was passed by the Parliament, and by it the Central Government was given the responsibility to control the development of atomic energy through the research and the use of any mineral which is or may be used for the production of atomic energy. This act provided for the legal framework of India's Nuclear Policy. On August 10, 1948 an Atomic Energy Commission under the chairmanship of Dr. H.J. Bhabha, was constituted to protect the interests of the country in connection with atomic energy and to launch a full-fledged atomic energy programme in the country. On January 3, 1954, a decision to establish a separate research institution at Trombay, in addition to the already existing the Tata Institute of Fundamental Research, was undertaken. On August 3, 1954, the Department of Atomic Energy was set up under the charge of the then Prime Minster, Pt. Jawaharlal Nehru with H.J. Bhabha as the Secretary. Thus, a bold initiation was made to guide and conduct research in peaceful uses of atomic energy. The Commission prepared a plan for establishing atomic power plants in India for meeting the power needs. In order to make the institutional arrangements fully operational and useful, the Government of India, in 1958, decided to set up an Atomic Energy Commission.

With a view to improving the working of AEC, the Government of India decided to reconstitute it and vest it with full executive and financial powers. Accordingly, in 1958, AEC was reconstituted to include at least three and not more than seven full time and part-time members with the Secretary to the Government of India in the Department of Atomic Energy as its ex-officio chairman. The Commission was entrusted with the power to formulate the policy of the Department of Atomic Energy, to prepare the budget, and to implement the policy of the Government in all matters concerning atomic energy. It was indeed made an institution responsible for guiding and utilising nuclear research and technology, particularly in the energy sector.

In 1962, the Parliament passed the Atomic Energy Act and laid down the Nuclear Policy of India. This Act gave statutory mandate to the Central Government "to provide for the development, control and use of atomic energy for the welfare of the people of India and for other peaceful purposes and for matters connected therewith". This act clearly laid down the objectives of Nuclear Policy of India. It squarely specified the development and use of nuclear energy for promoting the welfare of the people, and exploitation of nuclear energy for peaceful uses only.

Since 1948, India has been making rapid progress towards the establishment of atomic centres. In addition to the Tata Institute of Fundamental Research (TIFR) which had been in operation since 1945, the Atomic Energy Establishment was established in 1957. In 1967, it was renamed as Bhabha Atomic Research Centre (BARC). These two establishments — TIFR and BARC have been spearheading India's quest for nuclear technology. These two have rendered a yeoman's service in bringing India on the nuclear map of the world by training the nuclear scientists and by conducting nuclear research.

After the establishment of AEC in 1948, a number of institutions were established for helping India's nuclear energy programme. These institutions include: Rare Minerals Survey Units (1948); The Indian Rare Earths Ltd (1950); Uranium Corporation of India 1967; Heavy Water Plants at Nangal, Kota, Baroda, Tuticorin and Talcher; Nuclear Fuel Complex. Electronics Corporation of India, the Power Reactor Fuel Reprocessing Plant, the Variable Energy Cyclotron and the Reactor Research Centre Kalpakkam. Together with these establishments India has several nuclear reactors; Apsara (became critical in 1956), Cirus (became critical in 1960), ZERLINA (became critical in 1961), Pumima (became critical in 1972), Dhruv Reactor (1985) and Kalpakkam Reactor Second Unit (became critical in August 1985).

India has established several; atomic power plants: Tarapore Atomic Power Plant (TAPS); and Rajasthan Atomic Power Station at Rana Partap Sagar Kalpakkam Atomic Power Station. Narora Atomic Power Plant is under construction. Thus, India has developed a network of institutes, reactors and power plants which are helping India to conduct nuclear research and develop and use nuclear energy and technology for peaceful purposes.

BARC's and DHRUV atomic plant are fully operational and producing plutonium with a capacity of 100 MW. India has taken a big leap forward in nuclear technology. With a large, highly skilled and trained manpower, and a large team of nuclear scientists and electronics engineers, coupled with the existence of several atomic research institutes, reactors and power plants India has the potential to be a full nuclear power. The existence of adequate quantities of plutonium and thorium further strengthens the potential of India to be a nuclear power.

DEVELOPMENT OF ATOMIC ENERGY IN INDIA

Nehru Era

During Nehru era, India confined itself to the development of nuclear research for peaceful purposes. India strongly opposed the use of nuclear energy for military purposes, i.e. for the manufacture of nuclear weapons. It strongly criticised the nuclear weapon states for indulging into a dangerous nuclear arms race. India strongly favoured the cause of disarmament, particularly nuclear disarmament. It, however, accepted the need for developing and utilising nuclear energy for peaceful purposes. Nehru fully realised the potentials of nuclear technology as a means for the socio-economic development of the underdeveloped countries. He took several important steps towards the establishment of nuclear research centres, experimental nuclear reactors, nuclear reactors, nuclear power plants and the other establishments for guiding and helping India's drive for harnessing the atom for peaceful purposes. "Atoms for Peace" constituted the central theme of India's nuclear policy under Nehru. Inaugurating the Swimming Pool Reactor (APSAR) at Trombay — the first such reactor on Asian soil — on January 20, 1957, Nehru observed: "No man can prophesy the future. But I should like to say on behalf of my Government — and I think I can say with some assurance on behalf of any future Government of India — that whatever might happen, whatever the circumstances, we shall never use this atomic energy for evil purposes. There is no condition attached to this assurance, because once a condition is attached, the value of such an assurance does not go very far."

During Nehru era, India advocated the need for creating international safeguards against the misuse of nuclear technology, i.e. against use of nuclear technology for manufacturing nuclear weapons. These safeguards were demanded for all countries, whether in possession of nuclear technology/weapons or not. Nehru ascertained the right of every nation to have access to nuclear technology for peaceful purposes. India signed the Moscow Partial Text Ban Treaty because it was designed to prevent mankind from the hazards of increased atmospheric radiation that always results from uncontrolled and open nuclear explosions conducted by the nuclear states.

Shastri Period

Prime Minister Lal Bahadur Shastri kept up Nehru's nuclear policy. Despite the nuclear explosions carried out by China, and the continued stalemate and conflict in relations with Pakistan, Prime Minister Shastri did not think in terms of making atom bombs. Recognising the danger of a possible nuclear blackmail attempts on the part of a hostile nuclear power state, he did, once advocate the need to secure an international nuclear umbrella for non-nuclear states. However, realising the potential dangers of such a development, he did not hesitate to withdraw support to the proposal. He decided to keep up India's drive for the development of nuclear technology for peaceful and developmental purposes but at the same time accepted the fact that the Governments' policy was not static or rigid and that it would change according to the circumstances. He said: "I have no doubt that we cannot at the present moment think in term of making atom bombs."

Indira Gandhi's First Era

While maintaining the need for keeping up the development of peaceful nuclear technology, Mrs. Indira Gandhi, advocated the need to keep the Government's nuclear policy under constant review.

Keeping India's security in view, Mrs. Gandhi maintained: "The country's defence and security would be paramount consideration in the formulation of the Government's nuclear policy, which was under constant review." She decided to keep the option open. It was with this end in view that Mrs. Gandhi decided against the acceptance of Non-Proliferation Treaty (NPT).

NPT was regarded as a discriminatory treaty which sought to impose restrictions upon the non-nuclear states even when these were committed to pursue a peaceful nuclear policy, and which provided for no measures to check the growing nuclear arms race among the nuclear powers. Further, NPT provided neither for disarmament nor for nuclear disarmament/arms control, and nor even for checking the open violations of Moscow Test Ban Treaty by France and China. It arbitrarily sought to perpetuate the dominant position of the nuclear states and to make the non-nuclear states secondary states in so far as these were called upon to throw open all their nuclear establishments to international inspection. India, under Mrs. Gandhi, refused to sign NPT and decided to develop further the drive towards the development of peaceful nuclear technology.

Analysing India's attitude to NPT, K. Subramanyam, Director, Institute of Defence Studies, rightly observed: "The Indian objection was mainly against the unequal nature of the Treaty and the misuse of international public opinion to subserve a policy of vertical proliferation by a few powers and obfuscation of the dangers of nuclear first use. In India's view this was not a non-proliferation treaty but a measure designed to disarm the unarmed." When faced with the Bangladesh crisis and the resulting threat of Chinese intervention from the side of Pakistan, Mrs. Gandhi decided to strengthen India's nuclear options by allowing the AEC to prepare for an underground nuclear test — A Peaceful Nuclear Explosion (PNE). Under this policy India conducted its first PNE at Pokhran on May 18, 1974, and earned entry into nuclear club through self efforts. However, it was clearly stated and forcefully maintained by Mrs. Gandhi that Pokhran test was a peaceful and fully controlled explosion conducted to develop nuclear technology for peaceful purposes for the development of mines, construction of dams, harbours, search for minerals, etc. Despite strong criticism from abroad, particularly from USA, Canada, Britain, Pakistan and some other countries, Mrs. Gandhi's Government stoutly defended the right of every country like India to have access to peaceful nuclear technology through indigenous research and experimentation. Mrs. Gandhi once again, reiterated that India's nuclear policy was fully peaceful and that India was strongly opposed to the manufacturing of nuclear weapons.

The Pokharan explosion demonstrated the high level of scientific expertise attained by Indian scientists. It definitely reflected the progress made by India towards the development of indigenous nuclear technology for use in industrial and economic development of the country. It constituted a bold attempt towards the exploitation of advanced nuclear science and technology for commercial and economic benefits. While conducting its first PNE, India fully ensured conformity to the provisions of Moscow Partial Test Ban Treaty and made it a totally controlled nuclear explosion which did not increase the level of atmospheric radio-activity.

India's PNE, however, came to be the object of severe criticism by several countries, particularly by the Western powers, China and Pakistan. The critics challenged the utility of the PNE. The Western critics charged that since the borderline between a PNE and military nuclear explosion was very thin, India's PNE really constituted a step towards nuclear proliferation with strong military and non-peaceful potentials. Such apprehensions were also expressed by Pakistani leaders, many of whom even went to the extent of saying that India was already in possession of a nuclear bomb. Several other critics maintained that conducting of PNEs would cause a very serious strain on Indian economy and resources, and would in no way help the socio-economic reconstruction of the country. India, however, maintained that its nuclear policy was a peaceful policy and that PNE was essential in the interest of scientific and technological research. Mrs. Gandhi maintained that every country had the right to harness the atom for peaceful purposes and India's nuclear policy was designed to develop nuclear technology for peaceful, non-military, developmental purposes. India ascertained its right to conduct PNE for nuclear research and for the development of nuclear technology.

Janata Regime

India's Nuclear Policy underwent a change during Janata rule. Prime Minister Morarji Desai expressed his strong opposition to "India's going nuclear". He felt that PNE's were unnecessary and that India would not conduct another PNE. On October 4, 1977 the then External Affairs Minister, Atal Behari Vajpayee declared in the UN General Assembly that India was totally opposed to the acquisition and development of nuclear weapons and that it would not go in for them even if all the other countries of the world did so. Thus, Janata Government decided to abandon PNEs and make India's nuclear policy revert back to the position that was there during the Nehru Era. However, the Janata Government steadfastly refused to sign the NPT despite the strong pressure exerted by US President Carter because it considered this treaty discriminatory. Prime Minister Desai refused to sign the NPT. Janata Government maintained that though India was fully committed to a peaceful nuclear policy, it was fully justified in refusing to sign NPT as this treaty sought to limit India's sovereign rights without providing for any international treaty for disarmament or nuclear disarmament. It also rejected the Pakistani demand for denuclearization of South Asia on the ground that such a step was uncalled for at such a small sub-regional level.

From 1980 to 1985

With the return of Mrs. Indira Gandhi to power in January 1980, the confusions that had cropped up in India's Nuclear Policy during Janata's regime came to an end because the new government reiterated the view that India was fully committed to pursue a peaceful nuclear policy and it would not hesitate to conduct PNE's in case these were considered necessary for the promotion of indigenous nuclear research and technology. Mrs. Gandhi decided to step up the drive to increase the role of nuclear energy for meeting the growing power needs of Indian industries. After having experienced the American pressures over India's nuclear policy, particularly after experiencing a big difficulty in securing fuel for its Tarapore plant, India decided to step up nuclear research in nuclear fuel reprocessing technology alternative fuel for atomic plants, reactor technology, fast breeder reactor technology and other related areas of research. India kept up its drive to achieve as much self-reliance in nuclear technology as it could develop indigenously. However, in doing so it did not feel the necessity of conducting another PNE. Mrs. Gandhi, while strongly repudiating the thesis for the production of nuclear weapons in India, advocated the sovereign right and the primary need of the country to have access to peaceful nuclear technology which was vitally necessary for India's developmental, commercial and industrial needs.

Prime Minister Rajiv Gandhi's Government maintained the drive to keep up the development of peaceful nuclear options. With fully indigenous Dhruv Atomic Plant going into the production of Plutonium 239, and with the second unit of Kalpakam atomic plant going critical, India attained a high level of indigenous nuclear technology.

Addressing the Indian Association of Foreign Affairs Correspondents New Delhi, on November 1, 1985, Prime Minister Rajiv Gandhi observed that India had not closed its option on the question of producing a nuclear bomb. He categorically stated that Pakistan was heading toward a nuclear bomb and it was one of the responsibilities of the USA to prevail upon it to abandon the policy. The Prime Minister ruled out joint inspection of nuclear facilities of India and Pakistan, saying that it would not be effective since Pakistan would try to shift its nuclear materials which it was making clandestinely to another place.[4]

The governments subsequent to that of Rajiv Gandhi realised the need of harnessing nuclear energy for peaceful purposes and took a slew of measures to actively pursue the nuclear power programme. Although Prime Minister Deve Gowda shelved a nuclear explosion plan due to mounting international pressure, the BJP leader and head of the National Democratic Alliance (NDA) Government, Atal Bihari Vajpayee refused to sign the Comprehensive (Nuclear) Test Ban Treaty (CTBT). During his tenure, four state-of-the art 220 MW pressurised heavy water reactors — two each at Kaiga (Karnataka) and Rawatbhata, (Rajasthan) came online. Besides, solid storage surveillance facility under nuclear waste management was made operational in Tarapur. The nuclear power programme was given research and development support in various aspects of design manufacture, construction, commissioning, operation and maintenance of plants. Prime Minister Manmohan Singh was able to forge an unprecedented understanding with Washington

DC during his July 2005 visit which was followed by President Bush to New Delhi in March 2006.

INDIA AND NUCLEAR WEAPONS

Prime Minister Rajiv Gandhi was maintaining a status quo in respect of the nuclear policy. He time and again emphasized India's strong desire to keep up the development of peaceful nuclear policy but at the same time made it abundantly clear that India can be forced to reassess and revise its nuclear options in case Pakistan continued to keep up its current drive to acquire the nuclear weapons. In such an eventuality, the threat to the strategic security of India would become very grave and force India to change its nuclear policy. In fact, Pakistan's growing nuclear capability, which by all accounts appeared to be a programme for the development of nuclear weapons, became to be a major factor in the operationalisation of India's nuclear policy. There appeared an ambivalence between the options: to keep up the status quo or to go ahead with the manufacture of nuclear weapons.

On April 25, 1985, the then Defence Minister, P.V. Narasimha Rao, while intervening in the Lok Sabha debate on the grants for the Defence Ministry, stated that "the Union was seeking the opinion of Parliament on what it should do to meet the threat of Pakistan acquiring the nuclear capability." The need for reviewing India's nuclear policy was voiced, or course with concern, by Prime Minister Rajiv Gandhi himself. Expressing concern at Pakistan's growing nuclear capability, and the failure of the USA to dissuade Pakistan from acquiring nuclear weapons capability, Rajiv Gandhi remarked that such a development shall force India to revise its nuclear policy. While reiterating India's strong desire to avoid going nuclear (Nuclear Weapon Technology), speaking at New York, he observed: "... it will be difficult for us not to come out with some sort of counter to that. That counter need not be nuclear; it would be the last choice really." It was further clarified that India did not want to divert its resources from socio-economic development programmes to a nuclear weapons programme. Nevertheless, like every other country of the world, India cannot ignore the threat to its security resulting from the possession of nuclear weapons by Pakistan. India stands for peaceful nuclear technology and opposes fully and strongly the use of nuclear technology for making nuclear bombs. However, it cannot ignore threats to its own security.

On July 18, 1985 *The Tribune* in its Editorial analyzing the nuclear policy of the Government of India observed: "In these circumstances India's policy direction seems clear. With its infrastructure, know-how and progress in nuclear development, the country can hardly afford to go back. The Prime Minister seems to have pegged his nuclear options on the developments. India, according to him, will be forced to produce the bomb and divert the much-needed funds for economic development in the process if the ambitious neighbor in the north-west is known to possess the explosive device."[5]

Disarmament was then and continues to be a major plank in India's foreign policy. It was, in essence, and remains still, the natural course for a country that had waged a unique struggle for independence on the basis of 'ahimsa' and 'satyagraha'. Development of nuclear technology transformed the nature of global security. Our leaders reasoned that nuclear weapons were not weapons of war; these were weapons of mass destruction. A nuclear weapon-free-world would, therefore, enhance not only India's security but also the security of all nations. This is the principle plank of our nuclear policy. In the absence of universal and non-discriminatory disarmament, we cannot accept a regime that creates an arbitrary division between nuclear haves and have-nots. India believes that it is the sovereign right of every nation to make a judgment regarding its supreme national interests and exercise its sovereign choice. We subscribe to the principle of equal and legitimate security interests of nations and consider it a sovereign right.

At the same time, our leaders recognized early that nuclear technology offers tremendous potential for economic development, especially for developing countries that are endeavoring to leap across the technology gaps created by long years of colonial exploitation. This thinking was reflected in the enactment of the Atomic Energy Act of 1948, within a year of our independence. All the numerous initiatives taken by us since, in the field of nuclear disarmament have been in harmony and in continuation of those early enunciations.

NUCLEAR NON-PROLIFERATION

Virtually all responsible nations agree that the elimination of nuclear weapons is essential. However, there is no unanimity about how this can best be accomplished. India shares with most other nations the conviction that every effort should be made to eliminate the world's store of nuclear weapons, and it has demonstrated its commitment to this conviction in a variety of ways.

It was India that first proposed an end to nuclear testing in 1954. The principles for a Nuclear Non-Proliferation Treaty (NPT) were first proposed by India in 1965. India eventually refused to sign the NPT when it became clear that, instead of addressing the central objective of universal and comprehensive non-proliferation, the treaty only legitimized the continuing possession and multiplication of nuclear stockpiles by those few states possessing them.

Again, it was India that proposed in 1982 a convention to ban nuclear weapons, including a ban on the production of fissile materials for nuclear weapons.

Finally, it was India that put forward a comprehensive action plan for a nuclear-free world within a specific time-frame at the third United Nations Special Session on Disarmament, in 1988.

In a speech before the United Nations, Rajiv Gandhi, India's Prime Minister, argued: "We cannot accept the logic that a few nations have the right to pursue their security by threatening the survival of mankind...nor is it acceptable that those who possess nuclear weapons are freed of all controls while those without nuclear weapons are policed against their production. History is full of such prejudices paraded as iron laws: That men are superior to women; that white races are superior to the colored; that colonialism is a civilizing mission; and that those who possess nuclear weapons are responsible powers and those who do not are not."

India's nuclear programme is indigenous and entirely peaceful. In 1974, India carried out a peaceful nuclear explosion in the Rajasthan desert. As a responsible nation, it has never passed on this technology to another country.

In India's view, the fact that the NPT has now been extended permanently makes immutable a dangerous state of affairs. The treaty permanently legitimizes the continued possession by nuclear weapon states of stockpiles that can destroy the world many thousands of times over. It does so without any binding commitment from these nations to strive for the goal which India and others share, i.e. the complete elimination of nuclear weapons.

India's approach to the current nuclear debates is a product of both history and geography. Since gaining its independence from Great Britain in 1947, India has been attacked four times by its neighbours — three times by Pakistan and once by China. China has possessed nuclear weapons for over 40 years, and it is widely acknowledged that Pakistan also possesses nuclear weapons. Indeed, under the Pressler Amendment, the US was forced to cut off economic and military aid to Pakistan since the US President was unable to certify that Pakistan did not possess nuclear weapons.

In 1994, Pakistan was not only involved in international smuggling of plutonium but also received plutonium and long-range missiles capable of carrying nuclear warheads from China with which it has an ongoing military relationship. The US press has widely reported on hard evidence that Pakistan has obtained ring magnets, an item used for producing weapons-grade uranium, from China.

Indian Initiatives towards Pakistan

India has proposed to Pakistan that an existing agreement not to bomb each other's nuclear installations be extended to population centres and economic targets. At the same time, India has proposed to Pakistan that the two countries agree not to use or to be the first to use their nuclear capabilities against each other. Unfortunately, Pakistan has not responded to either initiative by India.

Comprehensive Test Ban Treaty

Since independence, pursuit of nuclear disarmament has been an important objective of India's foreign policy. India believes that the existence of nuclear weapons poses a threat to international peace and security. Creating a nuclear-weapon-free world by eliminating all nuclear weapons through a multilaterally negotiated treaty which is effective and verifiable, will enhance global security and the safety of every man, woman and child.

In pursuit of nuclear disarmament, India has taken many initiatives. India was among the first countries to call for a ban on nuclear weapon testing, as early as 1954. Such a ban would have prevented the nuclear arms race which the world has witnessed in recent decades. During this period, the UN General Assembly adopted nearly hundred resolutions on this, highlighting the concern of the world community on this issue.

India has always believed that such a treaty should be comprehensive and bring an end to the qualitative development of nuclear weapons. At the same time, a Comprehensive Test Ban Treaty should mark the first definitive and irreversible step in the process of nuclear disarmament. Therefore, the CTBT must reflect a commitment to achieving elimination of all nuclear weapons within a time bound framework.

During the negotiations on CTBT in the Conference on Disarmament in Geneva, India participated actively and constructively, putting forward its proposals, in keeping with its long-standing position. It is a matter of regret that the text, as has finally emerged, does not do justice to the negotiating mandate. It is not a comprehensive ban but merely a ban on nuclear explosive testing. It also lacks a definitive commitment to nuclear disarmament.

India remains committed to pursuing global, nuclear disarmament with a view to creating a nuclear weapon free world and a non-violent world order.[6]

As the first nation in the world to call for a Comprehensive Test Ban Treaty, India supported the idea behind the CTBT, but in discussions in the Conference on Disarmament, it also wanted to ensure that the CTBT did not legitimize existing nuclear arsenals as the Nuclear Non-Proliferation Treaty does.

India's then Prime Minister, Narasimha Rao, in a joint statement with the President of the United States, Bill Clinton, stated on May, 1994, that they both supported efforts towards "non-proliferation of weapons of mass destruction, their means of delivery and towards their progressive reduction with the goal of elimination of such weapons".

Our policy on the CTBT was succinctly and clearly restated by India's External Affairs Minister at the UN General Assembly on September 29, 1995:

> Two years ago, the international community at last agreed to negotiate a Comprehensive Test Ban Treaty. We are glad that negotiations are in progress, but we also note that nuclear weapon states have agreed to a CTBT only after acquiring the know-how to develop and refine their arsenals without the need for tests. In our view, the CTBT must be an integral step in the process of nuclear disarmament. Developing new warheads or refining existing ones after a CTBT is in place, using innovative technologies, would be as contrary to the spirit of CTBT as the NPT is to the spirit of non-proliferation. The CTBT must contain a binding commitment on the international community, especially the nuclear weapon states, to take further measures within an agreed timeframe towards the creation of a nuclear weapons-free world.

India's fundamental concern is that it does not want a "Nuclear Test Explosion Ban Treaty", which would merely allow the continuing expansion and refinement of existing nuclear arsenals through sophisticated laboratory techniques, but a genuine Comprehensive Test Ban Treaty without any loopholes. India holds that mere expression of intent has not been enough to make the nuclear-weapon states come to the negotiating table, and that the treaty should, therefore, clearly include a time bound framework for total nuclear disarmament.

The CTBT, as it emerged at the Conference on Disarmament, ignored all of India's concerns. India had no alternative but to stay out of that treaty, including opposing it in the UN General Assembly when the CTBT was sought to be legitimized through that forum through questionable legal sleight-of-hand.

There is significant support emerging now for India's stand from the quarters that are most knowledgeable on this subject.

Retired Air Force General, Lee Butler, Commander-in-Chief of America's strategic nuclear forces from 1991 to 1994 and the man in charge of America's nuclear weapons during this time, observed: "My experience as commander of America's strategic nuclear forces has pushed me to another conclusion: that a world free of the threat of nuclear weapons is necessarily a world devoid of nuclear weapons." He added: "Every President of the United States since Dwight Eisenhower has publicly endorsed elimination."

The "Canberra Group" of experts also issued a statement that nuclear weapons can and should be eliminated. Long time nuclear disarmament proponent, former Prime Minister David Lange of New Zealand termed the CTBT, as it was being negotiated, as "hypocritical" and added that "the Indians have it right."[7]

The decades of the 1980s and 1990s meanwhile witnessed the gradual deterioration the security environment as a result of nuclear and missile proliferation. In India's neighborhood, nuclear weapons increased and more sophisticated delivery systems were inducted. Further, there has come into existence a pattern about clandestine acquisition of nuclear materials, missiles and related technologies. India, in this period, became the victim of externally aided and abetted terrorism, militancy and clandestine war through hired mercenaries.

The end of the Cold War marks a watershed in the history of the 20th century. While it has transformed the political landscape of Europe, it has done little to address India's security concerns. The relative order that was arrived at in Europe was not replicated in other parts of the globe.

At the global level, there is no evidence yet on the part of the nuclear weapon states to take decisive and irreversible steps in moving towards a nuclear-weapon-free-world. Instead, the NPT has been extended indefinitely and unconditionally, perpetuating the existence of nuclear weapons in the hands of the five countries that are also permanent members of the UN Security Council. Some of these countries have doctrines that permit the first use of nuclear weapons; these countries are also engaged in programmes for modernisation of their nuclear arsenals.

Under such circumstances, India was left with little choice. It had to take necessary steps to ensure that the country's nuclear option, developed and safeguarded over decades not be permitted to erode by a voluntary self-imposed restraint. Indeed, such erosion would have had an irremediably adverse impact on our security. The Government was thus faced with a difficult decision. The only touchstone that guided it was national security.

Tests conducted on 11 and 13 May is a continuation of the policies set into motion that put this country on the path of self-reliance and independence of thought and action. Nevertheless, there are certain moments when the chosen path reaches a fork and a decision has to be made. The year 1968 was one such moment in our nuclear chapter as were 1974 and 1996. At each of these moments, we took the right decision guided by national interest and supported by national consensus. The year 1998 was borne in the crucible of earlier decisions and made possible only because those decisions had been taken correctly in the past and in time.

At a time when developments in the area of advanced technologies are taking place at a breathtaking pace, new parameters need to be identified, tested and validated in order to ensure that skills remain contemporary and succeeding generations of scientists and engineers are able to build on the work done by their predecessors. The limited series of five tests undertaken by India was precisely such an exercise. It has achieved its stated objective. The data provided by these tests is critical to validate our capabilities in the design of nuclear weapons of different yields for different applications and different delivery systems. Further, these tests have significantly enhanced the capabilities of our scientists and engineers in computer simulation of new designs and enabled them to undertake sub-critical experiments in future, if considered necessary. In terms of technical capability, our scientists and engineers have the requisite resources to ensure a credible deterrent.

Our policies towards our neighbors and other countries too have not changed; India remains fully committed to the promotion of peace with stability, and resolution of all outstanding issues through bilateral dialogue and negotiations. These tests were not directed against any country; these were intended to reassure the people of India about their security and convey determination that Government of India has the capability and resolve to safeguard their national security interests. India will remain committed to dialogue and reaffirm that preservation of its security creates no conflict of interest with these countries.

India is a nuclear weapon state. This is a reality that cannot be denied. It is not a conferment that we seek; nor is it a status for others to grant. It is an endowment to the nation by our scientists and engineers. It is India's due, the right of one-sixth of humankind. India, mindful of its international obligations, shall not use these weapons to commit aggression or to mount threats against any country; these are weapons of self-defence and to ensure that in turn, India is also not subjected to nuclear threats or coercion. In 1994, India and Pakistan jointly undertook not to be the first to use their nuclear capability against each other.

India remains committed to the basic tenet of the foreign policy — a conviction that global elimination of nuclear weapons will enhance its security as well as that of the rest of the world. It will continue to urge countries, particularly other nuclear weapon states to adopt measures that would contribute meaningfully to such an objective.

A number of initiatives have been taken in the past. In 1978, India proposed negotiations for an international convention that would prohibit the use or threat of use of nuclear weapons. This was followed by another initiative in 1982 calling for a 'nuclear freeze' — a prohibition on production of fissile materials for weapons, on production of nuclear weapons, and related delivery systems. In 1988, we put forward an action plan for phased elimination of all nuclear weapons within a specified time frame. It is our regret that these proposals did not receive a positive response from other nuclear weapon states. Had their response been positive, India need not have gone for the tests. This is where India's approach to nuclear weapons is different from others. This difference is the cornerstone of India's nuclear doctrine. It is marked by restraint and striving for the total elimination of all weapons of mass destruction.

India will continue to support such initiatives, taken individually or collectively by the Non-Aligned Movement, which has continued to attach the highest priority to nuclear disarmament. The collective voice of NAM countries reflects an approach to global nuclear disarmament to which India has remained committed. One of the NAM member initiatives to which we attach great importance was the reference to the International Court of Justice (ICJ) resulting in the unanimous declaration from the ICJ, as part of the Advisory Opinion handed down on July 8, 1996, that "there exists an obligation to pursue in good faith and bring to a conclusion negotiations leading to nuclear disarmament in all its aspects under strict and effective international control".

India was one of the countries that appealed to the ICJ on this issue. No other nuclear weapon state has supported this judgment; in fact, they have sought to decry its value. India has been and will continue to be in the forefront of the calls for opening negotiations for a Nuclear Weapons Convention, so that this challenge can be dealt within the same manner that has dealt with the scourge of two other weapons of mass destruction — through the Biological Weapons Convention and the Chemical Weapons Convention. In keeping with commitment to comprehensive, universal and non-discriminatory approaches to disarmament, India is an Original State Party to both these Conventions.[8]

NUCLEAR TESTS OF 1998

Prime Minister of India, Atal Behari Vajpayee authorized the tests on April 8, 1998, two days after the Ghauri missile test firing in Pakistan, and announced India's nuclear tests on May 11, 1998 in New Delhi. The Prime Minister said, "I have an important announcement to make: Today, at 15:45 hours, India conducted three underground nuclear tests in the Pokhran range. The tests conducted today were with a fission device, a low yield device and a thermonuclear device. The measured yields are in line with expected values. Measurements have also confirmed that there was no release of radioactivity into the atmosphere. These were contained explosions like the experiment conducted in May 1974. I warmly congratulate the scientists and engineers who have carried out these successful tests."[9]

The nuclear tests carried out at 3:45 pm on May 11, 1998 were claimed by the Indian Government to be a simultaneous detonation of three different devices — a fission device with a yield of about 12 kilotons (KT), a thermonuclear device with a yield of about 43 KT, and a sub-kiloton device. The two tests carried out at 12:21 pm on May 13, 1998 were also detonated simultaneously with reported yields in the range of 0.2 to 0.6 KT.[10] A synopsis is given below:

Test	Device	Date	Yield	Yield
	Fission device	18 May 1974	12-15 kiloton	4-6 kiloton
Shakti 1	Thermonuclear device	11 May 1998	43-60 kiloton	12-25 kiloton
Shakti 2	Fission device	11 May 1998	12 kiloton	
Shakti 3	Low-yield device	11 May 1998	0.2 kiloton	Low
Shakti 4	Low-yield device	13 May 1998	0.5 kiloton	Low
Shakti 5	Low-yield device	13 May 1998	0.3 kiloton	Low

In continuation of the planned programme of underground nuclear tests, this began on May 11, 1998 two more sub-kiloton nuclear tests were carried out at Pokhran range at 12:21 pm on May 13, 1998. The tests were carried out to generate additional data for improved computer simulation of designs and for attaining the capability to carry out subcritical experiments, if considered necessary. The tests were fully contained with no release of radioactivity into the atmosphere.

These tests established that India has a proven capability for a weaponised nuclear programme. They also provided a valuable database, which is useful in the design of nuclear weapons of different yields for different applications and for different delivery systems. Further, carried Indian scientists towards a sound computer simulation capability, which maybe supported by sub-critical experiments if considered necessary.

The Government was deeply concerned as were previous Governments, about the nuclear environment in India's neighborhood. These tests provided reassurance to the people of India that their national security interests are paramount and will be promoted and protected. Succeeding generations of Indians would also rest assured that contemporary technologies associated with nuclear option have been passing to them.

It is necessary to highlight today that India was in the vanguard of nations, which ushered in the Partial Test Ban Treaty in 1963 due to environmental concerns. Indian representatives have worked in various international forums, including the Conference on Disarmament, for universal, non-discriminatory and verifiable arrangements for the elimination of weapons of mass destruction. The Government would like to reiterate its support to efforts to realise the goal of a truly comprehensive international arrangement which would prohibit underground nuclear testing of all weapons as well as related experiments described as 'sub-critical' or 'hydro nuclear'.

India remains committed to a speedy process of nuclear disarmament leading to total and global elimination of nuclear weapons. India's adherence to the Chemical Weapons Convention and the Biological Weapons Convention is evidence of the commitment to any global disarmament regime, which is non-discriminatory and verifiable. India willingly participated in the negotiations for the conclusion of a fissile material cut-off treaty in the Geneva based conference on Disarmament.[11]

WORLDWIDE REACTIONS

United Nations

The United Nations Secretary-General Kofi Annan called for "maximum restraint" in the region. He said, "The tests are inconsistent with the pattern that has been firmly endorsed by the international community."

Pakistan

The then Pakistani Prime Minister Nawaz Sharif said, "I wish to assure the nation that Pakistan has the capability to respond to any threat to its security.... We will take all necessary measures to safeguard our security, sovereignty, territorial integrity and national interests." Foreign Minister Gohar Ayub Khan said, "Indian actions, which pose an immediate and grave threat to Pakistan's security, will not go unanswered." Abdul Qadeer Khan, father of Pakistan's nuclear research programme, said he only needed orders from the Government to carry out a nuclear explosion within 10 days. He said, "It is a political decision. Now it all depends on the Government." Former Prime Minister and Opposition leader Benazir Bhutto said, "India has now gone ahead conducting three nuclear tests and I expect Pakistan to follow suit."[12]

China

China expressed serious concern at India's initial conducting of three underground nuclear tests, saying it will hamper world peace and regional stability. The Chinese foreign ministry said the tests ran counter to progress that had been made in reducing nuclear arms. "India's conducting of nuclear test runs against international trend and is detrimental to the peace and stability of the South-Asian region," said foreign ministry spokesman Zhu Bang-Zao.

Japan

Japan has condemned the tests with some ministers calling for a suspension of economic aid. "The tests ran counter to the international ban on nuclear testing and pose a threat to regional stability. India's largest donor Japan cannot help but consider taking action to curb economic co-operation," said the Foreign Minister Keizo Obuchi. Prime Minister Ryutaro Hashimoto sees the tests as very regrettable. "I sent a letter to the Indian Prime Minister on March 31 urging his Government not to conduct nuclear testing. There has been no reply," Hashimoto said.

USA

The United States said that it would implement tough measures against India in response to its nuclear tests. United States President Clinton said that the measures would be taken under American laws governing nuclear tests by non-nuclear countries. "India's tests have made international efforts for a global nuclear test ban more difficult. While it was foreseen, given the electoral programme of the newly-elected party, that they might take this step, it still flies in the face of an international concensus about the need to promulgate and nurture the new regime on a comprehensive test ban," White House spokesman Michael McCurry said.

Russia

Russian President Boris Yeltsin said, "India has let us down with this explosion, but I think that through diplomatic efforts and a visit we should get them to change their position." The Deputy Atomic Energy Minister, Viktor Mikhailov said, "Moscow deeply regretted India's tests, it could lead to a new arms race in the region."

Canada

Canada Foreign Minister Lloyd Axworthy said, "The India's nuclear tests were very disappointing. The test blasts could have grave implications for global non-proliferation and nuclear disarmament and can only weaken regional security."

Australia

Australia said it would lodge a strong diplomatic protest with India and recall its top diplomat from New Delhi. Australia Foreign Minister Alexander Downer said, "The important thing is that we take measures that just aren't symbolic, that are going to be effective in stopping India continuing with this programme."

France

France said that it is not in a position to teach India a lesson. "Having said that, the Comprehensive Test Ban Treaty is going to be signed by most of the great developed countries, and I would of course approve of India signing it too," said the French Environment Minister Dominique Voynet.

United Kingdom

United Kingdom has expressed its dismay at the India tests. Defense Minister George Robertson said, "It is not a helpful move and not a good day for the world as a whole. The repercussions are obvious and ominous. It is very worrying for the international community." A Foreign Office statement said, "Reports of two further tests today were in flagrant disregard of the concerns already expressed by the international community and made matters yet worse."

Germany

Foreign Minister Klaus Kinkel of Germany said, "The tests are a slap in the face of the 149 countries which have signed the CTBT."

Denmark

Foreign Minister Niels Helveg Petersen said, "I have deeply deplored India's action warning that it will have negative effects on international help to develop the country."

Bangladesh

Bangladesh says that a nuclear arms race is not desirable in the interests of the poor people in the region. "We should all move forward for peace in the entire region. Poverty, illiteracy and human resource development warrant more attention, and we still hope that all countries will pay attention to this," said Minister of State Abul Hasan Chowdhury Kaiser.

International Atomic Energy Agency

"India is a great civilization, but that is not enough. They do not feel that they were treated as though they were in the same league [as the permanent five nations on the U.N. Security Council]. One could ask, if the outside world could have satisfied India's wish to be considered a great power in a different manner: Are nuclear bombs the only way to assert greatness," asked Hans Blix, former head of the International Atomic Energy Agency.[13]

G8

"We condemn the nuclear tests which were carried out by India on 11 and 13 May. Such action runs counter to the will expressed by 149 signatories to the CTBT to cease nuclear testing, to efforts to strengthen the global non-proliferation regime and to steps to enhance regional and international peace and security. It has been met by immediate international concern and opposition, from governments and more widely. We underline our full commitment to the Non-Proliferation Treaty and to the Comprehensive Test Ban Treaty as the cornerstones of the global non-proliferation regime and the essential foundations for the pursuit of nuclear disarmament. We express our grave concern about the increased risk of nuclear and missile proliferation in South Asia and elsewhere. We urge India and other states in the region to refrain from further tests and the deployment of nuclear weapons or ballistic missiles. We call upon India to rejoin the mainstream of international opinion, to adhere unconditionally to the NPT and the CTBT and to enter into negotiations on a global treaty to stop the production of fissile material for nuclear weapons. India's relationship with each of us has been affected by these developments. We are making this clear in our own direct exchanges and dealings with the Indian Government and we call upon other states similarly to address their concerns to India. We call upon and encourage Pakistan to exercise maximum restraint in the face of these tests and to adhere to international non-proliferation norms."[14]

NUCLEAR DOCTRINES

In August 1999, the Government of India released a draft of 'Indian Nuclear Doctrine'. The use of nuclear weapons in particular as well as other weapons of mass destruction constitutes the gravest threat to humanity and to peace and stability in the international system. Unlike the other two categories of weapons of mass destruction, biological and chemical weapons which have been outlawed by international treaties, nuclear weapons remain instruments for national and collective security, the possession of which on a selective basis has been sought to be legitimized through permanent extension of the Nuclear Non-proliferation Treaty (NPT) in May 1995. Nuclear weapon states have asserted that they will continue to rely on nuclear weapons with some of them adopting policies to use them even in a non-nuclear context. These developments amount to virtual abandonment of nuclear disarmament. This is a serious setback to the struggle of the international community to abolish weapons of mass destruction.

India's primary objective is to achieve economic, political, social, scientific and technological development within a peaceful and democratic framework. This requires an environment of durable peace and insurance against potential risks to peace and stability. It will be India's endeavour to proceed towards this overall objective in cooperation with the global democratic trends and to play a constructive role in advancing the international system toward a just, peaceful and equitable order.

Autonomy of decision-making in the developmental process and in strategic matters is an inalienable democratic right of the Indian people. India will strenuously guard this right in a world where nuclear weapons for a select few are sought to be legitimised for an indefinite future, and where there is growing complexity and frequency in the use of force for political purposes.

India's security is an integral component of its development process. India continuously aims at promoting an ever-expanding area of peace and stability around it so that developmental priorities can be pursued without disruption.

However, the very existence of offensive doctrine pertaining to the first use of nuclear weapons and the insistence of some nuclear weapons states on the legitimacy of their use even against non-nuclear weapon countries constitute a threat to peace, stability and

This document outlines the broad principles for the development, deployment and employment of India's nuclear forces. Details of policy and strategy concerning force structures, deployment and employment of nuclear forces will flow from this framework and will be laid down separately and kept under constant review.

Objectives

The objectives of India's foreign policy are enumerated below:

1. In the absence of global nuclear disarmament India's strategic interests require effective, credible nuclear deterrence and adequate retaliatory capability, should deterrence fail. This is consistent with the UN Charter, which sanctions the right of self-defence.
2. The requirements of deterrence should be carefully weighed in the design of Indian nuclear forces and in the strategy to provide for a level of capability consistent with maximum credibility, survivability, effectiveness, safety and security.
3. India shall pursue a doctrine of credible minimum nuclear deterrence. In this policy of "retaliation only", the survivability of our arsenal is critical. This is a dynamic concept related to the strategic environment, technological imperatives and the needs of national security. The actual size components, deployment and

employment of nuclear forces will be decided in the light of these factors. India's peacetime posture aims at convincing any potential aggressor that:

- any threat of use of nuclear weapons against India shall invoke measures to counter the threat; and
- any nuclear attack on India and its forces shall result in punitive retaliation with nuclear weapons to inflict damage unacceptable to the aggressor.

4. The fundamental purpose of Indian nuclear weapons is to deter the use and threat of use of nuclear weapons by any state or entity against India and its forces. India will not be the first to initiate a nuclear strike, but will respond with punitive retaliation, should deterrence fail.
5. India will not resort to the use or threat of use of nuclear weapons against States which do not possess nuclear weapons, or are not aligned with nuclear weapon powers.
6. Deterrence requires that India should maintain:
   - sufficient, survivable and operationally prepared nuclear forces;
   - a robust command and control system;
   - effective intelligence and early warning capabilities;
   - comprehensive planning and training for operations in line with the strategy; and
   - the will to employ nuclear forces and weapons.
7. Highly effective conventional military capabilities shall be maintained to raise the threshold of outbreak both of conventional military conflict as well as that of threat or use of nuclear weapons.

Nuclear Forces

India's nuclear forces will be effective, enduring, diverse, flexible, and responsive to the requirements in accordance with the concept of credible minimum deterrence. These forces will be based on a triad of aircraft, mobile land-based missiles and sea-based assets in keeping with the objectives outlined above.

Survivability of the forces will be enhanced by a combination of multiple redundant systems, mobility, dispersion and deception.

The doctrine envisages assured capability to shift from peacetime deployment to fully employable forces in the shortest possible time, and the ability to retaliate effectively even in case of significant degradation by hostile strikes.

Credibility and Survivability

The following principles are central to India's nuclear deterrent:

Credibility

Any adversary must know that India can and will retaliate with sufficient nuclear weapons to inflict destruction and punishment that the aggressor will find unacceptable if nuclear weapons are used against India and its forces.

Effectiveness

The efficacy of India's nuclear deterrent be maximised through synergy among all elements involving reliability, timeliness, accuracy and weight of the attack.

Survivability

(a) India's nuclear forces and their command and control shall be organised for very high survivability against surprise attacks and for rapid punitive response. They shall be designed and deployed to ensure survival against a first strike and to endure repetitive attrition attempts with adequate retaliatory capabilities for a punishing strike which would be unacceptable to the aggressor.

(b) Procedures for the continuity of nuclear command and control shall ensure a continuing capability to effectively employ nuclear weapons.

Command and Control

1. Nuclear weapons shall be tightly controlled and released for use at the highest political level. The authority to release nuclear weapons for use resides in the person of the Prime Minister of India, or the designated successor.
2. An effective and survivable command and control system with requisite flexibility and responsiveness shall be in place. An integrated operational plan, or a series of sequential plans, predicated on strategic objectives and a targetting policy shall form part of the system.
3. For effective employment the unity of command and control of nuclear forces including dual capable delivery systems shall be ensured.
4. The survivability of the nuclear arsenal and effective command, control, communications, computing, intelligence and information (C4I2) systems shall be assured.
5. The Indian defence forces shall be in a position to, execute operations in an NBC environment with minimal degradation.
6. Space based and other assets shall be created to provide early warning, communications, and damage/ detonation assessment.

SECURITY AND SAFETY

Security

Extraordinary precautions shall be taken to ensure that nuclear weapons, their manufacture, transportation and storage are fully guarded against possible theft, loss, sabotage, damage or unauthorised access or use.

Safety

Safety is an absolute requirement, and tamper proof procedures and systems shall be instituted to ensure that unauthorised or inadvertent activation/usc of nuclear weapons does not take place and risks of accident are avoided.

Disaster control

India shall develop an appropriate disaster control system capable of handling the unique requirements of potential incidents involving nuclear weapons and materials;

Research and Development

1. India should step up efforts in research and development to keep up with technological advances in this field.
2. While India is committed to maintain the deployment of a deterrent which is both minimum and credible, it will not accept any restraints on building its R&D capability.

Disarmament and Arms Control

1. Global, verifiable and non-discriminatory nuclear disarmament is a national security objective. India shall continue its efforts to achieve the goal of a nuclear weapon-free world at an early date.
2. Since no-first use of nuclear weapons is India's basic commitment, every effort shall be made to persuade other states possessing nuclear weapons to join an international treaty banning first use.
3. Having provided unqualified negative security assurances, India shall work for internationally binding unconditional negative security assurances by nuclear weapon states to non-nuclear weapon states.
4. Nuclear arms control measures shall be sought as part of national security policy to reduce potential threats and to protect our own capability and its effectiveness.
5. In view of the very high destructive potential of nuclear weapons, appropriate nuclear risk reduction and confidence building measures shall be sought, negotiated and instituted.[15]

The Doctrine says that nuclear weapons are solely for deterrence and that India will pursue a policy of retaliation only. The document also maintains that India will not be the first to initiate a nuclear first strike, but will respond with punitive retaliation, should deterrence fail, and that decisions to authorize the use of nuclear weapons would be made by the Prime Minister or his designated successor.

Despite the escalation of tensions between India and Pakistan in 2001-2002, India remains committed to its nuclear no-first-use policy, says NRDC. India is a member of the International Atomic Energy Agency (IAEA), and four of its 13 nuclear reactors are subject to IAEA safeguards. India objected to the lack of provision for universal nuclear disarmament within a time-bound framework. In February 1997, I.K. Gujral, Foreign Minister of India reiterated India's opposition to the treaty (CTBT), saying that "India favors any step aimed at destroying nuclear weapons, but considers that the treaty in its current form is not comprehensive and bans only certain types of tests". India has not signed both the Comprehensive Test Ban Treaty (CTBT) and the Non-Proliferation Treaty (NPT).[16]

The Indian Nuclear Doctrine has three clauses. One, the bomb would not be used against an enemy who does not have nuclear capability. Two, it will be used only after the enemy uses the weapon against India. Three, a conventional war can be waged against a nuclear-armed enemy and in that war the enemy can be nuclear-disabled.

Opposite to India's Nuclear Doctrine, Pakistan's Nuclear Doctrine states that when an Indian conventional strike reaches an unacceptable threshold, it will use nuclear weapons against India. In other words, because of a large disparity in the strength of conventional weapons of the two countries, Pakistan will not hesitate to make first use of nuclear weapons when it feels that its security is threatened.

India should drop 'no first use' policy against a country, which repeatedly threatens first use of nuclear weapons. The first use of nuclear weapons by Pakistan may be so massive and widespread that it may disable India to use the nuclear weapon.

Pakistan has been boasting that India is afraid of its nuclear option. In the wake of December 13 Parliament attack and Kaluchak massacre in June 2002 India rushed its forces to the border and called them back after ten months. Pakistan stated that India was deterred from venturing an attack by the former's nuclear weapons. Similarly, India went for a direct approach in Kargil at a heavy price in casualties when it could have launched a counter-strike elsewhere compelling Pakistan to vacate Kargil. In a counter-strike elsewhere the casualties would have been much larger for Pakistan than for India. If India drops its 'no first use' option of nuclear weapons, Pakistan would stop blackmailing India and may even be deterred venturing terrorism in India.[17]

India's nuclear policy has been marked by restraint and openness. It has not violated any international agreements either in 1974 or, in 1998. The restraint exercised for 24 years, after having demonstrated our capability in 1974, is in itself a unique example. Restraint, however, has to arise from strength. It cannot be based upon indecision or doubt. Restraint is valid only when doubts are removed. The series of tests undertaken by India have led to the removal of doubts. The action involved was balanced in that it was the minimum necessary to maintain what is an irreducible component of our national security calculus. This Government's decision has, therefore to be seen as part of a tradition of restraint that has characterized our policy in the past 50 years.

Subsequent to the tests Government has already stated that India will, now observe a voluntary moratorium and refrain from conducting underground nuclear test explosions. It has also indicated willingness to move towards a *de jure* formalization of this declaration. The basic obligation of the CTBT is thus met to refrain from undertaking nuclear test explosions. This voluntary declaration is intended to convey to the international community the seriousness of our intent for meaningful engagement. Subsequent decision will be taken after assuring ourselves of the security needs of the country.

India has maintained effective export controls on nuclear materials as well as related technologies even though we are neither a party to the NPT nor a member of the Nuclear Suppliers' Group. Nonetheless, India is committed to non-proliferation and the maintaining of stringent export controls to ensure that there is no leakage of our indigenously developed know-how and technologies. In fact, India's conduct in this regard has been better than some countries which are party to the NPT.

India has in the past conveyed the concerns over the inadequacies of the international nuclear non-proliferation regime. It has explained that the country was not in a position to join because the regime did not address our country's security concerns. These could have been addressed by moving towards global nuclear disarmament, our preferred approach. As this did not take place, India was obliged to stand aside from the emerging regime so that its freedom of action was not constrained. This is the precise path that has continued to be followed unwaveringly for the last three decades. That same constructive approach will underlie India's dialogue with countries that need to be persuaded of the serious intent and willingness to engage so that mutual concerns are satisfactorily addressed. The challenge to Indian statecraft is balancing and reconciling India's security imperatives with valid international concerns in this regard.

The overwhelming support of the citizens of India is a source of strength for the Government. It not only tells that this decision was right but also that the country wants a focused leadership, which attends to national security needs. This, the Government pledges to do as a sacred duty. The Government has also been greatly heartened by the outpouring of support from Indians abroad. The rationale for the Government's decision is based on the same policy tenets that have guided the country for five decades. The policies were sustained successfully because of the underlying national consensus. The present decision and future actions will continue to reflect a commitment to sensibilities and obligations of an ancient civilisation, a sense of responsibility and restraint, but a restraint born of the assurance of action, not of doubts or apprehension.[18] The Gita explains (Chapter VI-3) as none other can: "Action is a process to reach a goal; action may reflect tumult but when measured and focused, will yield its objective of stability and peace."[19]

INDIA-US CIVIL NUCLEAR DEAL

The Indian Prime Minister, Manmohan Singh's visit to the US in July 2005 was hailed "as a historic step forward" in their bilateral relations. A senior American official stated that the mutual interests of India and the United States were coinciding more than ever before. It was the time that the US began to see India as one of its most important partners worldwide, given the fact that India is a rising economic power and an established democracy. The PM's visit led to the Indo-US Joint Statement on July 18, 2005, announcing a series of bilateral measures on areas such as information technology, business, commerce, energy, space, disaster response, agriculture, science and technology and other economic issues.

One of the most important developments was to initiate the measure to strengthen energy security and promote the development of stable and efficient energy markets in India with a view to ensuring adequate and affordable energy supplies. Stage was set to start a US-India Energy Dialogue which led to the Civil Nuclear Cooperation Agreement between the two countries in March, 2006 following the US President George W. Bush's visit to India.

The development of close Indo-US relationship is said to be "one of the most important undertakings the US has embarked on in its foreign policy," and is considered to be the beginning of a new relationship. These relations, however, have not catapulted into closeness suddenly. Certain developments that took place in the international geo-politics have shaped these relations over a period of time. It is necessary to understand the finer points of these developments as a background to the Indo-US partnership.

Background

For nearly forty years, i.e. till the disintegration of the Union of Soviet Socialist Republics (USSR) in 1991, India's relations with the US were viewed through the narrow prism of Cold War. For geo-political reasons America considered Pakistan as its closer ally and had two alliances with it, first in the mid-fifties and second in the eighties, aimed at containing and fighting the erstwhile USSR. However, militarisation of polity in

Pakistan and nuclearisation of that country brought non-proliferation concerns in the American attitude.

The 9/11 attack by Islamic radicals on twin towers of World Trade Centre and the Pentagon made America see some congruence with India which had been facing such attacks through most of the preceding decade. In the months following 9/11 attack when India survived a body blow of terrorists to its Parliament, America began to realise India's security concerns and the rationale behind its nuclear tests. It started finding merit in India's arguments to refuse to sign Comprehensive Test Ban Treaty (CTBT). India's changing profile was written into the US National Security Strategy in 2002. For the first time, the US administration began to take cognizance of India's geo-political virtues, economic strength as well as genuineness of its security concerns. Experts feel that it was during that period that India began to emerge as a strategic partner to the USA.

The Indian Prime Minister had meeting with President Bush on the sidelines of United Nations General Assembly in New York in September 2004. The Joint Statement called: "US-India Partnership Cooperation Trust" was issued after the meeting laid out the directions for future relationship and noted that "bilateral relations had never been as close as they were in the present." The meeting served to underline the strategic areas including commitment to combat proliferation of Weapons of Mass Destruction (WMDs), terrorism and enhance global security. The leaders on both sides noted that the implementation of the first of the Next Steps in Strategic Partnership (NSSP) marked the beginning of a new era of cooperation and trust. Emphasis was also laid on advancing economic cooperation in multilateral institutions including Doha Development Agenda (DDA) of the World Trade Organisation (WTO) and also through other bilateral mechanisms, such as India-US Economic Dialogue, and the High Technology Cooperation Group.

At the political level, the high-level engagement continued throughout the year. India's External Affairs Minister visited Washington in June 2004. He also had meetings subsequently with the then US Secretary of State, Colin Powell on the sidelines of ASEAN Regional Forum in July 2004 and January 2005 in the aftermath of Tsunami, both held in Jakarta. Those meetings served to consolidate political contacts between the two countries after the formation of new Government in India under the prime ministership of Manmohan Singh. The response from the US came in the shape of visit of then Deputy Secretary of State, Richard Armitage and US Defence Secretary, Donald Rumsfeld to India on July 13-14 and December 8-9, 2004 respectively.

The US Secretary of State, Condoleezza Rice visited India in March 2005 as the first stop on her 6-nation Asian tour. She had meetings with the Prime Minister, the External Affairs Minister and the Chairperson of the United Progressive Alliance (UPA) and discussed the entire range of issues of bilateral, regional and global importance. Most importantly, there was a forward movement on starting an energy dialogue which cleared the pathway for the historic nuclear deal.

Global Nuclear Energy Partnership

The Bush Government launched a Global Nuclear Energy Partnership with an allocation of US$ 250 million during the year 2005-06. Under this initiative, the technologically advanced countries would supply small-scale nuclear reactors to the developing countries to help them meet their energy requirements and reduce their dependence on oil and other fossil fuels. The US disclosed plans to work with France, Russia and Japan and to co-opt India in due course.

In line with the above and in the context of India emerging as a global power, President Bush reached the historic July 18, 2005 agreement with Manmohan Singh. Manmohan Singh agreed to a separation plan of India's civil and weapons reactors, while Bush committed to provide New Delhi access to nuclear know-how, fuel and technology. The agreement is aimed to strengthen US-India relations, American security and the global non proliferation order.

After weeks of intense diplomatic activity, India and the US reached the historic Indo-US Civilian Nuclear Cooperation Agreement during President Bush's visit to India in the first week of March 2006. The Indian Plan to separate civilian and weapons reactors facilities met the United States' benchmarks of being creditable, verifiable and defensible from the non-proliferation standpoint. The main points of the deal are:

1. Fourteen of India's 22 reactors are to be separated as civilian and placed under safeguards. The US concedes that Breeder Reactor be kept outside until India decides otherwise.
2. The reactors once safeguarded will remain so permanently. India secures the right to take corrective action if the reactors' fuel supply is cut off.
3. India will decide whether it wishes to safeguard future reactors.
4. Enrichment and reprocessing plants can switch back and forth from safeguards, depending upon whether they handled safeguarded material or not.
5. The nuclear separation plan will be done in phases but will be concluded by 2014.

India would be provided with access to nuclear know-how, fuel and technology. It would integrate India into the global non-proliferation regime after having remained outside of it ever since the nuclear Non-proliferation Treaty (NPT) was signed in 1968.

Key Factors

The following five key factors explain why the US has pursued the agreement despite stiff opposition from some quarters including the Nuclear Suppliers Group:

1. It does not provide any assistance to India's nuclear weapons programme.
2. The supply of civilian grade fuel or building new power reactors does not free up fissile material for India's military programme.
3. It places nearly three-fourths of India's hitherto unsafe guarded fissile material and facilities under International Atomic Energy Agency (IAEA) safeguards.
4. India is non-signatory to the NPT but has maintained its impeccable non-proliferation credentials throughout

and was committed not to divert any nuclear material designated for civilian use or to export to other countries. Each time some foreign state such as Libya and Iran approached New Delhi for assistance in developing nuclear capabilities, they were firmly refused.

5. China and India represent the two biggest nuclear energy markets for the next two decades, estimated at US$ 40 billion and US$ 25-30 billion respectively. The provision of alternate energy options reduces New Delhi's dependence on regimes whose policies might undermine regional or global security.

Benefits for India

For Indian negotiators the deal ensures the following benefits:

1. It gives India the benefits of peaceful nuclear cooperation while transforming the unilateral Indian commitment to non-proliferation into a veritable international obligation. It creates the only viable international framework that can resolve India's nuclear 'outlier' status.
2. Despite creditable progress made by India on the basis of indigenous technology in the face of decades of technology embargoes, the Department of Atomic Energy's three-stage Civilian Nuclear Program faces an uncertain future. The Pressurized Heavy Water Reactors Program has constraints of limited supply of uranium. The operational validity and commercial viability of the Fast Breeder Reactor Program and the Advanced Heavy Water Reactor Program remain uncertain. In the absence of this nuclear deal, the scaling up of nuclear energy production as per growing requirements would be doubtful which may restrict the pace of India's economic growth.
3. The DAE has been successful in making weapons but when it comes to producing electricity, its record is abysmal. It needs both finance and technology to rectify this deficit. The separation plan as Manmohan Singh

has rightly agreed is the first step towards making India's nuclear power sector a genuine contributor to the economy as India's economic future is inextricably linked to its ability to produce power.

4. The pressure on India to burn its large reserves of coal which leads to rampant air pollution shall be reduced. The cause of environment shall be immensely helped.

Apprehensions

Despite widespread euphoria that followed the deal, serious apprehensions were expressed in some quarters. The scientists and officials at the headquarters of the Department of Economic Energy, Colaba and the Bhabha Atomic Research Centre (BARC), Trombay felt that the pact could mark the beginning of United States' domination of India's most important establishments and an attempt to downsize its nuclear military might. Placing as many as 14 reactors under international safeguards could have serious implications for our strategic programmes.

The deal could make the ongoing US negotiations with North Korea and Iran to stall their nuclear programs more difficult. Some American experts feel that this agreement may lead NPT signatories like South Africa and Brazil to seek nuclear weapons themselves.

It is also felt that a fierce political battle will be waged in Washington as well as within the Nuclear Suppliers Group over whether India has done enough to deserve a *de facto* nuclear power status. The obscure reasoning for keeping the breeders in the military list may also provide the dissidents a base to create an issue to sabotage the deal.

It is also apprehended that Washington shall be forced into entering a similar agreement with Pakistan at some stage which will be a dangerous development, given Islamabad's terrible record regarding WMD proliferation including A.Q. Khan's notorious activities. Though President Bush, on his visit to Pakistan, after completing his entourage to India refused to have a nuclear deal with Pakistan, in international politics equations change sooner than expected. Pakistan, viewed as a more useful ally to the US than India may strike a bargain in this regard, at some opportune time, in return for actively assisting the US in its policies regarding West Asia. If such a thing happens, the peace in the Indian subcontinent may be seriously disturbed.

Immediately after Bush's visit to Pakistan, General Pervez Musharraf said that Pakistan did not care about the US-India nuclear deal. He urged his countrymen not to be India-centric. However, Pakistan's reaction since then has become more visceral. Pakistan's Foreign Minister Khurshid Kasuri has stated, "If the Indian deal goes through, there are some things we will do," hinting that Pakistan will cadge a similar deal from China. In fact in the days leading to the Bush's Pakistan visit, Musharraf went to Beijing but returned empty-handed. It appears that China has become cautious about transactions with Pakistan, given its increasing fundamentalism under military rule.

Pakistan is asked for a 'package nuclear deal' along with India despite rejection from Washington that Islamabad was not eligible for such an agreement, given its proliferation history. Pakistan's ambassador to the US was quoted as saying, "Instead of a country specific deal on a subject as critical as nuclear technology, there should be a package for both India and Pakistan."

Pakistan's complaining made no visible impact on the US. But, Islamabad galvanised its lobby in Washington to derail the Indo-US nuclear deal. Pakistan's reaction to US-India nuclear deal has changed from feigned indifference to dismay and anger. But President Bush was able to beat the Pakistan lobby to see the deal through in Congress.

China has voiced its misgivings over the US offering nuclear fuel and technology to India. Qin Ganga, a spokesperson for China's Foreign Ministry, has asked India to abandon nuclear weapons and strengthen atomic safeguards. He said in a news briefing in Beijing that India should sign the NPT and dismantle its nuclear weapons.

It is pertinent to recall that NPT grants China, the US, Russia, France and Britain the status of nuclear weapons states but bars other signatory countries from having such weapons. Insisting India on signing NPT as sought by China may disturb the present arrangement and start fresh controversies.

The whole process of the deal, if it proceeds smoothly, shall take nearly two years to be formalised. In the meantime India will be under pressure from Washington to support its strategic objectives. One would recall that pressure started immediately after the Indo-US Joint Statement of July 2005 that made India support US and its European partners to seek punitive action against Iran for its nuclear fuel enrichment activities. Some circles believe that during his recent visit to India, Bush sought support for its position on the overthrow of military regime in Myanmar and a hardline towards Maoists of Nepal. This is the price that India seems to be willing to pay for the nuclear deal in utter disregard of neighborhood diplomacy.

Scientists' Concern over the Indo-US Nuclear Deal

Top Indian scientists have expressed four points to highlight their anxiety about the Indo-US nuclear deal:

1. that India's nuclear weapons programme should not come under any international security;
2. facilities developed indigenously should not come under safeguards;
3. indigenous research and development should remain autonomous; and
4. the parliament should uphold national interest in this regard.

The group included A.N. Prasad, M.R. Srinivasan, Placid Rodriguez, H.N. Sethna, P.K. Iyengar, S.L. Kati, A. Gopalakrishnan and Y.S.R. Prasad—scientists who have been directly involved with India's nuclear development at Bhabha Atomic Research Centre (BARC) and Department of Atomic Energy (DAE). They feel that on all four counts there is danger of crippling compromise. The statement issued by them says:

> It is important for our parliament to ensure that decisions taken today do not inhibit our future ability to develop and pursue nuclear technologies for the benefit of the nation. We therefore request you, the parliamentarians to discuss this deal and arrive at a unanimous decision recognizing the fundamental facts of India's indigenous nuclear science and technology achievements to date, the

efforts made to overcome the unfair restrictions placed on us and the imaginative policies and planning enunciated and followed in the years after independence.

P.K. Iyengar—the retired Chairman of Atomic Energy Commission (AEC), and recipient of Padma Bhushan award said, "From the various testimonies being presented about this agreement in Washington, we feel that India's atomic autonomy is now under a serious threat." A nuclear expert at the Department of Atomic Energy said that the opinion expressed by the eight nuclear chiefs was indeed legitimate and the government should consider it before initiating any further step. The nuclear scientists said: "We have all worked in the field of atomic energy from the very early years after India's independence. From the very small beginnings, we have now reached a stage where we are in possession of all the technologies."

The scientists pointed out that India should accept safeguards only on civilian entities: "We have agreed to this before and we can continue to agree to this in the future too, but strictly restricted to those facilities and materials imported from external sources." They have reservations on the bill piloted through the US House of Representatives, saying it would hamper Indian research and development. The scientists are insisting that the parliament should set the ground rules for the Indo-US nuclear deal.

The top level officials are doing their best to allay the fears of the scientists. A government spokesman said, "They are naturally anxious. Their insecurities have a lot to do with the experiences of the scientists who during the years that they were at the helm of India's nuclear affairs had to contend with a world busy tightening the nuclear noose around India. The current atmosphere of change is a difficult leap of faith for former nuclear denizens."

The scientists' objections about nuclear negotiations are dealt with in the Separation Plan that was agreed on March 2, 2006, the 123 Agreement and Safeguards Agreement currently being worked out. The essence of Separation Plan is that 14 of India's nuclear reactors were put in the civilian list and eight remained devoted to India's weapons program. This official said was intended to maintain India's minimum credible nuclear deterrence.

The government says that the perpetuity of safeguards is connected with the guaranteed fuel supplies including a strategic reserve for the lifetime of each nuclear reactor. The government officials said that Research and Development facilities had been kept out of the civilian list in the Separation Plan.

There are concerns in the US legislation about provisions on end-user verification, reprocessing of spent fuel by India and annual certification by the US President to the Congress. In this regard the government has told the US that India should be able to reprocess imported spent fuel for civilian purposes without being hindered. The annual certification should be removed to the non-binding part of the legislation.

However, those who are in favour of the deal argue that the deal puts no curbs on fissile material production by India. In fact, it gives India the option of piling up fissile material and making as many military reactors as it wants and developing its breeder reactor. The actual cause of concern would rather be a disrupted nuclear fuel supply. That is why India is negotiating a safeguards agreement with the International Atomic Energy Agency to gain commitment from third parties to supply fuel in case the US refuses to do so.

The deal does not stop India from conducting nuclear tests. Not even the fine print says so. What it says is that if India tests, the US will break off all civil nuclear cooperation. This is nothing new, nor exclusively for India. This has been part of US law since 1978 and applies to all countries including UK and Israel—ideologically, two closest countries to the United States.

Similarly, the idea of perpetuity is also not new. India first accepted the principle of perpetuity in 1978 when the Department of Atomic Energy let erstwhile USSR place Rana Pratap Sagar reactor in Rajasthan under safeguards. Thereafter, India also agreed to the same for its Koodankulam reactor in Tamil Nadu. Thus, India has been accepting perpetuity clauses in the past and that too for nothing. Through the deal it is required to do the same thing but getting international acceptance of its right to have both civilian and military nuclear programmes in return. Without perpetual safeguards, no country will provide India with nuclear fuel or technology as it is a global norm. In the absence of regular supply of nuclear fuel, we may end up with many idle nuclear power plants. Even China, one of the five nuclear weapons states places many of its atomic installations under perpetual safeguards.

It has been argued that setting up nuclear reactors is a million dollars affair, and India with a shortage of capital cannot afford them. But India has a powerful and thriving private sector. That is why private players are being brought in. Reliance, Tata and others feel that they have the funds and are lining up to forage into the nuclear power sector. The critics are also ignoring the fact that once a reactor is up and running, the per unit cost of its electricity is among the lowest and least volatile in the industry.

In order to ensure that the concerns of the scientific community are addressed, the Prime Minister held an internal high level review of the deal. Those present at the meeting included Atomic Energy Commission Chief, Anil Kakodkar; Principal Secretary to Prime Minister T.K.A. Nair; scientific advisor R. Chidambaram; and Foreign Secretary Shyam Saran. However, there is no provision within the Constitution for Parliament to review an agreement that the government enters into with another government. Nevertheless, the Prime Minister tried to dispel the misgivings and gave a clear message that the government will not compromise on its strategic program. Discussing the issue in the Rajya Sabha, he said, "We will not accept any condition that goes beyond the parameters of July 18, 2005 joint statement and the March 2, 2006 Separation Plan agreed to between India and the US The proposed US legislation on nuclear cooperation with India will not be allowed to become an instrument to compromise India's sovereignty." Allaying the scientists' concern on the likely loss of autonomy in indigenous Research and Development, he said, "There will be no external supervision of our R&D work in the nuclear field." He continued that there was no question of India's foreign policy on autonomy becoming subservient to US interests as a result of the deal. No legislation enacted in a foreign country can take away from us that sovereign right to solely determine what is in our national interest. Thus, there is no question of India being bound by a law passed by a foreign legislature. He assured the house that if the US legislation or the Nuclear Suppliers Group imposes extraneous conditions, the government will draw the necessary conclusion consistent with the government's commitments to Parliament and the people. "In this uncertain and unpredictable world in which nuclear power provided security, the autonomy of India's nuclear program was the cardinal principal of our nuclear policy," he said.

Further Requirements

Though the deal has been done, many hurdles still need to be crossed before it is formalised and implemented. The US Congress has to make amendments to American laws regarding non-proliferation. The support of the Congress and an early amendment of the laws cannot be taken for granted.

The US has to get the approval from the Nuclear Suppliers Group before the deal can be implemented. The Chinese opposition either at its own instance or to please Pakistan cannot be ruled out at this stage.

The International Atomic Energy Agency (IAEA) also needs to prepare India-specific safeguards so that nuclear rules and regulations that apply to NPT countries won't apply to India. The formalisation of the deal shall be based on India's acceptance of the principle of irreversibility of its decision irrespective of the future threats to its security.

Another roadblock that the implementation of the deal is likely to hit is the supply of uranium. Australia, the largest supplier of uranium, has made it clear that it would stick to its policy of not selling uranium to non-NPT countries like India. A committee is being set up to study India's specific position despite being a non-NPT country. Much will depend on the findings and final report of that committee.

The pro-Pakistan lobby will do its best to sabotage the deal. Many US legislators find it contradictory that Bush is doing his best to deny nuclear capability to Iran which is an NPT signatory and favouring India which refused to sign the NPT.

Nuclear Deal—An Attempt to Create a New Balance of Power

The Indo-US nuclear deal can be seen as an attempt by the United States to create a new balance of power in the world. It is America's third attempt. The first attempt was in the shape of formulation of the containment policy, creation of NATO and other alliance systems. The second attempt was through weaning away of China from communism and embracing the free market economy, following Henry Kissinger's visit to Beijing in 1989. And now, this third attempt is to focus on India as a balancer of power in Asia and the world.

The first two attempts were under the situation of a bipolar world order—an order that came to an end with the disintegration of the erstwhile Union of Soviet Socialist Republics (USSR) and collapse of the international communism.

Bush also accepted that the new policy towards India was necessary because of changes that have come about in the international system. The US remains the foremost power in a world of balance of power which, besides the US, is comprised of the European Union, Russia, China and India. The US, however, is no longer an unchallenged superpower. Though it is militarily still indomitable, its dominance in many areas—economy, science and technology, industrial and agricultural production, etc. is declining. Other major countries no longer cower behind it to seek security protection in case of a perceived threat from another superpower. Four of the six balances of power are in Asia: the focal point of global economy is shifting from trans-Atlantic areas to Asia; the threat to the US homeland is posed by terrorists hailing from West Asian countries; Asia holds most of the oil and gas reserves in the world; the region is the storehouse of cheap labour and a large manpower which is gaining in literacy rate and acquiring more and more technical skills. The two most important countries in Asia for geo-political reasons are China and India. Japan, though most developed of all Asian nations is politically not as influential as these two.

China vs India

In early 2005, America's National Intelligence Council, a think tank associated with the CIA noted in a report that China and India would emerge as major global forces by the year 2020 and that their impact on the world at large would be similar to that of the emergence of the US in the early 20th century. The report observed that "the combination of high economic growth, expanding military capabilities and large population will be at the root of the expected rise in economic and political power for both the countries."

America played a significant role in China's economic development. During the latter half of the Cold War period, China's economic growth was propelled by its closeness to the US. Without United States' help, influence and encouragement China would not have received flows of huge investment from other countries. The US itself allowed China to have high trade relations with its chainstores, in high proportion.

Now China has embarked on such a stage of its economic development that it threatens to overtake US in the next two to three decades in terms of GDP growth. The US is afraid that unless a stable balance of power is promoted in Asia, it will be dominated by China. In order to counter the rising power of China, the US is looking to establish India.

Promoting balance of power does not necessitate direct conflict with China. In the present-day world, violent fights between major powers are ruled out. The US also cannot think of bringing about China's containment because the magnitude of China's annual trade with the US and that with Japan is as high as US$ 200 billion each. Moreover, the essence of balance of power lies in having a number of major nations competing with one another in peace and harmony and having a proper equation of power. Bush's announcement of issuing technology licence exemption for India, launching of Rs.1000 crore, Agriculture Knowledge Initiative, Indo-US Space Cooperation for blast off, and initiatives to develop a bilateral business climate supportive of trade and investment encompassed in the Indo-US CEO Forum Report are some of the measures that the US is taking to bring India at par with China.

The US has the experience of building up Germany, Japan and China. Now the US is attempting to help India become a world class power. Just as building China helped the US too, building India will be beneficial to the US in terms of reviving the US nuclear industry, providing it with opportunities for export of technology and services to the Indian nuclear market. India is a software giant. It has made rapid strides in Information & Communication Technology (ICT). The Indian software companies have since long been on the American radar. A large number of US companies need to outsource their business through India to remain competitive. A stronger India will be more helpful for American software companies. These primarily are the reasons why Bush administration is tilted in favour of India. Moreover, building a balance of power in Asia is good both for Asia and the world stability.

Some people also believe that the balance of power that the United States is trying to create through this deal will only serve American interest. It is global dominance which is the underlying goal of the United States as elaborated in the various security documents and not what Condoleezza Rice may say of balance of power. Creating a regional balance of power through this "concession" will mean that there is no peer competitor for the US. America's building up of Pakistan's offensive capabilities against India bears testimony to this fact. While continuing to peddle superstardom dream to India, the United States has been regularly selling arms, aircraft and weapons worth billions of dollars to Pakistan. The latest arms package for Pakistan includes advanced targeting systems, satellite-guided bombs and the upgrading of 26 F-16s already in its arsenal. Besides, the US has also announced the sale of 130 Harpoon anti-ship missiles with command launch systems and 10 P3C Orion dual purpose aircraft to Pakistan to monitor India's entire western flank and hunt down Indian submarines. It is thus quite clear that the US wants to build and maintain Pakistan as a military counterweight to India. The challenge is, therefore, to preserve Indian interests in the context of global security and foreign policy objectives. Most of the concerns about the Indo-US nuclear deal have been assuaged by those who favour it as a win-win situation for India and the world.

An Alternate Model—China-Russia-India Cooperation

Some experts have suggested an alternate model to the above equation for establishing a balance of power—that of China-

Russia-India Cooperation. What goes against this model is China's nuclear proliferation to Pakistan. It is also difficult to imagine how India acquiesces into this partnership with countries having roots of communist ideology. India having a sizeable number of English-speaking people is naturally inclined towards the US as its students approach American Universities for higher education; they get outsourced jobs and outsourced Research & Development centres from the US. Its noisy democracy that vows liberal values is in proximity with America which is another great democracy. It is, therefore, doubtful if India's relation similar to the US is possible with either China or Russia.

Global Energy Issue

Although the US opposed the Kyoto Protocol which advocated that greenhouse gas emissions should be cut down, Bush continues to show concern towards environment and advocates the use of cleaner fuel. The US realises that fast economic development in China has made it step up greenhouse gas emission. It has become the second major contributor to global warming with 18 per cent of world's greenhouse gas emissions after America with 25 per cent of world's emissions. India's gas emissions produced at present stand at 4 per cent. Pursuit of higher economic growth is likely to push this percentage much higher. The US wants that India should not follow China's route of energy generation by excessive use of hydrocarbon fuels which will exacerbate the problem of environmental pollution. Bush feels that nuclear energy and other new technologies are the solution to the problem of excessive greenhouse gas emissions.

Rising Oil Prices and Nuclear Energy Option

The global prices of petrochemical products are fast increasing every year. The developing countries which cannot bear the burden of higher oil import bill have to cut down their imports and are facing energy crisis. The developed countries have also begun to feel the pressure due to limited supply, higher prices and diplomatic policies of the oil-exporting countries. It is apprehended that the persistent demand would raise the oil prices by $ 10 barrel or more per year, and the prices may reach $ 150 a barrel by 2009. Under these circumstances, nuclear energy has become an evocative article of faith—an obvious answer to the world's rapidly increasing energy demand.

The total quantities of crude oil and petroleum products imported by India during 2003-04 were 90.434 MMT and 7.897 MMT valued at Rs. 83,528 crore and Rs. 9,677 crore respectively. In the same period 14.620 MMT of petroleum products valued at Rs. 16,781 crore were exported.

During the first three-quarters of the financial year 2004-05, 71.818 MMT valued at Rs. 85,695 crore of crude oil and 5.610 MMT valued at Rs. 9,164 crore of petroleum products were imported and 13.025 MMT valued at Rs. 20,705 crore of petroleum products were exported.

There was an increase of 7.3 per cent in quantity and 41.8 per cent in value of crude oil imported during April-December 2004 over the preceding year. Crude oil imported during April-December 2003 amounted to 66.941 MMT valued at Rs. 60,450 crore *vis-à-vis* 71.818 MMT valued at Rs. 85,695 crore during the period April-December 2004.

Crude oil and Petroleum products continue to be the single major item of import with its share jumping over 40 per cent to $ 68 billion in 2007-08 as a consequence of relentless rise in international prices.

India imported 121.672 million tonnes of crude oil in 2007-08 as opposed to 111.502 million tonnes in the previous year. In rupee term, the import bill has risen 24.5 per cent to Rs. 2,72,699 crore as against Rs. 2,19,029 crore previously. In 2006-07, the country imported 17.66 million tonnes of products for Rs. 41,160 crore. Fuel consumption in the country grew by a healthy 7 per cent during the period.

During the year 2004-05, the public sector refineries purchased crude oil on term contract and spot basis. The countries from where term contract purchases were made included Saudi Arabia, Kuwait, UAE, Iran, etc.

The World Economic Forum organized in January 2006 in Davos focused on nuclear energy. Companies like Areva and GE gave several presentations to India and Chinese delegations sensing the two countries' massive energy requirements. India's power demand is projected to increase five-fold by 2030. The Government aims to increase production of nuclear energy from the present 3,000 MW to 20,000 MW in the next fifteen years. The Bush Government took an initiative in the form of Global Nuclear Energy Partnership with an allocation of US$ 250 million for the year 2005-06.

World Nuclear Power Scenario

There is a revival of the nuclear industry worldwide. Rising energy demands, limited fossil fuel, increasing oil prices and environmental concerns have put back nuclear energy on the energy mix. The global installed capacity has increased since 1990 till now from 327 GW to about 400 GW. Globally there are 439 reactors in operation in 31 countries and produce 16 per cent of the world's electricity. The nuclear energy industry, at present worth US$ 125 billion, is growing. The nuclear energy as a percentage of total energy generated in some major countries of Europe, Asia and in the US is shown in the Table below:

Table: 7.1 Nuclear Energy generated in Major Countries

Country	Nuclear Energy as a Percentage of Total Energy Generated
France	78
Sweden	52
Germany	32
Japan	29
Spain	23
US	20
UK	19
Russia	16
India	2.8
China	2.2

Source: MNA

The data reveal that India produces only 2.8 per cent of its total energy generation through nuclear reactors. In this context the Indo-US Civil Nuclear Cooperation assumes great significance in bringing India's nuclear energy production to a higher level to meet its increasing demand.

Disadvantages of Producing Nuclear Energy

Some people find India's euphoria over its nuclear deal puzzling, given that producing nuclear power is beset with several problems. The major such problems are discussed below:

Producing nuclear power involves high investment and long gestation period as compared to production through coal, gas or hydro sources. Building nuclear plants takes 10-15 years—the benefit comes after about two decades after the operation of reactors. According to International Energy Association (IEA), the capital cost for nuclear power is around US$ 2,500 per kw while for coal it is US$ 1,000 per kw. Nuclear electricity proves 60 per cent costlier than power from gas-fired plants. Nuclear-generated power is so expensive that the Britain's Liberal Party has rejected it as uneconomic.

The public opinion in Europe is against nuclear plants because they generate radioactive waste whose storage can kill or injure future generations. About 20 per cent of Britain's electricity is nuclear. It has decommissioned nearly half its nuclear reactors and is not keen in replacing the ones whose life is ending.

If nuclear energy is good for India, so should it be for the US. But, the US has not built a single nuclear plant since 1979. Ninety per cent of the electricity plants it is building are gas-fired. The West European countries are far more dependent on nuclear power than India. Only about 3 per cent of our electricity is nuclear as compared to 52 per cent of Sweden's, 32 per cent of Germany's and 23 per cent of Spain's. All these nations are decommissioning their nuclear plants due to concerns of safety and economics. Why is India going overboard for developing nuclear energy while most other countries are denouncing it, needs to be looked into.

The experts have tried to find the reason in a mix of secrecy, patriotism and methods of discussion. The economics of nuclear power is not publicly discussed in India. There is an unspoken consent because it is considered unpatriotic to question the DAE's advocacy of nuclear-generated electricity.

Only about 3 per cent of our electricity is nuclear—it is understandable because huge coal reserves and large water resources make economic sense for us to produce thermal power and hydroelectric power which at present constitute 71 per cent and 26 per cent, respectively, of our total electricity. Yet, DAE has set for itself a goal of producing 20,000 MW of nuclear generated power by 2020 which is nearly seven times our current production of nuclear power. But nobody has questioned the wisdom of such a stiff target.

India's opacity is well contrasted with the transparency of the western world where opinion makers freely discuss the economics of producing electricity from different fuels like coal, oil, gas, uranium, etc. On the other hand, there was no open discussion on the relative merits and demerits of India producing nuclear electricity—before, during or after Bush's visit to India. We have failed to separate commerce from patriotism.

Handling nuclear waste is another big hazard connected with the production of nuclear power. India has chosen to ignore this significant aspect. In the UK, robotic arms safely handle nuclear waste inside the nuclear plants. India obviously lacks such technology, which is also very expensive. In America, the nuclear waste is stored deep inside a rocky mountain in Nevada. Some people feel that America is interested in setting up small nuclear reactors in the developing countries to dispose of its nuclear waste through them. We must guard ourselves against such a move. However, producing nuclear power is not without arguments in favour, some of which are summarised below:

The fuel cost in nuclear power is much lower at 15 per cent as compared to 60 per cent and 74 per cent in coal and gas respectively. India has abundant supply of coal but its technology of producing thermal power is outdated. Our coal is high on ash content and has to be mixed with imported low ash coal. The thermal plants are cheap to operate if they are near the mines which are not the case in India. A Nuclear Power Corporation reveals that if the thermal plant is more than 1,000 km away from the coal pithead, as most of our power plants are, then nuclear power may be a cheaper option.

Burning of coal remains a big environmental hazard. Release of tonnes of smoke in the atmosphere not only leads to various diseases in human beings and livestock but also contributes to global warming which in turn leads to fast melting of glaciers—the reservoirs of water; rise in the level of seas, submerging many coastal areas and islands; change in the precipitation pattern, causing harm to natural ecosystems and hence species of flora and fauna. Nuclear energy, on the other hand, is clean and environment friendly. It produces no sulphuric acid or greenhouse gases. According to the Nuclear Energy Institute, in the year 2004, the US nuclear power plants prevented 3.43 million tonnes of sulphur dioxide, 1.11 million tonnes of nitrogen oxide, and 696.6 million metric tonnes of carbon dioxide from entering the earth's atmosphere. The IAEA estimates that a 10,000 MM(e) coal burning plant produces about 3,000,000 tonnes of radioactive ash annually, as compared to a similar nuclear plant producing 800 tonnes of low and medium level radioactive waste and about 30 tonnes of high-level waste that can be isolated from the biosphere.

Nuclear waste decays faster than chemical waste. Advanced countries like America are finding innovative solutions for its quick disposal. Finland will have an operational facility by 2010 for placing nuclear waste underground in a geological repository. Thus, the problem of storing disposable nuclear waste may not be as acute in future as it is today.

Gas plants with uninterrupted fuel supply have a cost advantage over coal and nuclear energy. These benefits, however, remain elusive to India as it imports 75 per cent of its gas without even a single pipeline in place.

Nuclear energy is therefore a viable option for India. The countries that are hesitant in setting up new nuclear plants have their own reasons. Many countries like France, Finland and Japan remain enthusiastic about nuclear energy after decades of use. Their economic growth has been greatly helped by nuclear power. They have been benefited by other applications of nuclear physics in medical sciences, agriculture and industry. Russia and China are also expanding their nuclear plans. In order to maintain a growth rate of 9-10 per cent on a consistent basis, India needs to produce much larger amount of power. The Indo-US nuclear deal has provided us an opportunity to meet our energy requirements to pursue this high growth path. As the share of nuclear power is set to grow in India, it is necessary to ensure safety and efficiency by adopting best international practices and following security guidelines.

India and the NPT

India has remained outside of the Non-proliferation Treaty (NPT), which was signed in 1968. America and other leading nations have been putting pressure on India to sign the Treaty. NPT grants China, the US, Russia, France and Britain the status of nuclear weapons power. India's argument has been that if these countries are stockpiling nuclear weapons, how they can stop other countries that have their own security concerns, from acquiring such weapons. In the 1990s, the US came up with some regional and global initiatives like Comprehensive Test Ban Treaty (CTBT) to stop India and Pakistan from pursuing their nuclear programs, but the efforts failed when both these countries tested nuclear weapons in May 1998.

Through the nuclear deal, the US aims to bring India into a modified non-proliferation regime. The move of India's exceptionalisation from NPT will virtually enforce non-proliferation norms through separation of its civilian nuclear reactors and placement of nearly three-fourths of India's hitherto unsafe guarded fissile material and facilities under International Atomic Energy Agency (IAEA) safeguards.

The gain for India is handsome in terms of power generation. In the 1970s we set a target of having 10,000 MW of nuclear power by 2000. As of now, the generation stands at 3,310 MW. The reason is US-led embargo on India's nuclear program which became tighter by the year. In 2001, Russia supplied fuel for the Tarapur nuclear power plant and agreed to construct two new reactors at Koodankulam but could not help further because of restrictions of Nuclear Suppliers Group. Though a non-signatory to the NPT, India has an impeccable record of 32 years since its first nuclear test in 1974, of behaving very responsibly and observing non-proliferation norms more rigorously than China which proliferated to Pakistan and West-European Companies. Pakistan, in turn proliferated it to Iran, North Korea and Iraq, and also offered it to Libya. Out of the three countries which are non-signatories of NPT, i.e. Israel, India and Pakistan, the energy needs of India are many times more than those of the other two, and they also fail to match India's non-proliferation record.

India's Stand on Iran

According to a report by a UN agency, Iran has accelerated its nuclear fuel enrichment activities and rejected demands of international inspectors to explain evidence that had raised suspicions of nuclear weapons program. The US and its European partners have been seeking punitive action against Iran in the Security Council. IAEA, which customarily takes decisions by consensus, brought a resolution on Iran at Vienna which was adopted by vote. Out of the thirty-five countries on the board, twenty-two including India voted for the resolution. Apart from Russia and China, ten other countries belonging to the non-aligned movement such as South Africa, Brazil, Mexico and Sri Lanka abstained.

The left allies of the ruling UPA criticized the Government for supporting the IAEA resolution on the following counts:

1. It was thought to be an act taken under US pressure and that the US had given a blunt message that the nuclear cooperation agreement will not be ratified by the US Congress if India takes an independent stand.
2. Till the eve of the vote, the Government was in favour of deciding the issue through discussions and consensus. By voting in favour of the resolution, the Government backed on its stand.
3. India has broken ranks with the non-aligned countries which had decided not to support the US stand on Iran.

The Government set aside these allegations saying that the decision was based on 'very careful consideration' and aimed at averting 'a major confrontation' between Tehran and the International Community. Denying any US pressure, Manmohan Singh said in the Parliament that India cannot turn a blind eye to the security implications of Iran's nuclear program. The resolution of the IAEA board states that, "the history of concealment" of nuclear activities and the "resulting absence of confidence that Iran's nuclear program is exclusively for peaceful purposes have given rise to the questions that are within the competence of the Security Council." India feels that Iran, as a signatory of the NPT, should develop its nuclear technology only under international safeguards. The Indo-Asian News Service called India's stand on Iran issue "difficult but principled". The vote in Vienna caused disquiet in some sections in both the countries. The two countries shared centuries of close cultural and civilization affinities. The prospects of working together on Iran-Pakistan-India gas pipeline were an opportunity for greater and permanent interdependence. India ran the risk of this project being jeopardized by voting against Iran, though Dr. Manmohan Singh remained hopeful that India's stand on Iran would not derail the Iran-India gas pipeline.

India's stand was also bold in the sense that it broke away from the non-aligned countries which had decided not to support the US on the issue. Even Pakistan which is considered to be a close ally of the US could not muster courage to vote against Iran and hence abstained.

India's stand on Iran expresses its concern over the proliferation of nuclear technology and the need to enforce IAEA safeguards in developing nuclear technologies. It also underlines India's firmness in taking important decisions as well as the confidence to withstand peer pressure from home and abroad. The US must have taken cognizance of these qualities while deciding about entering into a nuclear deal of such magnitude with India.

Pakistan vis-à-vis India

The US President's visit to India projected a sense of comfort and mutual understanding between Bush and Manmohan Singh which was not dimmed by demonstration from some quarters. But his visit to Pakistan presented a different mood.

Pervez Musharraf is regarded in Washington as a close ally in the fight against terrorism. Notwithstanding, the divergence between the US and Pakistan on the key issues of democracy and proliferation was visible. Pakistan was viewed as a problem country—required for war on terror but also most prone to pass on nuclear secrets and material to al Qaeda and other groups.

Refusing to extend the historic Indo-US civil nuclear deal to Pakistan, President Bush clearly stated that India and Pakistan had different history—referring to Pakistan's clandestine nuclear proliferation to North Korea and India's unblemished non-proliferation credentials. Pakistan's contrast with India was obvious and heavily in India's favour. While Bush's visit to India was widely acclaimed and much celebrated, his visit to Pakistan was tense and censorious. There was also not much to encourage Pakistan to expect a more active US role on Kashmir as it invariably seeks. The clearly differentiating American approach to the two South Asian countries shows that India has pulled away into a different orbit and is not to be linked with Pakistan.

The US is not likely to find in India a military ally in the European or Japanese sense. But it will find it a country with largely similar views on global issues and common threat perceptions, a similar political and economic ethos despite the big asymmetry in their geographical positions.

Bonds of Democracy

Bush and his advisors have become aware that the hegemony they are seeking to establish could not be based on military power. After the Vietnam fiasco way back in the 1960s and the denouncement of almost the entire world for invasions of Afghanistan and Iraq in 2001 and 2003 respectively, there has been a progressive loss of the hegemony the US enjoyed since the end of the World War-II. The findings of the Pew Research Center's survey of global attitudes towards the US, released recently confirm this view.

According to the survey:

1. Ten out of seventeen countries surveyed had an overall unfavourable impression of the US.
2. Fifteen expressed a lack of confidence in Bush and all seventeen believed that the US made policy solely in its own interest.

A majority ranging from 53 per cent in Canada to 70 per cent in France in eighteen of the twenty-one countries believed that removing Saddam Hussein from power had made the world a more dangerous place. The only way the US administration has known of dealing with nations that confront its will is through unrelenting confrontation. But this policy has only brought disaster. Iraq is a case in example which was a staunch secular state run by Saddam Hussein before the US invasion and now shows a fusion of religious fanaticism and nationalism against the US

With these experiences and suffering after 9/11, the US has started believing that the promotion of democracy is the only means to ensure liberty. Bush in one of his speeches, states:

> The survival of liberty in our land increasingly depends on the success of liberty in other lands. The best hope for peace in our world is the expansion of freedom in the entire world. So, it is the policy of the US to seek and support the growth of democratic movements and institutions in every nation and culture with the ultimate goal of ending tyranny in our world.

This vision of a democratic peaceful world draws Bush to India like a magnet. His unstinted praise of India's multi-ethnic democracy reflects his realisation that the country is an example of the post-national global-State. India's proud self-image is of a country committed to peace, fairness and democracy. Bush feels that "India's leadership is needed in a world that is hungry for freedom."

Both India and the US recognise that cooperation among the countries will lay the foundation for a peaceful political structure in future. This shared political interest is as important as other interests—security, energy and economic growth. During one of his speeches in India, Bush referred to Woodrow Wilson's liberal internationalism, which envisaged a democratic world, less prone to war. Bush also spoke of restoration of democracy in Nepal and the release of Aung San Suu Kyi—the Burmese leader fighting for democracy. As of now the approach to fighting terrorism is by replacing hatred with hope using the force of human freedom. Democracy is a great bond that ties India and the US. The US President is excited most by India's democratic policy. In his Purana Qila speech, Bush declared, "India in the 21st century is a natural partner of the United States because we are brothers in the cause of human liberty."

Joining the US in the cause of spreading democracy as a means of resolving ethnic conflicts and fundamentalism globally will bring high responsibilities on India. The following factors must be considered carefully in this regard:

1. We must know what India will be required to do as a member of the Budapest-based International Centre for Democratic Transition following our agreement to cooperate in the promotion of democracy. This organisation which is an offshoot of the National Endowment of Democracy (NED) of the US, formed in 1983 to "support democratic institutions throughout the world", has a history of meddling in the internal affairs of other countries.
2. As "a responsible major power", India might be required to provide foot soldiers to tackle *jehad* because the US possesses the means but lacks manpower to deliver.

These factors reveal that we may be get caught in situations over which we have no control. So far, we are not a major target in the radar screen of international *jehadis*. One wrong step can attract the wrath of international terrorists towards India. In aligning with the US in the spread of democracy, India therefore, must draw its limits so that our internal security is not threatened.

Shared Philosophy

Both India and the US have shared the same philosophy. Bush acknowledged that Mahatma Gandhi moved generations of Americans with his non-violence. While Gandhi was himself influenced by the great American philosopher—Thoreau, Martin Luther King made the Gandhian thought of non-violence as "the only logical moral approach" to fight prejudices. These values made India and the US natural partners long ago. During the pre-independence period, India's freedom fighters were moved by American visionaries like Thomas Jefferson who stood against "every form of tyranny over the mind of man" and Abraham Lincoln who dedicated his life for the abolition of slavery.

Economic Cooperation between India and US

Bush's visit to India has chalked out a new order of relationship between India and the US, not only in the nuclear area but also in business and economic relations. Both the countries have agreed on a bevy of initiatives regarding economic cooperation. The US has shown a commitment to help India achieve the 10 per cent economic growth rate that Manmohan Singh thinks necessary to lift India from poverty. The initiatives announced by Bush government in this regard are:

Issuing of Technology License Exemption

Reversing years of a US policy of technical denial, Bush has agreed to develop a positive list of Indian firms and agencies which would be given automatic access to US know-how. The US Commerce Department has consented to create a license exemption for items that would otherwise require an export licence to end users in India enjoyed solely in civilian activities. The Indian officials have described the exemption as similar to the "green channel" in customs. The US will also benefit in increased hi-tech exports to India.

Agriculture Knowledge Initiative

The US has undertaken to launch a Rs. 1000 crore Agriculture Knowledge Initiative with a three-year commitment to link our universities, technical institutions and businesses to support agriculture education, joint research, and capacity building projects including those in the area of biotechnology. Bush and Singh see this as an opportunity to launch a second Green Revolution to service India's agriculture which has been showing low and volatile growth rates.

The Agriculture Knowledge Initiative may prove to be the harbinger of the second Green Revolution that India is seeking. It may be recalled that it was the great American Norman Borlang who was instrumental in launching the first Green Revolution in India through insect resistant high-yielding varieties of wheat and other foodgrain crops.

The first Green Revolution has left behind a legacy of increased irrigation and unrestrained fertilizer and pesticide usage-practices which being extremely harmful for the environment are no longer sustainable. The second Green Revolution requires a qualitative change in agricultural technology, like development of genetically modified crops. The Agriculture Knowledge Initiative may prove to be an important instrument of bringing the required technology change.

US-India CEO Forum

The US-India Chief Executive Officers' Forum was launched during the Indian Prime Minister's visit to Washington in July 2005. The Forum arose out of recognition that in today's world, trade and investment were driven by the private sector. The top executives of both the countries were involved to outline how to accelerate the Indo-US economic relationship.

The US-India Joint Statement on Trade issued during President Bush's visit to India expressed the determination and readiness of both the countries to contribute in global trade keeping the development dimension in focus. Both the countries welcomed the report of the Forum and agreed to work on its recommendations through economic dialogue. They endorsed the efforts of the US-India Trade Policy Forum to reduce barriers to trade and investment. The dialogue continued on various issues including further liberalization of investment restrictions, regulatory transparency, dispute settlement and reducing tariff and non-tariff barriers to trade.

In the high powered US-India CEO Forum co-chaired by Tata Sons Chairman Ratan Tata and William Harrison, Chairman and CEO of JP Morgan Chase, the SPC sectors including biotech and manufacturing were identified for strengthening Indo-US economic relations. The CEOs from the two countries mooted the creation of a US$ 5 billion fund to boost infrastructure development.

The Forum also endorsed the agreed work plan to promote bilateral trade in agriculture through agreements that keep open US market to Indian mangoes, recognize India as having authority to certify shipments of Indian products to US, meet USDA standards and provide for discussions on current regulations affecting trade in fresh fruits, vegetables, poultry, dairy, and almonds.

Innovative and Advanced Technologies

The United States and India are also working together to support the creation of innovative, dynamic and knowledge-based economies. Realising the importance of knowledge partnerships, the two countries announced the establishment of the US$ 30 million Bi-National Science and Technology Commission which the US and India will co-fund. It will generate collaborative partnerships in science and technology and promote industrial research and development.

The two governments agreed to work together to promote innovation, creativity and technological advancement through the Intellectual Property Rights (IPR) regime—by taking up capacity building activities, human resource development and public awareness programs. The US is funding IPR training programs to strengthen the enforcement and patent examination because the IPR regime is crucial for the promotion of a creative, technologically advanced economy.

India and the US agree that trade is essential for promoting global economic growth, development, freedom and prosperity. They shared the goal of completing the WTO Doha Development Agenda before the end of 2006 and agreed to work in partnership to help achieve this goal.

Cooperation in Civil Space

India and the US also agreed to continue to extend mutual cooperation in civil space, including space exploration, satellite navigation and earth science. The two countries entered into agreements that will permit the launch of US satellites containing US components by Indian Space Launch Vehicles, opening up new opportunities for commercial space cooperation between the two countries. India welcomed the inclusion of two US instruments in the Indian lunar mission Chandrayaan-1. The memorandum of understanding to be signed between ISRO and NASA would be a significant step forward in this direction.

Public Health

The United States and India are also cooperating to expand efforts to combat and prevent HIV/AIDS by harnessing resources, knowledge and expertise. The following steps have been taken in this regard since then:

1. The United States increased funding in the Financial Year 2005-06 for HIV/AIDS prevention, care and treatment program to US$ 29.3 million.
2. An Indo-US Corporate Sector Fund for HIV/AIDS has been established. This is a partnership among US and Indian businesses to fight AIDS. Six companies have already pledged a total of US$ 1.2 million to the Fund.
3. The US Food and Drug Administration have given approval to 13 genetic antiretroviral drugs produced by Indian pharmaceutical companies. These drugs can now be purchased as part of Bush's Emergency Plan for HIV/AIDS for use around the world.

The US and India have also agreed to expand bilateral efforts to control Bird Flu which has emerged as a major threat to the poultry industry. The initiative includes: reaching out to the private sector; developing regional communications strategies and planning in-region containment in case of outbreak of the epidemic; and initiate quick response exercise. India will host the International Partnership on Avian and Pandemic Influenza meeting in 2007. These initiatives will prove extremely helpful to India after the confirmed cases of Bird Flu in Nandurbar and Jalgaon in Maharashtra.

Divided Opinion

India is a democratic country where each individual group or party has the liberty to express their opinion on issues concerning India and Indian society. The majority feels that we must bandwagon with the US and gain the benefits that go with joining the most powerful. A large number of people, however, feel that India should balance against what they perceive to be a unilateral and imperial US.

Some people feel that the Indo-US nuclear agreement is an intrusion in India's strategic policy. There is an apprehension that the deal will lead us to the Non-Proliferation Treaty through the backdoor, cap our weapons potential and relegate India to a perpetual secondary status.

The US House of Representatives bill of June 26, 2006 states that the President would have to submit yearly reports to the Congress from January 2007 onwards, describing in considerable detail India's nuclear-related activities in the previous year and the extent to which the US has achieved its foreign policy objectives. Most of these objectives are such that have a direct bearing on India's defence strategies or foreign policies. They include: achieving a moratorium on the production of fissile material for nuclear explosion by India, China and Pakistan; adherence to Fissile Material Cut-off Treaty on which both the US and India will be signatories; India's full participation in Proliferation Security Initiative and its interdiction principles; India's conforming to the convention and dual-use weapons under Wassennaar Arrangements and chemical and biological weapons under the Australia Group Policies; and India's full compliance in the US policy on Iran's nuclear program. In the bill there is also a mandatory punitive clause, should India decide to test a nuclear device. The intention is clearly to control India's nuclear capabilities. It, therefore, appears that our foreign and strategic policies are being outsourced to the US through this deal.

The deal which started with India's growing energy needs is now being used as a bait to gain a hold over the country's strategic asset—its nuclear weapons program. It has been argued that the non-proliferation regime has been central to United States strategic interests. It has always taken a serious note of India's actions that stood against the United States' established order centred on a five-nation nuclear monopoly. It has presented the deal to bury the hatchet but is compelling India to agree to shut down Cirus—the research reactor that provided the plutonium for the 1974 test and now produces one-third of India's weapons-grade plutonium. The intention is to stop India from emerging as a full-fledged weapons state. India has to accept perpetual, legally irrevocable international inspections on 35 identified, mostly indigenous facilities. In the guise of the deal, India is being drawn into more stringent obligations than the NPT and without any right to exit. Homi Sethna, India's top nuclear scientist expressed similar views when he said that it would be better off signing the Non-Proliferation Treaty (NPT) which permits the exit of any signatory nation, rather than the nuclear deal with the US that will bind the country for perpetuity. Delivering a key-note address at the Forum of Integrated National Security (FINS) Sethna said:

> Therefore I prefer NPT...to signing the current deal with the US India is supposed to get only uranium for its nuclear program to expand. Simply for this, so much compromising is uncalled for. The Americans were out of the nuclear power reactor building business for the last 25 years. So where is the question of getting technology from them? Therefore, in order to end the current global sanctions on the nuclear program, we rather sign the NPT and it will give an escape route from going through all this trauma of separation and getting a special status agreement with IAEA under the additional protocol.

It is not easy to reach a consensus on the issue. To be allied with the US is not only to join what appears to be the winning side but also to balance against an increasingly powerful and allegedly dangerous neighbour, China, which invaded us in 1962 and is still holding a large Indian territory under Boundary Dispute. Another grand strategy suggested for India is to work with like-minded countries to promote a multipolar balance of power. Such a strategy, it is suggested, would be in line with India's non-alignment policy during the Cold War era. It can be argued in this regard that the countries within the group are governed by their economic compulsions, and their long-term allegiance to a single power or group cannot be taken for granted. While India's relations with Pakistan will always be under the microscopic eye, the differences exist with neighbours—Bangladesh, Myanmar, Nepal and Iran on many counts.

For many years, the United States and India were kept apart by the rivalries that divided the world. In the 21st century they are natural partners. Both these countries are linked by a deep commitment to freedom and democracy, a quest to expand prosperity and economic opportunity worldwide and to meet the common threats posed by terrorism, nuclear proliferation and environmental pollution. The strengthening of the US-India relationship will have a decisive and positive influence on the future international system as it evolves in this new century.

The Indo-US nuclear power deal is a historic breakthrough. It will enable both the countries to move forward towards their common objective of full civil energy cooperation. The partnership will enable India and the US to work together with other countries to pursue sustainable development and meet increasing energy requirements through cleaner, cost-effective and more efficient technologies. The US-India strategic partnership is rooted on shared values and is broad in nature and scope. The two countries will work together on global issues, expand economic freedom and ensure sufficient sources of clean energy. The nuclear deal has been made in mutual trust and a positive frame of mind. It is up to the Government of both the countries to nurture this trust and draw mutual benefits.

The detractors of the deal brought forward the following issues during the debate:

It will break the NPT and trigger arms race

The detractors of the Indo-US nuclear deal claim that the pact violates America's international obligations under the Non-Proliferation Treaty. According to them, India may not have to comply with the Treaty, but the US as a signatory to it, has a solemn responsibility to discourage proliferation by others and to refrain from assisting other states' nuclear weapons program in any manner. The deal would breach this central provision of the NPT.

The war cry of the non-proliferation lobby is that if India, a non-NPT signatory, gets to have both civilian and military nuclear arsenals, the NPT could begin to unravel and the nuclear rogue states will spread. The deal will open the door for people to say 'is non-proliferation program valid any longer?' and 'why is there different treatment for Iran and North Korea?' Some members echoed the views of China that India and the US should implement the nuclear deal within the framework of global non-proliferation mechanism. Seeking Congressional support to the agreement, Condoleezza Rice tried to clear the above apprehensions, saying, "This agreement is a path-breaking and really very important agreement because India is an anomaly in international politics. It is a country that never signed Non-Proliferation Treaty, did develop nuclear weapons, but did so of course, having never signed the NPT. It has been cut-off as a result of those decisions, from any kind of civil nuclear cooperation with the rest of the world." Setting forth the reasons why Washington wants to change this anomaly, Rice said, "First of all, because the US needs good strategic partners around the world who are democratic and India is a huge multi-ethnic, multi-religions democracy that is transparent and can play an extremely important role in the world as a strategic partner, a responsible strategic partner." Rice told lawmakers that there is a very big difference between the behaviour of India and that of Iran and North Korea, who callously signed the NPT and then did not remain in compliance with it. "India never signed the NPT," she said, "but we are asking India to adhere too many of the important elements of the guidelines that are making up the non-proliferation regime."

Even while seeing the Non-Proliferation Treaty as the cornerstone of its nuclear policy, the Bush administration is working on the rules that the Nuclear Suppliers Group has on certain standards of behaviour. Rice was firm in her belief that the deal would not trigger arms race saying that India's program has been 'restrained' over the years and that the political situation in the subcontinent has improved. She also believed that those who signed the NPT and then violated it and disregard it are really the ones who come under punishment from the international system. Rice told the members that the civilian nuclear deal will not lead to an arms race in the South Asian region, nor will it complicate American policy with respect to North Korea or Iran. She maintained that it was simply 'not credible' to compare India to North Korea or Iran. She pointed to the fact that the civilian energy initiative had the backing of the Head of the International Atomic Energy Agency, Mohammad ElBaradei and countries like Britain, France and Russia. The Secretary of State said that the nuclear deal does strengthen international nuclear non-proliferation regime.

The senior Democrat, Lantos felt that the real threat to non-proliferation did not come from democratic India, but from non-democratic states such as Iran and North Korea, and how the great powers decide to handle them.

India must stop fissile production

The separation plan puts fourteen of India's twenty-two reactors as civilian and brings them under safeguards. Some quarters feel that this allows too much freedom to India to pursue its nuclear weapons program and continue fissile production. Moreover, India's two developmental fast breeder reactors will remain unsafeguarded. With these facilities, India can produce enough nuclear weapons to significantly expand its nuclear arsenal. To quote Senator Richard Lugar, Chairman of SFRC whose endorsement and support is key to Congressional approval of the US-India civil nuclear agreement, "In pursuing a nuclear relationship with India, we must deal with some fundamental facts. India has not signed the Nuclear Non-proliferation Treaty; it has built and tested nuclear weapons; and it has declared its intention to continue its nuclear weapons programs and the production of fissile material. Although the US-India Civilian Nuclear Agreement would move India into a closer relationship with the International Atomic Energy Agency and would put more Indian reactors under safeguards, it would not prevent India from expanding its nuclear arsenal."

An editorial published in the April 2006 issue of *Arms Control Today* urged lawmakers not to approve the US-India nuclear deal unless India stopped production of fissile material for weapons purposes. It stated that the US diplomats have failed to secure any new commitments from India to restrain its nuclear weapons program as called for in a 1998 UN Security Council resolution. Daryl G. Kimball of the Arms Control Association (ACA) suggested a fissile raw material production cut-off that would stop the production that the five original nuclear weapons states are understood to observe, and also cap the growth of arsenals of India, Pakistan and Israel. Kimball is of the opinion that the controversial proposal for full civil nuclear assistance to India would inadvertently put the fissile material cut-off back in the spotlight. He added, "To leverage action on a Fissile Material Cut-off Treaty and begin to address the flawed proposal for nuclear assistance to India, Congress and Nuclear

Suppliers Group member state should refuse to relax nuclear trade rules with India until it halts production of fissile material for weapons purposes." Raising objection to what he termed as Bush's "controversial proposal," Kimball pointed out that the deal would allow India to exclude from safeguards all of its military production facilities plus as many as eight additional power reactors and existing spent nuclear fuel. India's fast breeder reactors which are particularly well suited for weapons-grade plutonium production would be kept off limits. Many Congressional members and NSG states believed the administration gave up too much and got few non-proliferation benefits. They were concerned that the proposal would implicitly endorse, if not indirectly assist the growth of India's nuclear arsenal.

Seeking to allay the above apprehensions, the US Embassy said it realized that India will continue to maintain its strategic program but believed that majority of its future growth will be on the civilian side. The Embassy also stated that Washington believed that India will not join NPT as a non-nuclear weapon state.

Restrain India from detonating a nuclear device

A controversy cropped up over the proposed US text of the new bilateral cooperation accord that warned that the agreement would cease to exist if India were to detonate a nuclear device. The US Assistant Secretary of State for South and Central Asian Affairs, Richard Boucher declared that as far as the US is concerned, India's public moratorium on further nuclear weapons testing is the linchpin of the US-India civilian nuclear agreement. In the draft law introduced in the Congress and elsewhere, the fact that the Indian decision to have a moratorium on nuclear testing is one of the bases on which we can undertake this civilian nuclear cooperation. Washington has given New Delhi a draft of the legislation it had presented to the US Congress incorporating a new suggestion — that the preliminary draft of the bilateral civilian nuclear cooperation agreement called for a cap on nuclear testing, warning that cooperation would be immediately suspended if India were to detonate a nuclear explosive device.

Immediately after the draft agreement containing this provision was handed over to the Foreign Secretary Shyam Saran by the US, when he visited the US towards the end of March 2006 for discussions on the deal, New Delhi came to know of the provision. The External Affairs Ministry spokesman Navtej Sarna said, "In preliminary discussions on these elements, India has already conveyed to the US that such a provision has no place in the proposed bilateral agreement and that India is bound only by what is contained in the July 18 Joint Statement, that is, continuing its commitment to a unilateral moratorium on nuclear testing." The Indian circles reacted sharply and categorically stated that such substantial changes or revisions were not acceptable to India. The deal was about India's civilian nuclear programme, the sources said, and the strategic program cannot be part of a bilateral treaty. The bilateral agreement will be prepared alongside the passage of the draft legislation to amend the US Atomic Energy Act's Article 123 in the US Congress. The US had shared with India a preliminary draft agreement on the Indo-US civil nuclear cooperation under Article 123 of the US Atomic Energy Act.

The Foreign Secretary Shyam Saran said he hoped that the new US legislation to implement the agreement will be framed within already agreed parameters. "What we have at this point of time is an extremely carefully delicately balanced understanding. Whatever legislation that is passed must remain within those parameters", he said. Owing to the new provision, some internal sources have alleged that this is Washington's *modus operandi* to commit India to the Comprehensive Test Ban Treaty (CTBT) through the backdoor.

Condoleezza Rice sought to allay the fears of Senators that by signing on to the changes in the Atomic Energy Act of 1954 to formalize the civilian nuclear deal, the United States is not encouraging an arms race in the region. "On the question of India's nuclear weapons program," she said, "first of all, the Indian program we believe, just in terms of what India's incentives or disincentives are to grow its nuclear programs, its strategic program, are more related to the political-military conditions in the region, than to any quantity of available nuclear material." She emphasized that India's program has been restrained over the years; moreover, the region is one in which the political situation has improved and we hope it is going to continue to improve. She further said, "I think the assessment that we have, that India has some 50,000 — give and take — tons of uranium available to it in its reserves and it would need a very small percentage of that on the military nuclear side."

The US Assistant Secretary of State, Richard Boucher said that India has a moratorium on nuclear testing and has made a public commitment based on its own decision to continue that moratorium. He added that it was not surprising to find that encoded in various formats in documents and statements. Asked if there was any pressure by the US to cajole India into making the commitment contained in the US text of the bilateral agreement, now rejected by India, Boucher reiterated that the Indian decision to have moratorium on nuclear testing is one of the bases on which the civil nuclear cooperation can be undertaken. Boucher has acknowledged that the position on the text is not the same, but we have to talk about it which is normal part of diplomatic life, "It is not something complicated — you have to negotiate the agreement. It's going to be something that we have to negotiate, we have to discuss. We are not going to start posturing based on positions ascribed to us or pieces of paper that may have leaked. We look forward to hearing from the Indian government and sitting down with them to negotiate," said Boucher.

Back home, the additional provision was severely criticized. Former Prime Minister Atal Behari Vajpayee said that the obligations under the bill are far more stringent than those under the Comprehensive Test Ban Treaty. The proposed bill when passed, will convert a voluntary moratorium on further tests by India into a legally binding commitment for all times to come without any possibility of withdrawal under special circumstances, as provided for in the CTBT.

Prime Minister Manmohan Singh has ruled out placing all of India's nuclear reactors under safeguards and reaffirmed commitment on unilateral moratorium. Given the circumstances, India needs a strategic nuclear weapons program: "In our neighbourhood, we have China, which is a nuclear power and

Pakistan that has developed its weapons through clandestine proliferation". Singh said, adding that he could not imagine the circumstances that would require India to resume its nuclear testing which many in India have said was the country's sovereign right. The Indian scientists have told the Prime Minister that they don't need further nuclear tests. But as for the distant future, a prediction cannot be made. India's commitment is to continue its unilateral moratorium.

Condoleezza Rice, who has presented India's case persuasively, is of the opinion that owing to the political-military conditions prevailing in the region, India needs its strategic program. She feels India would never accept a unilateral freeze or cap on its nuclear arsenal, though some Congress members have suggested that the US should have negotiated that. The plans and policies of India take into account regional realities and no one can credibly assert that India would accept what would amount to an arms control agreement unilaterally that did not include other key countries, mainly China and Pakistan. The unilateral moratorium about which India has made a public commitment is no less important than that of the P5 which are the original weapons states—the US, Russia, and the UK, France and China have decided not to test a nuclear weapon, but they have not signed any agreement or treaty in this regard.

India should define minimum nuclear deterrent

Amid efforts by the Bush administration to push the Indo-US civil nuclear deal through the Congress, Richard Boucher created another controversy by asking India to "further define its credible minimum nuclear deterrent," saying it was absolutely necessary for alleviating tensions in Asia. He said that it has long been the position of the US to think that all the parties in the region need to consider strategic stability. The US has welcomed the discussions that the Indians and Pakistanis have had on the subject. The US also had its own discussions with each of the parties on the questions of strategic stability in the region. This issue is "worth pursuing and important to talk about," said Richard Boucher.

The US Assistant Secretary of State for South Asia said that New Delhi and Islamabad should work out mutual understanding to build confidence in both conventional and nuclear areas. "As in the past, we continue to look to India for leadership in stabilising nuclear and defence relations with its neighbours," Boucher said. He added that the previous US governments have "pushed for India to further defines its minimum credible deterrent in the nuclear field and we continue that today." He further said that Washington understood the complexity of this task having spent 40 years in discussions with the erstwhile Soviet Union over the nuclear programs of the two countries. The discussions are "complicated by China's intentions and by Iran's energetic pursuit of technologies that underlie nuclear weapons," said Boucher.

Following reports of Boucher's remarks, the Indian Foreign Secretary Shyam Saran asserted that India has no obligation to define its credible minimum nuclear deterrent to anybody, saying, "What our credible minimum deterrent would be is really for India to decide." He continued that India had on various occasions pointed out to the US that there is no responsibility on the part of India to declare what its minimum deterrent is. Saran said, "We have a strategic dialogue with the US where we have agreed to exchange views on our respective nuclear doctrines as well as issues like missile defence." On Bush administration's contention that it was pushing India and Pakistan for moratorium on missile tests, Saran said that New Delhi's position was that it would work with Washington in the conference on disarmament in Geneva on a multilateral Fissile Material Cut-off Treaty.

The US is pushing for an Asian moratorium on nuclear weapons production in view of the relationship between India, Pakistan and other countries of the region. To use the words of Condoleezza Rice: "We would obviously like to see, in the relationship between India, Pakistan and others, a regional moratorium on fissile material production. We have made it very clear that we would encourage that; we would encourage India and Pakistan to look at their nuclear relationship and the way that in some earlier days people were concerned about safety and security between the US and the Soviet arsenals". To a question by Senator Kerry, Rice explained that earlier we could not achieve a restraint unilaterally by any one state. But the idea that has been pursued in new arrangements and discussions is not just absolute levels but also safety, security and confidence-building measures which are so important.

Is India giving military training to Iran?

As mentioned earlier, Iran, in utter disregard of NPT terms to which it is a signatory, has declared to pursue a nuclear weapons program—an act which has irked the US and its allies which have referred it to the UN Security Council to take suitable action against Iran to deter it from making nuclear weapons.

Any positive gesture by India towards Iran is seen with suspicion and blown out of proportion. Many false stories are added to reality. According to Senator Barbara Boxer, two Iranian warships were docked in Kochi as part of a training program under a 3-year old military cooperation agreement India has with Tehran. She went on to say that this was not in the best interest of America when they were going to do this extraordinary special deal. At the SFRC hearing, Boxer stated that some lawmakers wanted India to end any such relationship with Iran as a precondition to the Indo-US civilian nuclear deal.

Condoleezza Rice said that the Defence News report on a military to military relationship between Iran and India on which Senator Boxer made her statement was incorrect. "There have been Iranian ship port calls in India. The assertion that they train Iranian sailors is not right", she said. She also mentioned that the US has made very clear to India its concerns about their relationship with Iran, about the pipeline and about their initial vote in IAEA. However, the Secretary of State's replies did not seem to satisfy Boxer who said that her remarks left a 'big hollow' and that the nuclear deal needed more 'checks and balances'.

Tom Lantos, the top Democrat in the HIRC, whose support is considered crucial to get the deal through Congress, said that India's military links with Iran could hinder the work of approving the Indo-US nuclear deal. He also construed the report of two Iranian ships making a port call in Kochi, as India training Iranian forces. Lantos' spokeswoman told a wire service: "Congressman Lantos pointed out that episodes of conflict in relations between US and India, such as India's early wavering in its commitment to refer Iran to the UN Security Council and more recent concerns raised about Iranian troops receiving training from India will only undermine Congressional support for the deal."

The Indian officials denied that there was any training program with Iranians and said that the port call was a standard goodwill visit. Foreign Secretary Shyam Saran stated that he had alleviated the latest misplaced Iran-India obsession of Congressman Tom Lantos. In a press conference of the Indian Embassy following his three-day meetings with senior administration officials, Saran said, "The concern expressed was about a ship to one of the southern India ports and somehow, somebody had given the impression that India is engaged in training the Iranian navy or there were some exercises that took place, which is completely misleading.

It is quite obvious that the reports of India training the Iranian navy were misconceived. The presence of Iranian vessels in Indian ports was nothing more than ship visits involving cadets. This was a limited type of event and does not in any manner suggest Indian training or Indian contribution to Iranian military capabilities. Iranian naval ships visit a number of countries which have close relations with the US A minor and a normal event of ship visits to its port should not call into question India's commitment to non-proliferation. It should be remembered that India voted to report Iran's safeguards agreements violations to the UN Security Council and has a very responsible record as an international actor.

The Iran issue came to haunt the deal when Democratic lawmaker, Tom Lantos, took exception to India's remarks about lending support to a statement by Non-Aligned Movement (NAM) that all countries including Iran had a right to nuclear research and production of energy. Lantos said that the statement issued by NAM was diametrically opposed to the approach taken by the five permanent members of the UN Security Council. Calling it a negative phenomenon, he warned that if India wants the nuclear deal to get through and become a reality, such things should not be repeated. He added that a blanket endorsement of

NAM statements regarding Iran could be a deal breaker and have to be carefully avoided. The Indo-US nuclear deal called for responsibility along political statements as against "signing mass statements of 117 countries that couldn't care less about the US-India nuclear agreement except perhaps that some of them wanting to torpedo it."

Indo-Iran Oil Pipeline

India has oil and gas relationship with Iran. India and Iran signed a Memorandum of Understanding (MoU) in 1993 to get US$ 6 billion (Rs. 28,200 crore) pipeline project off the ground. Under this project, gas will be transported from Assuliyeh fields in southern Iran to India via land and deep-sea routes. The pipeline which will traverse 707 km of Pakistan territory makes an economic sense to Pakistan as the country would earn between US$ 200-400 million as transit fee. The project will not only alleviate energy problem in India but also emerge as an enduring symbol of peace in the subcontinent.

Some members of the Congress do not consider India's dependence on Iran for supply of natural gas as a positive sign and are seeking amendments to the Atomic Energy Act, 1954. Condoleezza Rice stressed before the lawmakers of the SFRC that even if the amendment goes through, the administration cannot give any guarantee that India's reliance on Iranian energy will go away or that the pipeline will not be built.

India is not the only country with an oil and gas relationship with Iran. One of the USA's closest allies, e.g. Japan have an oil and gas relationship with Iran. Italy is Iran's largest trading partner. Many European countries have trade relations with Iran. If India acquires access to civil nuclear energy, it does not mean that it will forgo other relationships. It may give India a better option for a more reliable energy supply, but breaking the energy association between India and Iran could not be accepted as the rationale behind the Indo-US nuclear deal. Bush himself had remarked in a joint news conference, "Our beef with Iran is not the pipeline; our beef with Iran is in fact they want to develop a nuclear weapon...." Reliable energy supply is a problem for countries like India that are growing at 8 per cent. They need energy supply and are looking for it anywhere they can. Some circles also believe that by voting in favour of referring Iran's nuclear weapons program to the UN Security Council, India ran a great risk of its pipeline project being shelved by Iran. The Congress appreciated India's spirit of siding with the international community against nuclear non-proliferation risking the pipeline project that would fulfill its energy needs and boost its economy.

Pakistan has been trying hard to spoil the Indo-US nuclear deal ever since President Bush visited India and Pakistan in March 2006, although it stated initially that its problems were not India-centric. Islamabad has said that a civilian nuclear energy deal between India and the US would destroy international agreements to stop the spread of nuclear weapons. Pakistan's Foreign Minister Khurshid Mehmood Kasuri said that the United States' decision to give nuclear technology to India—which likes Pakistan has a military nuclear program—would encourage other nations to follow suit. "The whole Nuclear Non-Proliferation Treaty will unravel. It is only a matter of time before other countries will act in the same way," Kasuri said. He added that nuclear weapons are currency of power and many countries would like to use it. If this deal goes through, the NPT will be finished. "It is not just Iran and North Korea. Brazil, Argentina and Pakistan will think differently," he continued to say.

Stepping up its campaign against the Indo-US nuclear deal, Islamabad has sent a letter to all NSG members, urging them not to make an exception for India. This has been followed up with persuasive diplomacy in various world capitals against the agreement. The letter states that the deal with India would adversely affect the strategic stability and security environment of the region. This was re-emphasized by Khurshid when he visited Berlin in the wake of Manmohan Singh's visit to Germany. Despite Washington's continued rejections of its demand for parity in civil nuclear ties, Pakistan claimed that it qualified for an arrangement similar to the Indo-US nuclear deal, pleading that there still was time to rectify the situation. Prime Minister Shaukat Aziz asked the US to adopt 'a package approach' for India and Pakistan, saying that it would help prevent a nuclear arms race and promote restraint while ensuring that the legitimate needs of both the countries for power generation are met.

The Pakistan's letter to NSG members weighed heavily against the India agreement, stating that the NSG should instead consider a package deal which would include Pakistan. Kasuri also briefed the Dutch Foreign Minister on the latter's visit to Islamabad: "Pakistan merits the support of the international community, including the Nuclear Suppliers Group to acquire nuclear technology for peaceful purposes.

Pakistan, in the past had proposed a nuclear restraint regime to India, which did not show much interest, saying that its nuclear program was not Pakistan-centric.

Shaukat Aziz further pleaded his case by saying that Pakistan was determined to prevent terrorists and extremists from acquiring weapons of mass destruction or know-how. He claimed a major role for Islamabad in dismantling its former top scientist A.Q. Khan's network of international nuclear black market.

Pakistan's envoy to the US has claimed that Islamabad's criticism of the US-India deal does not amount to interference. He said, "We are not interfering, we are merely putting on the table that we also have an energy requirement and that we would very much like that the US has a package approach to South Asia, so that Pakistan is not left out."

Despite all these claims, it is an open secret that Pakistan is trying hard to scuttle the Indo-US nuclear deal due to sheer rivalry if nothing else. Special efforts are being made to exhort the Government of China to oppose this agreement at the Nuclear Suppliers Group just as it had in the past tried to sabotage India's claim for permanent membership of the UN Security Council when the issue of reforms of the United Nations came up. The US has already rejected its demands for a similar deal or a package deal and for right reasons. Pakistan's nuclear proliferation, support to terrorism and suppression of democracy are too well-known. International community including the Nuclear Suppliers Group fully understands Pakistan's intentions. The US Congress would do well not succumb to pressure from these quarters.

NRI's Role in Indo-US Nuclear Deal

The Indian American community is one of the wealthiest and best-educated minorities in the country. According to a

Washington daily, it played a pivotal role in pushing forward the Indo-US nuclear deal. New Delhi gave a clarion call to Indian Americans with political connections to reach Washington when US Congress reconvened in the last week of April, 2006, and meet their Senators and Congressmen to firm up support for the bill on Indo-US nuclear deal. The core group of 20 Indian Americans made a splash by giving a full page ad in *The Washington Post* costing upwards of one hundred thousand dollars, on why Congress must approve the pact. They raised two and a half million dollars for this cause. The US-India Political Action Committee — a formation having some clout in the Capitol Hill — brought together 20-odd Senators and Representatives for an event to turn the spotlight on the nuclear deal.

Republican Senator John Cornyn from Texas took initiative to form the Friends of India Caucus at the behest of a Dallas-based influential NRI—Ashok Mago. The latter remained in touch with a dozen Congressmen from Texas, who were willing to co-sponsor the bill in the House of Representatives. The pro-India groups believed that the supportive announcements made by Senator Joseph Biden and John Kerry would make many skeptics to revise their stand.

Science and Technology Minister Kapil Sibal who visited Washington for a series of meetings with Senior Bush administration officials and US lawmakers said that the India American community's role was imperative to persuade Congress to approve Indo-US civil nuclear agreement. Addressing the Overseas National Congress in Washington, he said that they had a very important role to play by convincing the American people as to how important this relationship was to the rest of the world.

The role of the Indian American community attracted a lot of attention within Capitol Hill as well as from official Indian visitors who acknowledged that much depended on the community which is no longer seen as a political polygamy. The Indian Americans have been the fastest-growing ethnic group since the 1990s and remained one of the largest sources of legal immigration to the United States. Indian-American entrepreneurs own nearly 20 per cent of all Silicon Valley high-tech start-ups and an estimated 55 per cent of all US motels are owned by Americans of South Asian ancestry. In 2000, one out of every nine Indian-Americans was a millionaire. Nearly 60 per cent of Indian-Americans over 25 have graduated from college. Politically, this has meant that the Congressional India Caucus, which began in 1992 with eight members, now has more than 180 members—among the largest on Capitol Hill — a fact that helped in getting the deal through.

As the Bush administration was seeking Congress support for the Indo-US nuclear deal, several lawmakers asked the Indian-American community to launch a massive effort to get the packet approved. Frank Pallone, the founder of the Congressional Caucus on India and Indian-Americans, asked the Indian-American community to set up a 'war room' and launch a massive effort to get the draft legislation on the deal through Congress.

Despite opposition from some members, the Indo-US nuclear deal is considered by many others to be in the US interest. Some of them recounted the benefits during the SFRC debate.

In her speech before the House International Relations Committee, Secretary of State Condoleezza Rice said that American exports to India have doubled in only past four years. India is a rising global power and can be a pillar of stability in a rapidly changing Asia—it is a natural partner for the United States. In her speech before that Senate Foreign Relations Committee, Rice said that the initiative would benefit that environment.

Nuclear energy is clean energy. Providing India with an environmentally friendly energy source is an important goal of the deal. India's carbon emission increased 61 per cent between 1990 and 2001, next only to China. America's own energy problems will be exacerbated if it does not forge energy partnership with India, China and other nations experiencing rapid economic growth. The United States has an interest in expanding energy operation with India to develop new technologies, cushion supply disruptions and prepare for the declining global fossil fuel reserves.

The initiative will enhance energy security. India is a nation of over a billion people. Its economy is growing at approximately 8 per cent each year. It has a massive and growing requirement for energy which is expected to double by the year 2025. It is now the sixth largest consumer of energy in the world. Diversifying India's energy sector will help it meet its energy needs and also ease its dependence on hydrocarbons and the unstable sources of energy like oil, gas, coal and countries like Iran. This will be good for the United States as well as for India.

Senator Joseph R. Biden, the ranking Democrat on the SFRC, also suggested that helping India to meet its energy needs will be in the interest of the United States. He pointed out to the fact that in the 1960s the US helped bring the Green Revolution in India which boosted foodgrains production in India. "That was good for India and that was good for Americans' business. Now India faces a burgeoning need for energy, and so too, I believe, presents an opportunity for the US," says Biden. He views the competition created by the phenomenal growth of India and China as a real opportunity for the United States. Richar Lugar, a Republican Senator also said that the SFRC is cognizant of the fact that a closer relationship with India is very valuable for the United States: "I believe that we will find little argument in Congress with the general premise that the national security and economic future of the United States would be enhanced by a strong and enduring partnership with India," he said.

The initiative will create opportunities for American jobs. Nuclear cooperation will provide a new market for American nuclear firms as well as assist India's economic growth. The initiative could add as many as five thousand new direct jobs and about fifteen thousand indirect jobs as America engages itself in nuclear commerce with India. By helping India's economy to grow, America will help its own.

The larger bilateral relationship is being viewed through the prism of Indo-US nuclear deal. The HIRC sources say that if the law doesn't get passed, it will negatively impact bilateral relationships. Lantos asked the lawmakers to view all the benefits in the still larger and greater context of how this initiative elevates the US-India relationship to a new strategic level.

OPINION OF OTHER COUNTRIES ON INDO-US NUCLEAR DEAL

China

China remains non-committal on backing the Indo-US nuclear deal. It feels that the international community is working on enhancing the authority and effectiveness of the international non-proliferation regime. China hopes that the cooperation of relevant countries can contribute to these efforts. A Chinese spokesperson said that the growing Indo-US relations would be helpful for regional stability but insisted that the two countries should implement the historic deal within the framework of global non-proliferation mechanism.

China's stand on the Indo-US nuclear agreement could be crucial as there should be consensus within the NSG members to amend its rules to clear the way for the implementation of the deal. Earlier, China, a member of the 45-nation Nuclear Suppliers Group, had critically questioned the US efforts to push through the nuclear deal at a meeting of the NSG in Vienna.

The Chinese Foreign Ministry sources said that Beijing was of the view that the countries can develop nuclear cooperation for peaceful purposes while conforming to the regulations of the international non-proliferation regime.

Two major factors may cause China to work out diplomacy against the Indo-US nuclear deal: The first is its apprehension that a closer relationship between India and the US, cemented by the deal will weaken its position in Asia. If India is developed into a world power through US help, China stands to suffer. With sufficient energy supply and latest technology provided by America, India might become a hub of manufacturing electronic goods and capture bulk of the trade which is currently flowing to China. The second factor is that China and Pakistan have been partners in nuclear proliferation.

Russia

India has important strategic and economic relations with Russia. In fact, our relations with Russia have the strength of tradition and content of mutual cooperation. Recognizing India's energy needs, Russia called for making an exception for the country in the Nuclear Non-Proliferation Treaty to give it access to civilian nuclear technology. Anatoly Antonov, Director of Russia's Foreign Ministry's Security and Disarmament Department said: "We cannot ignore India's energy requirements. It is a rapidly developing country with good non-proliferation record. We should probably make an exception in this case without adopting new norms that may erode the non-proliferation regime." Antonov opined that NPT is an important element of international security and stability. However, it must be used to deal with new challenges and threats to non-proliferation regime.

Russia has played a significant role in India's establishing nuclear reactors to harness nuclear energy. It has been supplying fuel for our Tarapur plant. India has received the first part of a promised supply of 60 MT of enriched uranium fuel from Russia for two units of Tarapur Atomic Power Plants in the first week of April 2006. The first consignment of about 25 MT of uranium which arrived from Russia at the Nuclear Fuel Complex of the Department of Atomic Energy was promptly delivered to Nuclear Power Corporation of India Ltd. The fuel supply to Units I and II of the US-built reactors lasted for 8 months in one unit and 18 months at the other. The Russian Prime Minister said that the supply was within the international framework and Russia had informed the Nuclear Suppliers' Group about it. However, Washington expressed reservations to the move saying such a step should have been taken only after India fulfils its obligations under the Indo-US civil nuclear deal.

Apart from its tilt towards India because of decades of friendly relations, Russia plays an important part in solving global problems even in the unipolar world. It is using its influence to find out a mutually acceptable solution to Iran imbroglio

UK

India has historical relations with the UK Both the countries have a mutual desire to deepen and diversify bilateral relations. UK warmly welcomed the Indo-US civil nuclear cooperation initiative. It indicated that on the basis of Joint Statement, it was "ready to discuss with our international partners the basis for the cooperation in civil nuclear matters with India."

France

France is one of the countries that coordinated diplomatic moves at the NSG to make an exemption for India. In fact, India banked on French support to deliver the European Nations' support on the India exemption issue.

For France, piloting the India deal was important because it felt that it was necessary to muster support to make a nuclear exemption for India. The French officials were of the view that since India had already announced its separation plan, the India debate should continue as a positive gesture and it should be given emergency fuel for Tarapur. France had not incorporated a specific termination clause with India in the bilateral nuclear cooperation pact, signed during President Chirac's visit to India in February 2006. However, the French officials hold that any testing by India would have a very negative impact and could jeopardise the NSG's acceptance of the deal. Yet, France remained a key supporter of India's ambitions to emerge from decades of nuclear outcast status.

Australia

The Australian Prime Minister John Howard has stated that there were a lot of good things about the Indo-US nuclear deal in particular the fact that for the first time India's civil nuclear facilities will come under international inspections. However, he refused that Australia will be selling nuclear fuel to India. "We do have a long-standing policy of selling uranium only to countries that are part of the NPT regime...." Howard said.

Prime Minister Manmohan Singh hopes that Australia, as a member of the Nuclear Suppliers' Group, would endorse what India and America have worked out — an arrangement that would help the cause of nuclear non-proliferation. He reminded that India has an impeccable record of not entering into any unauthorized arms proliferation.

Australia, with 29 per cent of the world's medium cost uranium reserves, operates three mines and is a big exporter of uranium to non-nuclear weapons states and the NPT signatories. India does not fit into either category. For nuclear weapons states, Australian uranium must be covered under a safeguards agreement with the International Atomic Energy Agency.

John Howard, during his visit to India in March 2006 had detailed discussion with his Indian counterpart. Both the countries agreed that a group of officials will discuss a possible supply of uranium to India.

There have been positive signals from Australia about the Indo-US nuclear deal. The Australia's Minister for Foreign Affairs Alexander Downer stated that some of the proposals put forward by India, even if they don't amount to signing the NPT but only adhering to the transparency of the regime, may not be optimal but it is a step in the right direction.

Although India and Australia share a common colonial history and a common language, yet their strategic interest have rarely converged. They also lack high-level approval for joint military exercises, military and technical cooperation and regular service to service contacts and intelligence cooperation.

A report on India by the Australian Strategic Policy Institute in Canberra revealed that the Howard administration continues to treat terrorism in India more as a "secessionist and ethnic conflict rather than part of a so-called *jehadist* and global Islamic struggle." Australia was once called by Howard as US "deputy" in the Asia Pacific region, but it departs from Washington where it is in its own interest to do so. While the US is focusing on using India as a possible means of containing China which it views as a strategic threat, Australia is less inclined to look at India from the same angle.

European Union

The European Union is of the opinion that the India-US nuclear issue should address the basic issue of non-proliferation. Andris Piebalgs, the European Commissioner for Energy, said on his visit to New Delhi, "We are looking with interest at the debate on the India-US nuclear deal in the US Congress. We want the basic issue of non-proliferation answered." He added however that, "we should be extremely ambitious about nuclear fusion." Till we get a sustainable answer to energy security, coal has an important potential for supplying energy resources. But a lot of research and development is necessary in the coal sector so that the disadvantage in the form of carbon dioxide emissions is mitigated. Energy efficiency, renewable energies, clean conversion technologies and fusion energy are therefore extremely important.

Germany

Initially, Germany was a non-believer in the Indo-US civil nuclear cooperation. It was not in favour of making an exemption for India at the NSG. Thanks to Indian diplomacy, particularly to Prime Minister Manmohan Singh who visited Germany in April 2006, Germany became more open on the issue and supported the deal.

Scandinavian Countries

Norway, Sweden, Denmark, Iceland, Finland and Faroe Islands comprise Scandinavian countries. They have their non-proliferation agenda and are likely to remain the last holdouts at the NSG discussions. They expressed substantial doubts about the Indo-US nuclear deal for fear of inadvertent damage to the nuclear non-proliferation regime.

New Agenda Coalition

Group, including countries like Brazil, Egypt, Ireland, Mexico, New Zealand, Slovenia, South Africa and Sweden formed a New Agenda Coalition which raised "NPT concerns"—asking for fullscope safeguards from India, in line with the 1995 declaration during the NPT extensions.

Cyprus

Cyprus, a member of the Nuclear Suppliers Group, backed the Indo-US civil nuclear deal lending a boost to efforts to achieve a mandatory endorsement of the agreement by the US nation world body. As a member of the NSG, Cyprus welcomed the Indo-US civil nuclear cooperation declared on March 2 during the visit of President George W. Bush. Cypriot President Tassos Padadopoulos stated that such cooperation would be helpful in addressing concerns relating to global energy security and environmental protection.

International Atomic Energy Agency

It is pertinent to remember that IAEA Director General, Mohamed ElBaradei had welcomed the announcement of nuclear cooperation agreement saying that it was an important step towards satisfying India's growing need for energy, including nuclear technology and fuel as an engine for development. Later, the IAEA Director General gave the deal a shot in the arm by giving some compelling arguments in its support. He said that it would be illogical to deny civil nuclear technology to India—a country that has not violated any legal commitment and never encouraged proliferation of nuclear weapons.

ElBaradei commented that the US has come to treat India as a valued partner and a trusted contributor to international peace and security. It is, therefore, difficult to understand "the logic that would continue to carve out civil nuclear energy as the single area of non-cooperation." Setting forth his views in *The Washington Post* Op-Ed piece, the IAEA Chief termed the deal as a creative break with the past, making India a part of international effort to combat nuclear terrorism and rid the world of nuclear weapons.

Replying some critics, ElBaradei clarified that there was no such thing as a 'legitimate' or 'illegitimate' nuclear weapons state. The fact that five states, i.e. the US, UK, Russia, France and China, are recognized in the Non-Proliferation Treaty as holders of the nuclear weapons was regarded as a matter of transition. The Treaty does not in any sense confer permanent status on those states as nuclear weapons holders. He said that it was also important to consider the implications of denying peaceful nuclear energy to India—a country with one-sixth of world's population and an enormous energy demand.

US NON-PROLIFERATION LAWS AND THE NUCLEAR DEAL

The US undertook an obligation to "seek agreement from the Congress to adjust the existing US laws and policies to achieve full civilian nuclear energy cooperation." Therefore, the historic Indo-US nuclear agreement should, *inter alia*, bring some changes in the legal regime governing nuclear proliferation in the United States.

The primary legislation involved in the initiative is the Atomic Energy Act, 1954. A civil nuclear cooperation between the two countries took place in the 1950s and 1960s. Following a nuclear test conducted by India in 1974, the US amended this Act by the

Nuclear Non-Proliferation Act (NNPA) in 1978. The main condition imposed by this amending legislation was that it barred nuclear exports to non-nuclear weapon countries that did not sign the so-called "fullscope safeguard agreement" with the International Atomic Energy Agency. This blocked fuel supplies to the Tarapur Reactors which, though safeguarded, were barred from receiving fuel supplies because India's entire nuclear program was not under safeguards subject to international inspections.

The Section 123 of the Atomic Energy Act states that an agreement of cooperation must exist between the US and the importing country as a precondition for any significant nuclear cooperation. The Section further specifies that there are nine criteria that such an agreement has to fulfill. Out of these, the following three are relevant for India:

1. IAEA safeguards have to be maintained by non-nuclear weapons states;
2. Safeguards continue in perpetuity, irrespective of termination or suspension of the agreement; and
3. There should be no enriching or reprocessing of nuclear fuel without prior approval.

If an agreement falls short of these criteria, the President can grant exemption—if imposition of this requirement would be "seriously prejudicial to US non-proliferation objectives or otherwise jeopardise the common defence and security." However, the Export Administration Amendment Act, 1985 brought an amendment which introduced a further requirement that the Presidential exemption would only be effective if both chambers of Congress adopt a joint resolution stating that it favors such an agreement.

Section 129 provides for stopping nuclear exports to non-nuclear weapon states that have indulged in nuclear proliferation activities after March 10, 1978. India falls under the provisions of this Section, having conducted its nuclear test series in 1998. However, the President has again been empowered to waive this termination on the basis of Section 123. This determination must be submitted to Congress from where it would be referred to the Senate Foreign Relations Committee and the House

International Relations Committee for a 60 days' continuous session. Moreover, the President is required to report annually to Congress under Section 601 of NNPA, on federal efforts to prevent proliferation.

The other option that is being resorted to in this case is to bring about amendments in the IAEA and the NNPA to relax the criteria for cooperation and make the process of approval from Congress of a Presidential determination less stringent. It is apprehended that such amendment would bring about a general relaxation in non-proliferation rules and regulations and may result in similar agreements being signed by the administration with countries like Pakistan and Israel. The best option would therefore be to enact another law which would state that the relevant provisions of the Atomic Energy Act and the Nuclear Non-Proliferation Act would not apply to India, while providing for adequate safeguards at the same time.[20]

The historic agreement on civil nuclear cooperation aims to address India's surging energy needs for its growing economy. This will also ease the burden on other countries as the world's energy needs continue to rise:

1. The US and India have agreed to pursue civil nuclear cooperation to allow India to cooperate and trade in this key area.
2. India has agreed to take steps that will bring it into the international non-proliferation mainstream, including placing its civilian nuclear facilities and programs under IAEA safeguards and adhering to the guidelines of the Nuclear Suppliers Group and the Missile Technology Control Regime.[21]

On 26 June 2006, the US House International Relations Committee passed a Bill H.R. 5682 titled: "United States and India Nuclear Cooperation Promotion Act of 2006" with a strong majority of 37-5. Later the US House of Representatives passed the Bill with an overwhelming majority of 359-68 on 26 July 2006. Similarly, US Senate Foreign Relations Committee approved by a vote of 16-2 its version of the Bill S.3709 entitled the "United States and India Peaceful Atomic Energy Cooperation Act" on June 29, 2006. On 16 November 2006, the US Senate in its lame duck session passed the Bill by an overwhelming majority of 85-12.

The nuclear understanding has been discussed with the US side in several meetings since July 18, 2005. Notable meetings, apart from the meetings referred elsewhere in the note, *inter alia,* include:

- Meeting between Prime Minister and President Bush in New York on September 25, 2005.
- Meeting between President Bush and Prime Minister Manmohan Singh on March 2, 2006 in New Delhi.
- Meeting between Foreign Secretary Shyam Saran and US Under Secretary Burns in Washington DC in April 2006.
- Meeting between Foreign Secretary and US Under Secretary Burns in London on May 23, 2006.
- Meeting between Prime Minister and President Bush in St. Petersburg on July 17, 2006.
- Meeting between Foreign Secretary and US Under Secretary Burns in Paris in July 2006.
- Meeting between Foreign Secretary and US Under Secretary Burns in New York in September 2006.
- Meeting between Raksha Mantri Pranab Mukherji and US Secretary of State Condoleezza Rice in New York on September 21, 2006.

The above meetings were used to exchange views and take stock of the process underway to bring about full civil nuclear energy cooperation, and to convey India's concerns on some aspects of the legislation under consideration in the US Congress.

Earlier, an India-US Working Group was set up for implementation of the nuclear understanding and met four times: in Delhi from October 21-22, 2005, in Washington DC from December 21-22, 2005, in Delhi from January 19-20, 2006 and again in Delhi from February 23-24, 2006.

India-US Bilateral Nuclear Cooperation Agreement

Both sides held one round of 123 negotiations from June 12-14, 2006 during which substantial progress was registered.

Foreign Secretary also met Under Secretary Burns in July and September 2006 to discuss US legislation and the next steps on the 123 Agreement negotiations. Thereafter, an informal meeting between teams of the two countries took place in New Delhi from November 6-8, 2006 to discuss various concepts pertaining to the legislation and unresolved issues in the agreement.

Discussions with IAEA

Discussions with IAEA on the Safeguards Agreement were initiated when the Chairman of the Atomic Energy Commission, A. Kakodkar visited Vienna in early March 2006 for a meeting with the Director-General of the IAEA. Subsequently, an IAEA team visited New Delhi for discussions with the Indian side on July 8, 2006.

Adjustment of NSG Guidelines

As part of its commitments, US circulated a statement in the NSG in March 2006 proposing to adjust NSG Guidelines with respect to India to enable full civil nuclear cooperation. An Indian delegation made a presentation to the NSG meeting in Vienna in October 2006.

Prime Minister Manmohan Singh had made a statement during a Short Duration Discussion in Rajya Sabha on August 17, 2006 and in Lok Sabha on August 23, 2006. The statements made clear that anything that went beyond the parameters of July 18, Joint Statement would be unacceptable to India. There were elements of concerns with regard to what is in the current version of the Bills, and these had been conveyed to the US Government.

The India-US nuclear understanding is as laid out in the July 18, 2005 Joint Statement and the Separation Plan tabled in Parliament by the Prime Minister on March 7, 2006. There is no question of accepting any additional requirements beyond those contained in July 18, 2005 Joint Statement and March 2006 Separation Plan. This has been conveyed to the US side. The US side in its Statement of Administration Policy of July 26, 2006 issued after the passage of the House version of the Waiver Bill has clarified that any conditions imposed by the waiver bills to be passed by US Congress that goes beyond the July 18, 2005

Joint Statement would not be acceptable to the US Administration.

India finalized its Separation Plan in March 2006 and the Prime Minister tabled it in the Parliament on March 7, 2006. The full and complete version of this plan was once again laid on the table of the Parliament by Prime Minister on May 11, 2006. The Separation Plan has laid out the schedule of placing India's nuclear reactors under safeguards beginning from 2007. As Prime Minister stated in the Parliament on August 17, 2006, India would not place its nuclear facilities under safeguards till all restrictions on India are lifted.[22]

Henry J Hyde India-US Civil Nuclear Cooperation Act

The US President George W Bush signed on December 18, 2006 the Indo-US Nuclear Co-operation Bill dubbed the Henry J Hyde India-US Civil Nuclear Cooperation Act into law at a special White House ceremony. "The deal will help keep America safe by paving the way for India to join the global efforts to stop the spread of nuclear weapons. After 30 years outside the system, India will now operate its civilian nuclear energy programme under internationally accepted guidelines and the world is going to be safer as a result," the US President said with Secretary of State Condoleezza Rice standing by his side.[23]

Indian-American community leaders and activists were present at the historic signing, along with several senior Bush administrational officers and Congressional aides including Nick Burns, the chief negotiating officer, Assistant Secretary of State for South Asian Affairs Richard Boucher, and several lobbyists. Deputy Chief of Mission Raminder Jassal represented the Indian government. But the biggest supporters of the bill were absent due to ill health and other personal reasons; they were retiring Congressman Henry Hyde, after whom the bill was named, Senator Joseph Biden, Senate Minority leader Harry Reed and Congressman Tom Lantos.[24]

"Another important stage in this process has now been reached with the passage of legislation by the US Congress, with substantial bi-partisan support, in pursuance of the undertakings of the United States in the July Joint Statement that it would seek to adjust US laws and policies to achieve full civil nuclear cooperation with India. This Act is necessary for the United States to resume civil nuclear cooperation with India and also an important step leading to the lifting of international restrictions currently applicable to India," Prime Minister Manmohan Singh's said in the Lok Sabha during discussion on India-US Civil Nuclear Cooperation on December 18, 2006. "We appreciate the efforts made by the US Administration and the bipartisan support in the US Congress, which has led to the passage of this legislation. This law has several positive features, which take into account our concerns. However, there are areas, which continue to be a cause for concern, and we will need to discuss them with the US Administration before the bilateral cooperation agreement can be finalized. The House can rest assured that in these negotiations, the commitments and assurances I gave to Parliament on August 17, 2006 will constitute our guidelines," Singh added.

The passage of the legislation enables the US Administration to follow up on another commitment made by the US in the July 18 Joint Statement, viz. approaching its international partners, particularly in the NSG, to lift restrictions to allow full civil nuclear cooperation with India.[25]

"It is an honour to sign this bill that will strengthen the relationship between the two largest democracies in the world. The relationship between the US and India has never been so vital," Bush said. "We recognize that clean energy is going to be important for the advancement of our economies. During my visit to India, we concluded this historic agreement that will allow us to share civilian nuclear technology and bring India's civilian nuclear programme under the safeguards of IAEA. As part of the agreement, the US and India have committed to take a series of steps to make nuclear cooperation a reality and we are going to fulfill these commitments," Bush added.

The India-US Civil Nuclear Cooperation Act will help America achieve four key goals:

1. This Act will help strengthen cooperation between India and the United States on energy, one of the most important challenges of the 21st century. India is now the world's fifth largest consumer of energy, and its demand for electricity is expected almost to double by

2015. The United States has a clear interest in helping India meet this demand with nuclear energy. By helping India expand its use of safe, clean nuclear energy, this Act lays the foundation for a new strategic partnership between our two nations that will help ease India's demands for fossil fuels and ease pressure on global markets.

2. This Act will help promote economic growth. This Act helps open an important new market for American businesses by paving the way for investment in India's civilian nuclear industry for the first time. This new trade will help American companies gain new customers abroad and create new jobs here at home.
3. This Act will help make it possible for India to reduce emissions and improve its environment. Today, India produces nearly 70 per cent of its electricity from coal. Burning coal produces air pollution and greenhouse gases, but nuclear power can generate massive amounts of electricity without producing any air pollution or greenhouse gases. By sharing advanced civilian nuclear technology, we will help India meet its growing demand for energy and lower emissions at the same time.
4. This Act will help keep America safe by paving the way for India to join the global effort to stop the spread of nuclear weapons. India has conducted its civilian nuclear energy program in a safe and responsible way for decades. Now, in return for access to American technology, India has agreed to open its civilian nuclear power program to international inspection. After 30 years outside the system, India will now operate its civilian nuclear energy program under internationally accepted guidelines, and the world will be safer as a result.[26]

America and India are allies in the war on terror, partners in global trade, and stewards of our environment. India is a democracy that protects the rule of law and is accountable to its people, and an open society that defends freedom of speech and freedom of religion. Both countries are working together to expand economic opportunities in both countries. India's economy has more than doubled in size since 1991, and it is one of the fastest-growing markets for American exports. This trade is creating new jobs in America and raising the standard of living for millions throughout India. This Act is also an important step that will help in sharing civilian nuclear technology and bring India's civilian nuclear program under the safeguards of the international atomic energy agency. The Nuclear cooperation will help the people of India produce more of their energy from clean, safe civilian nuclear power, help both countries economy grow, and make America more secure.

India is interested in long term, stable and predictable cooperation in civil nuclear energy with the United States and other members of the international community. Such a partnership with the United States can be facilitated if the legislation- its scope, content and implementation — were to strengthen the hands of the Administration to fulfill all the commitments agreed to by the US in the July 18 Joint Statement and the March 2, Separation Plan.

On the other hand, this objective can be hindered by extraneous issues that were not part of the understandings in the July 18 Joint Statement and the March 2 Separation Plan.[27]

Main Features of the 123 Agreement

1. The Agreement could be a major contributor to our energy security. For India it is critical that we maintain our current economic growth rate of 8 to 10 per cent per annum if we are to achieve the goal of eradicating poverty. Inadequacy of energy supply is one of the primary constraints on accelerating India's growth rate. We are trying to expand all forms of energy production in a manner which takes care of concerns about environment. Nuclear energy is a logical choice in this context and can make a larger contribution to our overall energy mix. At present its share is only about three per cent. We have an ambitious program to increase our nuclear energy generating capacity to 20,000 MWe by 2020 and double this by 2030. While our domestic three stage program continues, using our

own uranium resources, this Agreement, by adding additional capacity quickly, would help us to reach that target soon.

2. The Agreement also opens the door for cooperation in civil nuclear energy with other countries. We are already discussing with France and Russia similar bilateral cooperation agreements on civil nuclear energy. Once the NSG adopts an exemption to its Guidelines we hope to operationalize all these agreements.
3. The Agreement places India in a special category as a "State possessing advanced nuclear technology", like the United States, with both parties "having the same benefits and advantages".
4. The Agreement provides for full civil nuclear energy cooperation covering nuclear reactors and aspects of the associated nuclear fuel cycle including enrichment and reprocessing.
5. The Agreement provides for nuclear trade, transfer of nuclear material, equipment, components, and related technologies and for cooperation in nuclear fuel cycle activities.
6. The Agreement contains a full reflection of the March 2, 2006 supply assurances, its linkage to safeguards in perpetuity and the provision for corrective measures in case of disruption of fuel supply.
7. The Agreement provides for the development of a strategic reserve of nuclear fuel to guard against any disruption of supply over the lifetime of India's reactors.
8. The Agreement provides for the application of IAEA safeguards to transferred material and equipment. There is no provision that mandates scrutiny of our nuclear weapons programme or any unsafeguarded nuclear facility.
9. The Agreement explicitly provides that it will not affect the unsafeguarded facilities of either party and that it shall be implemented in a manner so as not to hinder

or otherwise interfere with any military nuclear facilities or nuclear material produced, acquired or developed independent of this Agreement.

10. The Agreement grants prior consent to reprocess nuclear material, transfer nuclear material and its products. To bring this into effect, India will establish a national reprocessing facility to reprocess safeguarded nuclear material. Consultations on arrangements and procedures will begin within six months of a request by either party and will be concluded within one year.
11. The 123 Agreement does not affect India's right to conduct nuclear tests in any manner.

India's nuclear installations have not been separated between the military and civil programs. Thus, when nuclear tests were conducted in 1974, the belief that these were fuelled by nuclear fuel supplied for civil nuclear energy led to sanctions being imposed against India. This resulted in denial of technology, fissile material and related support for our nuclear program. Our first nuclear power plant at Tarapur, built with US help and based on US uranium supplies, was crippled without uranium supplies. It was a major setback to the three-stage program as it imposed restrictions on imports of high-technology products, denied access to uranium from the US and other countries, prohibited transfer of nuclear technology-reactors, reprocessing, etc. The US, Japan and some other countries imposed economic and financial sanctions, withdrew bilateral assistance and restricted support from multilateral financial agencies like World Bank and International Monetary Fund.

Our nuclear policy has been marked by restraint and transparency. India has maintained effective export controls on nuclear materials as well as related technologies even though we are neither a party of the NPT nor a member of the Nuclear Suppliers' Group. India is committed to non-proliferation and the maintaining of stringent export controls to ensure that there is no leakage of our indigenously developed know-how and technologies. In fact, India's conduct in this regard has been better than some countries party to the Nuclear Non-Proliferation Treaty. India has not violated any international agreements and its record on non-proliferation has been unblemished.

Subsequent to the nuclear tests in 1998, the Government worked towards re-engaging countries like US to end India's nuclear isolation, project itself rightfully as a country with advanced nuclear technology and work towards greater international cooperation in areas of high technology and initiate measures to do away with technology denial regimes. The importance of the 123 Agreement is that it allows us to develop our civilian nuclear energy program without hindering in any way our strategic nuclear weapons program. The 123 Agreement does not stop India from proceeding further with its strategic nuclear program, which will remain separate, its indigenous three-stage program, and her independent nuclear R&D.[28]

With regard to the recently enacted US law on civil nuclear cooperation, India made it clear on January 10, 2007 that it will 'walk out' of the deal if at any point it seems to undermine its national interest. "There are concerns, of course.... If at any point, it becomes apparent that it (deal) is something which would undermine India's national interest, we will walk out, no matter how much political investment has been made," the Prime Minister's special envoy on nuclear issue Shyam Saran said while delivering a lecture on 'India-US Understanding on Civil Nuclear Cooperation and Future'.

However, New Delhi expressed confidence that the elements over which it has 'genuine' reason for concern, including conditional access to reprocessing technology and reprocessing of spent fuel, would be addressed in the 123 Agreement being negotiated to operationalise the deal.

The civil nuclear deal, Saran pointed out, will become a reality only after the 45-nation NSG changes guidelines to allow civil nuclear cooperation with India and New Delhi concludes a safeguards agreement with the IAEA. Shyam Saran said, "India continued to lobby for support among the NSG countries and was now 'better placed' in the grouping. But that does not mean that problems are over and we need to work with all members."

On the provision that US will end the agreement if India were to conduct a nuclear test, he said as India was not ready to give any legal commitment in this regard, Washington also was doing the same.

On what will happen to the agreement if the regime changes and formed a new administration in the US, he said the bipartisan support given to the bill on it augurs well.

Prime Minister Manmohan Singh returning from the India-ASEAN and East Asia Summits in the Philippines on January 16, 2007, told accompanying journalists that 'there are issues, and concerns, we have to discuss (these) with the US administration'. Manmohan Singh said, "Negotiations will commence 'very shortly' with the US on a bilateral agreement to operationalise the civil nuclear deal during which India will flag its concerns with regard to the law passed by the American Congress on the issue." New Delhi has made it clear that India will not accept any legally binding provision on future nuclear testing in the 123 Agreement and that it will 'walk out' of the deal if it seems to undermine its national interest at any point.

NOTES

1. India's Nuclear Weapons Program: The Beginning: 1944-1960 http://nuclearweaponarchive.org/India/IndiaOrigin.html
2. India and Weapons of Mass Destruction en.wikipedia.org/wiki/India_and_weapons_of_mass_destruction -- 68k
3. Evolution of India's Nuclear Policy — May 28, 1998 www.indianembassy.org/pic/nuclearpolicy.htm - 27k
4. N. Jayapalan, *Foreign Policy of India*, Atlantic Publishers and Distributors Pvt. Ltd. New Delhi (2003), pp. 472-79.
5. *Ibid.*, pp. 479-82.
6. Comprehensive Test Ban Treaty http://www.indianembassy.org/policy/CTBT/ctbt_index.htm
7. Nuclear Non-Proliferation http://www.indianembassy.org/policy/CTBT/embassy_non-proliferation.htm
8. Evolution of India's Nuclear Policy May 27, 1998 http://www.indianembassy.org/pic/nuclearpolicy.htm
9. The Text of Prime Minister Vajpayee's Announcement of Nuclear Tests http://www.indianembassy.org/pic/vajpayee1198.htm
10. Nuclear Weapons — India Nuclear Forces www.fas.org/nuke/guide/india/nuke/ - 20k
11. Planned Series of Nuclear Tests Completed http://www.indianembassy.org/pic/PR_1998/May98/prmay1198.htm
12. Pakistan *AP*, 12 May 98, *Reuters*, 13 May 98, *The Times*, 13 May 98, *AP*, 13 May 98.

13. World Concern at Nuclear Tests
http://newsvote.bbc.co.uk/1/hi/world/91288.stm
14. Official Statement Following the Birmingham Summit, 15 May, 1998
www.g7.utoronto.ca/summit/1999koln/finalcom.htm - 33k
15. Draft Report of National Security Advisory Board on Indian Nuclear Doctrine
http://www.indianembassy.org/policy/CTBT/nuclear_doctrine_aug_17_1999.html
16. Nuclear Weapons — India Nuclear Forces
www.fas.org/nuke/guide/india/nuke/ - 20k
17. K.R. Gupta, (ed.), *India and Pakistan Relations with Special References to Kashmir,* Vol. 1. Atlantic Publishers and Distributors, Pvt.Ltd. New Delhi, pp. 28-29.
18. *Ibid.*, No.8.
19. Gita (Chapter VI-3).
20. R.K. Bhonsle, (ed.), "Special Issue on Indo-US Civil Nuclear Deal", *The Atlantic Journal of World Affairs,* Volume. 2 Number 2-3, April-June & July-September 2006, pp-127-85.
21. United States and India: Strategic Partnership
http://www.state.gov/p/sca/rls/fs/2006/62422.htm
22. Reply of the External Affairs Minister, Mr. Pranab Mukherjee in Lok Sabha to a Parliament Question on the Current Status of India–US Nuclear Deal, New Delhi, November 23, 2006
http://www.indianembassy.org/newsite/press_release/2006/Nov/6.asp
23. Fact Sheet: The United States-India Peaceful Atomic Energy Cooperation Act
http://www.whitehouse.gov/news/releases/2006/12/20061218-2.html
24. President Bush Inks Indo-US Nuclear Deal
http://www.rediff.com/news/2006/dec/18ndeal3.htm
25. Excerpts of Prime Minister Dr. Manmohan Singh's Intervention in the Lok Sabha during Discussion on India-US Civil Nuclear Cooperation
www.indianembassy.org/newsite/press_release/2006/Dec/7.asp - 27k
26. *Ibid.*, No. 23.
27. *Ibid.*, No. 25.
28. India's Nuclear Energy Programme and the 123 Agreement with United States
www.aicc.org.in/documents-detail.php?id=29 - 80k